09 - 2008

# CHIPETA

## Queen of the Utes

## A BIOGRAPHY

### BY CYNTHIA S. BECKER & P. DAVID SMITH

WESTERN REFLECTIONS
PUBLISHING COMPANY®
Lake City, Colorado

ISBN 1-890437-79-4

Library of Congress Control Number: 2003108210

Cover: Left photo, Matthew Brady Photo Courtesy of Main
Street Photography, Montrose, CO; Right photos, Courtesy of
Ruth Gregory Collection
Cover and text design by Laurie Goralka Design

Second Edition
Printed in the United States of America

Western Reflections Publishing Company®
P.O. Box 1149
Lake City, CO 81235
www.westernreflectionspub.com

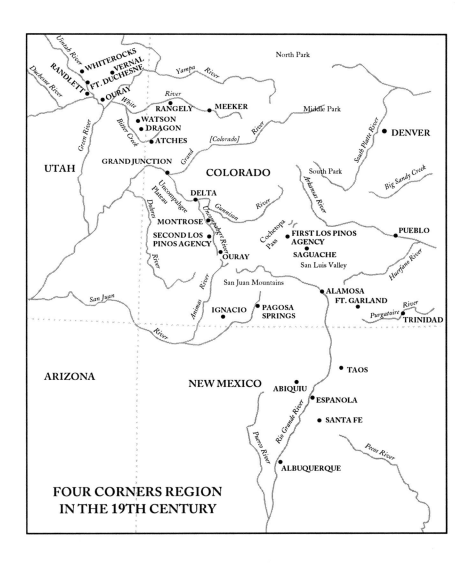

FOUR CORNERS REGION
IN THE 19TH CENTURY

# TABLE OF CONTENTS

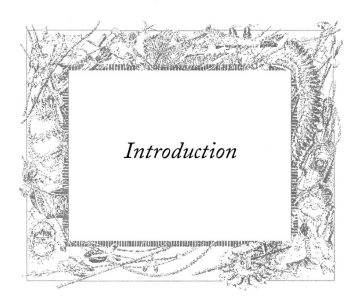

# Introduction

◎ "Dear Mom, The brownies were great. Thanks from all the girls in Chipeta lodge." — *Child's letter home from Cheley Camp, Estes Park. Colorado*

◎ The Chipeta Chapter, Colorado Archaeological Society meets at 7:00 p.m. on the third Wednesday at the United Methodist Church, Montrose, Colorado. — *Colorado Archaeological Society Directory*

◎ "We are the first Girl Scout troop in Western Colorado to have our own webpage." — *Chipeta Girl Scout Council, Grand Junction, Colorado, Junior Troop #80 <www.gj.net/~jholton/act.htm>*

◎ Chipeta Canyon is the gateway to Utah's 15,200 acre Cripple Cowboy wilderness area where deep canyons, high ridges, and sheer cliffs create spectacular scenic vistas. — *Utah Wilderness Inventory*

✳ ✳ ✳

Three-quarters of a century after the death of the well-known Ute Indian woman, Chipeta still ranks among Colorado's historic elite. Roads and parks, schools and organizations are named for her. Yet, if a poll were taken, few people could describe anything about her life or explain why her name is so venerated. She is usually identified only as the mate of the great Ute chief, Ouray. Other information about Chipeta is often based on a few romanticized and distorted incidents.

The story of Chipeta and Chief Ouray is a love story. It is a tale of two special people who sought, against formidable odds, to preserve the way of life of their people. They earned respect and, eventually, honor from the very society that sought to wipe them from the face of the earth, or at least from the confines of the state of Colorado. Chipeta was a typical shy and submissive Ute woman who grew to be Ouray's partner and confidant. She became his eyes and ears, even his emissary, among the Utes. After his death she joined their people in a forced exodus from the land of their ancestors to live and die in the traditional way. The *rediscovery* of Chipeta by early twentieth century Coloradans propelled her to folk heroine status.

Frontier history is difficult to reconstruct. In researching his biography of Crazy Horse, Larry McMurtry identified a problem common to recreating lives of people whose existence was generally undocumented until fate thrust them onto center stage in national events. "Fact withers in the heat of myth," McMurtry notes. Chipeta is a case in point.

Like Crazy Horse, Chipeta's legend has been related to us through oral history. Any written records of places, dates, and events of her life were created by the white culture. Nineteenth century public interest in "the Ute problem" and her husband's prominence in Ute/white relations generated newspaper records that span several decades. Although sometimes tainted by the sensationalized writing style of the period and pervasive anti-Ute sentiment, these accounts identify events in Chipeta's life. Ouray's activities were documented more factually by federal, territorial, and state officials; Chipeta's own words were captured in U.S. congressional transcripts. Yet, these records, for the most part, collected dust while the passage of time and retelling of tales created the romantic myth of Chipeta, Queen of the Utes.

This book is a companion to the earlier publication *Ouray, Chief of the Utes*. The previous work details the life of Chief Ouray in the context of Ute history. This book is an account of Chipeta's life as a Ute woman, the mate of a bold leader, and a compassionate peacemaker. Her life has been traced from recorded events and personal recollections of individuals who knew her. Some of these accounts provide conflicting information. In such cases the authors have recreated the most probable scenarios and, in some instances, projected Chipeta's likely responses to events that were recorded in limited detail. A considerable amount of new information, uncovered since publication of the Ouray biography, has been included. Both books should be read together for a complete view of Ouray, Chipeta, and Ute life.

The use of Chipeta's name to identify places and organizations originated, at least in part, from a sense of guilt on the part of citizens who stole her homeland. Her name is used throughout the Rocky Mountain region today to recall the spirit of a woman who once passed this way and made a difference. Perhaps most remarkable, she remained a kind and loving individual during all of the turbulent ups and downs of her life. What better epitaph could one have?

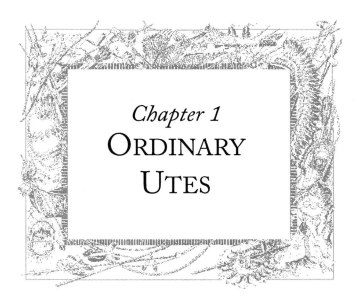

# Chapter 1
# ORDINARY
# UTES

A mile-long procession crossed the broad Colorado valley to the grave site near the crumbling remains of a lone adobe house. Dignified civic leaders in dark suits and Sunday dresses and a handful of buckskin-clad Ute Indians rode in open cars behind the casket. A brass band and formations of men and women sporting regalia of military, patriotic, and civic societies marched behind, followed by a parade of automobiles filled with curious citizens. Five thousand people gathered to hear dignitaries speak of the loyalty and bravery of the deceased as they placed flowers and an American flag at the grave. The pallbearers lifted the casket into a concrete sarcophagus positioned beside a cast cement replica of a teepee. Rev. M. J. Hersey pronounced the Episcopal funeral rights, and the band struck up "The Star Spangled Banner."

The subject of all this attention was a woman who had been banished from the state for nearly half a century. The adobe house was once her home. As far as the eye could see in every direction through the valley and over the ridges of the distant mountain ranges, the land once belonged to her people. In their eyes it was, and is still, their land.

Her name was Chipeta. No surname. No title. Simply Chipeta. The newspapers called her burial a triumphant return. Whether it was a moment of victory or the final insult inflicted by an alien culture is a matter for individual interpretation.

❋ ❋ ❋

Stories of Chipeta's origin are almost as numerous as the legends of her deeds. According to some tales she was the eldest daughter of a mighty Ute chief who cared for her father and the household when her young mother died. In other stories she was identified as a niece of the great Chief Nevava of the Weeminuche. Legend made her a hereditary Ute princess. Perhaps the most common tale bears the truth:

A small Ute hunting party crept cautiously toward the circle of Kiowa-Apache teepees nestled in a grove of cottonwoods. Thin ribbons of smoke rose from the camp, but there was no movement. No dogs barked. No horses stood ready to ride. As they moved closer the Utes were convinced the camp was abandoned. Then they spotted a body sprawled face down in the grass. Circling the camp they saw more and more bloody, contorted bodies of men, women, and children who had died with weapons in hand. The attack had been swift and thorough.

The Ute hunters turned to slip quickly away from this place of death when a child's wail broke the stillness. A terrified girl no more than two years old toddled among the bodies. One man ventured into the camp to gather the child in his arms and comfort her. She was the sole survivor of a massacre.[1] The man took the child home to his piwan, Watawoop. They named her Chipeta, and she became their daughter.

Children, regardless of their origins, were much revered in Ute society. Abandoned children and those taken captive in raids or received in trade were accepted as full members of the family. Regardless of her bloodlines, Chipeta was raised in the Tabeguache band of Utes, and she was considered to be a Ute for all purposes.

· Chipeta was born about 1843. The meaning of her name is as disputed as her origin. It has been variously translated as "White Singing Bird," "Charitable One," "The Jewel,"

"Spring of Clear Water," or identified as a derivative of the Spanish "Guadalupita."

As a Ute girl Chipeta grew up among a nomadic people who roamed ancestral paths through the Rocky Mountains in what is now Colorado and northern New Mexico. They followed the seasonal foods offered by nature and the grazing patterns of game animals. Everything they needed to sustain themselves was available within their annual circle of travel. The sun and the moon were their clock and compass; the changing seasons were their calendar.

Life was not easy in this rugged terrain. Survival required a distinct division of labor between men and women. Men were hunters and protectors. They made tools and weapons, maintained the horses, tracked and killed game, stood guard, fought off enemies, and trained the young boys for these same duties. Women kept the home. They gathered and preserved fruits, vegetables, and grains and dried meat for winter survival. They made the family's clothing and bedding and even their shelter (the teepee covering) from the skins of animals. Women nurtured the babies and taught the young girls the work of women. Moving frequently from place to place was a family affair. Everyone helped with the packing, transportation, and setup of the new camp.

Chipeta's family of twenty to twenty-five people was matrilineal and multi-generational. Her grandmother, her mother, and her aunts formed the nucleus. Daughters took mates and remained with the family to raise their children. Sons joined new families when they found women to accept them as partners.

Each spring Chipeta's family returned to their favorite meadows. After living on dried foods all winter the family craved the taste of fresh vegetables. Brake fern, asparagus, and onions grew wild in the runoff from high mountain snowmelt. Often they plopped stomach down in the wet grass to nibble the first tender, green shoots without pulling them from the ground. Her mother pried roots of sego lily, fritillary, and wild carrots from the earth with a long stick. Ducks and mud hens and the eggs of many waterfowl were abundant. Her father caught fish with willow baskets and occasionally trapped river wildlife. Their favorite delicacy was roasted beaver tail.

The family worked their way to higher elevations as the strawberries, raspberries, currants, chokecherries, and plums ripened. They ate the first pickings of fruit then dried the rest for winter. They camped high on the mountainside where small herds of deer, elk, and mountain sheep grazed and offered plentiful fresh meat.

*Three Ute girls posed about 1860 for a French journal,* La Conguete Blanche. *P. David Smith Collection*

By late summer they made their way into South Park, a wide plain surrounded by mountains, to join other Ute families for a buffalo hunt. They dried and stored the meat with the preserved fruits of summer for their winter sustenance. The hides, the bones, and all the parts of the great animals had some use. They gathered wild grass seeds — pigweed, lamb's quarter, millet, and broomrape — to grind for flour. After the first frost they harvested and roasted piñon nuts. Then they packed the supplies and returned to the sheltered valley where they made winter camp with other families. As many as six hundred people wintered near the junction of the Gunnison and Uncompahgre Rivers. And the seasonal cycle began again.

Winter was the season for storytelling. Seated around the fire the elders recounted the history of the Utes, the *Nuche*[2] ("the People") as they called themselves. They told tales of their ancestors, created to inhabit the mountains, who learned to survive with respect for the spirits of the living earth. The origins of prayer songs for birth and death, successful hunts, and safe journeys were woven into tales of wars and victories, enemies and friends. They marked time by memorable events — the great snow that trapped the people in their villages, the forest fire that cleared the trees from the pass of the buffalo, the fever sickness that wiped out whole families. With no written language the Utes preserved their history and tradition in the collective mind of the people. They repeated stories over and over, committing them to memory so that the children would one day tell their own children.

Like most Ute children Chipeta loved the stories with animal characters that taught the children lessons — to tell the truth, to share, to respect their elders. She was not so fond of the frightening tales that warned of the fates that awaited disobedient children. Anusacutz was a creature with a hairy face, big eyes and ears, long nails on his fingers and toes, and skin like tree bark. He roamed about in search of little children who did not do as they were told. On his back he carried a large basket to hold captive children. In one story a patient and resourceful boy outwitted the beast. Every time Anusacutz stopped, the boy reached out of the basket and grabbed a stone. When the basket was filled with stones, the boy latched onto a tree branch, pulled himself out of the basket, and escaped.[3] Perhaps little Chipeta hoped she might be so clever and brave.

Children were much indulged by everyone in the family. Chipeta played with carved wooden animals and dressed buckskin dolls that she carried in miniature cradleboards. With other children she built child-size camps where they mimicked adult routines. The girls tossed willow hoops and had contests to see who could find the longest stalk of a particular kind of grass or who could juggle clay balls without dropping them. In summer they splashed in streams and bubbling hot springs; in winter they slid down snowy banks on pieces of rawhide. The Utes kept many dogs so there were often new puppies to cuddle. Some children kept pet owls in cages made of willow branches.

By her sixth summer Chipeta cared for the family's babies while their mothers did chores. She began to learn women's skills from her mother. Joining the women of the camp as they gathered wood, dug root vegetables, and picked nuts and berries, she fixed in her memory the locations and seasons for each food. The edible plants and medicinal herbs became familiar by their shape, color, texture and scent. She learned to slash a willow or aspen tree and extract the sweet sap that flowed in springtime to use as a painkiller and also how to use piñon pitch as an adhesive and a sealer. Chipeta practiced cooking in a pitch-lined basket, using heated rocks to boil the contents, and roasted meat and vegetables in a shallow pit lined with hot stones and sealed with damp grass.

Chipeta's mother also taught her to sew. Small purses made from soft doeskin scraps were her first projects. Then she learned to create moccasins, leggings, shirts, and dresses from the tanned hides. She punched sewing holes along the edges with a sharpened bone awl and joined the pieces with sinew stripped from the backbone of a deer or buffalo. Chipeta found her calling in the design and decoration of garments. She became known among the greater Tabeguache band of Utes for her skill and patience with intricate beadwork. It became a lifelong art and source of great pleasure.

As she grew Chipeta graduated to more challenging tasks — butchering the deer, elk, and buffalo her father killed and preserving the hides. Kneeling on the ground to scrape fur and flesh from a hide made her back ache and her fingers grew stiff from clutching the sharp bone used as a scraper. The heavy work followed after the hide was soaked in a pit of water. The hide of a deer weighed thirty to forty pounds even before it was soaked; a wet bull buffalo hide was more than a hundred-pound load.[4] It was a struggle to drag the waterlogged hide from the pit and spread it flat to dry. Chipeta massaged the hide with the tanning agent — the brains of the animal. She cured the hide in the sun, soaked it again, and stretched it flat to dry once more. To soften the great piece of leather Chipeta held one end and her mother held the other as they pulled it back and forth over a tree limb. Sometimes they smoked it over the fire to color the hide and make it waterproof. Pine branches created a light yellow tone; greasewood resulted in dark yellow; willow limbs turned the hide a rich brown. Pounding a hide with chalk made it white. The whole process was strenuous — and messy — but Chipeta loved the soft comfort of expertly treated animal hides. She soon learned that her work was a valuable trade commodity.

The Ute families of the nineteenth century measured their wealth by the size and quality of their herd of horses. The Utes were the first of all the North American tribes to acquire horses from the Spanish. The animals were vital to the Ute way of life and horse racing was a favorite pastime. A race pitted just two horses and riders against each other. Families gathered in an open meadow to make wagers and judge the outcome. Often multiple races were settled at one gathering, thus prolonging the entertainment.[5] An expert rider herself, Chipeta was an eager spectator when her father or older brother was challenged to a race. The Utes were known for their fine horses, grown strong and fast on the rich high-country grass. They usually won their races against other tribes and, by winning, increased the number of their horses.

Chipeta was a slender, athletic girl who grew to about five feet three inches tall. Her slim face boasted well-defined cheeks and an aquiline nose. The dark-skinned Utes were called "the black people" by many other tribes, but Chipeta's skin was light colored. Her Kiowa-Apache heritage made her stand out from the stocky, round-faced Ute women.[6]

Like most girls, Chipeta looked forward each year to *mama-kwa-nhka-pu*, the Bear Dance that signaled the beginning of spring. It was an exciting event that drew scattered groups of Utes together for three days of feasting and socializing. As the weather warmed, Chipeta watched for the arrival of

*A diorama from the Ute Indian Museum at Montrose represents the Bear Dance — a traditional spring dance.*
*Colorado Historical Society, F-19672*

runners who traveled between camps with news. She pestered her father to tell her how many sunrises she must wait.

Chipeta could hardly sleep the night before they broke camp. She was eager to help load the horses and get under way. Travel was slow because several horses pulled travois — two poles tied together above the horse's shoulders. The poles dragged behind the horse and supported cross pieces that held family possessions. As they topped the last hill Chipeta's eyes danced with excitement. Hundreds of teepees dotted the valley below. She began to list in her mind the friends she had not seen since last spring. When they arrived in camp, Chipeta had a hard time keeping her attention on the unpacking and setting up the teepee. She was eager to make the most of the brief gathering.

In a flat area the men built an *avinkwep* — a large circular cave of sticks surrounded by a brush fence. Musicians gathered on the west side, the source of thunder and lighting and rain, facing the east through the cave entrance. Their voices joined in a vocal chant to the rhythm of the drum. The honored bear was represented by its growl, produced by a morache, a piece of hardwood notched to resemble a washboard. The sound was made by vigorously rubbing a short stick or bone over the notches.

The women chose their dancing partners. The men lined up shoulder-to-shoulder on the north side of the cave. An equal line of women faced them from the south with partners across from each other. They stepped forward and back to the music in increasingly faster and more complex steps. When someone fell down from exhaustion, that dance ended and a new one began.

While adults danced inside the cave, the children and nondancers watched through the fence. During the festivities old friends greeted each other and caught up on news. The children played games. Young people who had entered puberty flirted and courted and often found marriage partners. After three days the Utes separated into their family groups and once again began their trek in search of food.

Although she spent her childhood in the isolation of the mountains, Chipeta occasionally encountered non-Utes, including a few white men. The Utes maintained active commerce with other tribes and with Spanish colonists from as far south as Santa Fe. When her family traveled south, Chipeta watched her parents bargain their fine tanned hides for Navajo rugs, blankets, and silver jewelry. With the Pueblo Indians they bartered for clay pots and woven, patterned baskets. Spanish traders offered guns, knives, metal cooking pots, and beautiful beads and buttons. By the time of Chipeta's birth, white mountain men had for many years ventured into Ute territory to hunt and trade for furs that commanded high prices in eastern cities. They made friends with the Utes and sometimes were invited to winter in Ute camps.

During Chipeta's childhood a few Spanish and American adventurers established trading posts on the plains, in the San Luis Valley, and among the foothills east of the mountains. Traders like Dick Wooten and Alexander Barclay made regular trips to the high country to do business with the Utes.

In October 1846, Barclay found a large Ute hunting camp along the Arkansas River midway between the present-day towns of Salida and Buena Vista. Chipeta might have been among the children who gathered around Barclay to get a close look at his strange pale skin. He did big business that day trading guns and ammunition, knives, tobacco, vermilion, and beads for mules, ponies, buckskins, buffalo robes, and Navajo blankets. He also gained permission to dig a load of salt from the natural beds just over Trout Creek Pass. Barclay could sell the salt in his store in the rude settlement of Hardscrabble.

John C. Fremont's exploration party crossed Cochetopa Pass in 1848 and might have traded with Chipeta's family for fresh horses. Though she encountered a few white men, such brief experiences provided Chipeta only rudimentary knowledge of the world outside her secluded mountain homeland.

In June 1846, tensions between Mexico and the United States over the land that is now New Mexico and southern Colorado erupted in war. In a week's time the American army took control of Santa Fe. Stories of the battles circulated among the Utes but the conflict was of little concern to the Tabeguache band in their far away high country. The Mouache band of Utes, who lived in the southern mountains, made an informal treaty with the white men, and the Utes expected no trouble. Then the following year the Pueblo Indians revolted against the domineering whites. One hundred fifty Indians were killed as the American army swept in to quell the revolt. Word of the fearsome firepower of the Americans spread from camp to camp as Ute chiefs discussed the situation in councils.

The war ended in February 1848. Much to their surprise, the Utes discovered that the territory they occupied had become part of the spoils of war. The Arkansas River was the northern boundary of the vast tract of land given to the United States by the defeated Mexico. The Utes had always known that the mountains were their lands, just as they knew which parts of the plains belonged to the Commanche, the Kiowa, and the Apache. But the U.S. government had another perspective.

The United States invited all of the southern Ute chiefs to Abiquiu, near Taos, for a treaty council. The government representatives knew little about the reclusive Utes and failed to understand that they had no major form of organization. The Utes were a group of seven loosely allied bands that shared overlapping territories and spent much of the year in small family groups working the food-gathering circuit. Each band had a council of elders, or headmen, and chiefs with special responsibilities for coordinating wars, buffalo hunts, and ceremonial dances. At times any Ute who could gain the support of more than his own family might assume the title "Chief." More than one hundred fifty chiefs plus their families (every Ute of any importance in what is now southern Colorado or northern New Mexico) showed up in Abiquiu for the council.

A few Tabeguache families, including Chipeta's, traveled from the central mountains to attend the gathering. Sapovanero, Chipeta's seventeen-year-old brother, was old enough to sit beside their father in the formal meetings. Six-year-old Chipeta passed her first council with the United States government enjoying games with the assembled children. She also had a particular new interest, a baby brother, McCook, who was born the year of the Abiquiu Treaty Council, 1849.[8] She was devoted to helping her mother care for him.

The council concluded on December 30, 1849, with a treaty signed by twenty-nine Ute chiefs. They agreed to stay in their usual territory, return any captives or stolen property, remain at peace, and let white travelers pass safely through their lands. They would allow the government to build military posts and agencies in Ute Territory. The chiefs also agreed to devote themselves to agricultural pursuits — whatever that meant. In return the government promised to give the Utes annual gifts of blankets and food (known as annuities).[9] As a result of the treaty, the Utes were assigned a government Indian agent who was stationed at the very southern edge of their territory in the little Spanish town of Taos.

Chipeta was eight years old when a new family arrived in winter camp. The father, a Tabeguache man, was well known among the adults. His Jicarilla Apache wife had died, and he decided to return to his own people with his three sons and two daughters.[10] The two oldest boys, powerfully built Ulay and slender Quenche, drew much attention from the girls, who whispered in private about the handsome pair.[11] Ulay was eighteen, and Quenche was a year older.[12] Growing up near Taos, they were hired out as sheepherders for a Spanish rancher. Catholic friars baptized the boys, trained them as Catholics, and provided them some basic education.[13] They became fluent in Spanish and also learned some English. By the time they joined their Ute family, these cosmopolitan young men understood Spanish customs and white men's ways.

Bright and aggressive, Ulay gained a reputation as a skilled hunter, quick thinker, fierce warrior, and a young man

*This very early photograph shows Ouray (left) and his brother Quenche (referred to as Yulé and Quincy).*
Denver Public Library, Western History Department, X-30707

*Although a Tabeguache Ute, Ouray was born near Abiquiu, New Mexico.*
*P. David Smith Photograph*

not shy about recounting his accomplishments. His most out-standing battle took place when he was twenty-two. As he told the story, a band of thirty-eight Arapahos and Cheyennes stole forty horses from a Ute named Colorow. Ulay, Colorow, and eight other braves tracked the thieves to their camp on the south side of the Arkansas River just below its juncture with the Huerfano. Although outnumbered almost four to one, the Utes attacked, overpowering the enemy in a short round of hand-to-hand combat. The battered Cheyenne and Arapaho warriors fled leaving the Utes with eight scalps, the stolen horses, and several extra horses.[14]

In 1853 Ulay took a mate named Tukukavapiapi (also identified as Black Mare).[15] The couple met at the Bear Dance, and having demonstrated his prowess as a warrior, Ulay courted her in the traditional way, serenading her with his flute and wooing her in the seclusion of the woods. To cement the relationship he killed a deer and placed it in front of her family's teepee. Black Mare butchered the animal, prepared a meal, and invited Ulay to share it with her family. With this ritual they became a couple.

Ulay moved into the teepee of Black Mare's family, where they lived until their first child was born. During this time Black Mare tanned and collected the hides of the buffalo that Ulay killed. When she had ten hides the women held a "sewing party" to prepare the teepee cover for the couple's new home.

Black Mare delivered two children — a daughter who lived only a short time and a son born about 1858. Ulay dearly loved the little boy who became "a child of many names." Ulay named him Cotoan, but called him by nicknames — Pahlone and Queashegut. This latter name, meaning "little left hand," described a particular trait of the boy. The child reminded Ulay of his own left-handed brother, Quenche. *Pahlone* (often written as Paron) referred to an apple. According to Ulay, he gave his son this nickname because he had a round face like an apple — and he certainly was the apple of his father's eye.

Naming a child was not an urgent matter to the Utes. Parents often waited a long time for the right name to appear, based on some action or characteristic of the child or a material object the child favored. Ulay said that his own name had no meaning. His first word, or sound, had been "oo-ay," and he made that noise so constantly that his parents began to use it for his name.[16]

In the case of Ulay, his name evolved to Uray or Ouray on the tongues of white men. The Utes had no *r* in their language and had difficulty pronouncing that sound in Spanish and English words. It came out sounding like an *l.* To the non-Ute ear "Oo-ay" or "Oo-lay" sounded like an attempt to say "Oo-Ray." It was by the name *Ouray* that he became known in the white culture and subsequently in Colorado history.[17]

A Ute's name could be changed later in life based on some deed or event and nicknames were common and numerous. The boy Pahlone gained a new nickname at the age of five when he showed considerable skill and bravery like his father. The boy was fearless on horseback and loved to race his small mare over any terrain. One day in the spring, he climbed on his father's most spirited warhorse. The stallion bolted and ran wild. Pahlone clung desperately to the horse for some distance until knocked off by a tree limb. The incident marked him permanently with a forked

*A typical young Native American mother and her baby take time together at home.*

Harper's Weekly, *June 20, 1868*
*P. David Smith Collection*

scar on his right shoulder. His bravery throughout the event earned him a new name: "Little Chief." [18]

Not long after the birth of their son, Black Mare died. The grief-stricken Ouray needed someone to watch his child and attend to his domestic chores. Chipeta was chosen. Time and legend have created many versions of how Chipeta entered Ouray's household. In one story Ouray saw Chipeta gathering water and was so smitten with her beauty that he brought her home as a second wife (an occasional Ute practice) while Black Mare was still living. [19] In a more likely account Sapovanero's wife had delivered a baby shortly before Black Mare's death and could provide Ouray's baby with milk. [20] Sapovanero's little sister, Chipeta, was conveniently available to take care of the child. It is also quite possible that Chipeta was a relative, perhaps a sister, of Black Mare. It was common practice when a young woman died that her sister or a cousin took her place as wife and mother.

Whatever the reason, at age fifteen Chipeta began to care for Ouray's child. She expanded her duties to care for the father as well. She cooked for him, sewed his clothes, carried firewood, fetched water, set up his teepee, and tanned his deer, elk, and buffalo hides.

Ouray liked having the charming Chipeta around. Shy and unassuming (desirable traits to Ute men), she was also a happy person and a tireless worker who loved his precious son. Best of all, she was intelligent, and Ouray discovered he could talk to her for hours at a time. As his grief over the loss of Black Mare diminished, Ouray discovered that a soul mate had come into his life. By 1859, Chipeta and Ouray decided to become a couple. She was sixteen, and he was twenty-six.[21]

---

[1] Saunders, William F., "The Joy of the Frontier," unpublished manuscript in possession of author (Smith), Chapter VIII, 83.

[2] Wroth, William, Editor, *Ute Indian Arts & Culture*, (Colorado Springs: Colorado Springs Fine Arts Center, 2000), 35; also found spelled as Noochew, Nuciu, Nu'tsi, Nuntz.

[3] Monaghan, J., CWA Interviews Moffat County 1933-34, Colorado Historical Society, interview 356/24, 94.

[4] Davis, Jim, Taxidermist, Trails End Taxidermy, Pueblo West, Colorado, interview January 4, 2002.

[5] Russell, James, "Conditions and Customs of Present-Day Utes in Colorado," *Colorado Magazine*, VI, 3 (May 1929) 107.

[6] Ibid.

[7] There were seven primary Ute bands: the Capote and the Mouache (now jointly known as the Southern Ute Tribe); the Weeminuche (now the Ute Mountain Ute Tribe); the Tabeguache (or Uncompahgre), the Yampa (or White River), the Uintah, and the Grand River (now jointly known as the Northern Ute Tribe occupying the Uintah-Ouray Reservation in Utah).

[8] U.S. Indian Census Roles, 1885-1940, NARA Record Group 75.

[9] Kappler, Charles J., *Indian Affairs: Laws and Treaties*, II, U.S. Statutes at Large, Vol. 9 (Washington, D.C.: U.S. Government Printing Office), 984.

[10] There is much conflicting information about Ulay's parents. Some sources say the father was Guera Murah, a Jicarilla-Apache who was raised by the Utes and married a Tabeguache woman. Other sources say the father was Ute and the mother was Jicarilla-Apache (*Denver Post*, August 28, 1880). According to Val J. McClellan in *This Is Our Land* (Vol 1, pages 399 & 401), Major Andrew Jonathan Alexander, who attended a conference with Ute Chiefs in August 1872, reported in a letter that "Ouray's father was a Ute warrior of some importance, his mother a sister of Wherro-Moondo (Guero Murah) a chief of the Jicarilla Apaches." Typically, a Ute man joined the family of his spouse. This practice, and the fact that Ulay grew up in New Mexico where the Jicarilla-Apache lived, suggests that Ulay's mother was Jicarilla-Apache and after her death the father returned to his own people, the Utes.

[11] *Denver Daily Times*, Oct 9, 1873, 2.

[12] McClellan, Val, *This Is Our Land*, Vol 1, (New York: Vantage Press, 1977), 341-2.

[13] Ochoa, Maria, Director Historic-Artistic Patrimony and Archives of the Archdiocese of Santa Fe, correspondence with author 1996; Tom Dunlay, *Kit Carson & the Indians*, (Lincoln: University of Nebraska Press, 2000), 202-203; *Denver Post*, August 28, 1880.

[14] *Denver Daily Times*, Oct 9, 1873, 2.

[15] Wroth, William, 17.

[16] Dawson, Thomas F., "Major Thompson, Chief Ouray and the Utes — An Interview with Major James B. Thompson, May 23, 1921," *Colorado Magazine*, Vol. VII, No. 3, (May 1930), 12; *Denver Daily Times*, Oct 9, 1873, 2.

[17] U.S. Government Documents 0246. Beside Ouray's name on the Treaty of 1863 an interpreter wrote "Arrow." Some inventive writer later concluded that Ouray was called "Arrow" because he was such a "straight shooter." Still others writers said that his name meant "Yes" in Ute.

[18] Hafen, Ann Woodbury, *Campfire Frontier*, (Denver: The Old West Publishing Company, 1969), 182.

[19] Lyman-Whitney, Susan, *Worth Their Salt: Notable But Often Unnoted Women of Utah* (Boulder, Colo: NetLibrary, Inc., 1999), 79, based on interviews with Ute Tribal Historian, Clifford Duncan.

[20] McClellan, Val, 359.

[21] Ibid.

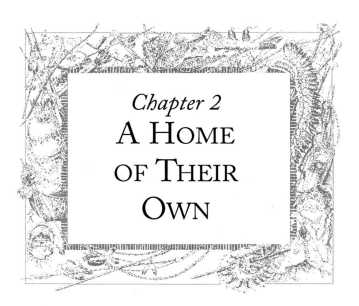

## Chapter 2
# A HOME
# OF THEIR
# OWN

Chipeta's youth, like that of all Ute girls, had prepared her to become matron of her own teepee. She slipped easily from child to woman and relished her adult station in life. Her handsome new husband was a fierce warrior who treated her with gentleness and respect. She worked hard to please him. Ouray's son had become like her own child and she adored the boy. Her own cherished little brother, McCook, spent so much time in their teepee that Ouray treated him like another son. Ouray's little sister, Tsashin, just two years younger than Chipeta, often came to visit and entertained Pahlone or helped about the teepee. As she did her daily chores with Pahlone strapped to her back or propped nearby in his cradleboard, Chipeta must have mused about the family she and Ouray would have. Before falling asleep at night, she perhaps spread her hands over her flat belly and wondered how soon she would grow big with her first baby.

While Chipeta and Ouray settled into their new family life, the outside world was rapidly encroaching upon their secluded mountain homeland. For many years trappers, traders, and explorers had enjoyed safe passage through Ute territory so long as they brought goods, traded fairly, and kept moving. When visitors attempted to take up residence, the Utes drove them out. Unknown to the Utes some of the explorers they welcomed and guided through their territory had secretly mapped the land and its resources for the U.S. government. These maps helped easterners to visualize the vast territory and untold riches available to people with adventurous and enterprising spirits.

Oddly enough, a ship sinking in the waters off the Pacific Coast spurred the invasion of Ute territory. The United States had suffered a series of business failures and investment losses that caused frightened people to withdraw their savings from eastern banks. The loss of the *Central America*, a ship loaded with gold, left many U.S. banks unable to fund their deposits. Banks failed and the country sank into economic depression.

When Horace Greeley's *New York Tribune* reported a gold strike along Cherry Creek in Kansas Territory (which included present-day Colorado), desperate men hurried west with visions of salvaging their financial futures in a few days. In a matter of months the eastern slope of the Rocky Mountains was overrun by fifty-thousand men, and a few women, expecting to scoop up gold nuggets by the fistful. Some were successful, but half the hopefuls returned home disappointed before the year ended. The persistent ones who remained behind soon spread out through the mountains to search beneath the surface for hidden treasures.

The stampede was on. Speculators and businessmen, seeing their opportunity to provide goods and services to the miners, established communities along the eastern foot of the mountains. Montana City, St. Charles, Auraria, and Denver City seemed to spring up overnight in the area that is present-day Denver. By April of 1860 William Byers circulated his newspaper, *The Rocky Mountain News*. A school opened in October for the children of families who had followed their men west. A new stagecoach route from Leavenworth, Kansas, delivered mail and even more people. Indian trails became busy wagon roads servicing the mining camps that dotted the foothills and eastern mountains.

These interlopers planned to stay. They lobbied Congress to divide Kansas Territory roughly in half. The new Colorado Territory won approval in 1861. Colorado City became the territorial capital, a governor was appointed, and the wheels of the American system of government began to roll. The new territory had a population of a little more than 34,277 people.[1] Counting noses on the frontier was haphazard at best, and many estimates suggest that the number of residents was twice the official figure. Of course, none of the counts included Chipeta, Ouray, and the rest of the native inhabitants.

Some Utes welcomed the trade goods brought by the Americans and established friendly relationships with the newcomers. On occasion they rescued settlers trapped by erratic mountain weather and sent them on their way unharmed. Other Utes responded to this invasion of their territory by attempting to scare off the invaders. They raided miners' camps. They burned cabins. They stole horses and supplies. They killed prospectors and travelers. However, after awhile these intimidation techniques no longer worked because the balance of power had shifted.

Within the span of a single year white settlers outnumbered the Utes more than five to one,[2] and they were determined to go where they pleased in what appeared to them to be open and available land. Many of the new arrivals viewed the Utes as mere stumbling blocks in the road of progress, and stumbling blocks could be removed. Some newcomers embraced General Philip Sheridan's aphorism, "The only good Indian is a dead Indian."[3]

Complaints about the Utes became frequent. In September 1859, Ute Indian Agent Kit Carson announced that, as punishment for killing some white men, the Utes would not receive their annual government annuities. While Carson designed the announcement to diffuse white anger over the murders, he added a warning to remind the miners and settlers that they courted danger by intruding in Ute land. "The Tabewache (sic) are now on the waters of the Grand River. They are hostilely disposed and I would advise all to be cautious of their intercourse with them.[4] The Utes are the most

*Kit Carson became a
good and trusted
friend and advisor of
Ouray and Chipeta.
Colorado Historical
Society, F-44104*

dangerous of the mountain Indians, excellent shots with the
rifle and if hostile, will be likely to destroy many small
prospecting parties and solitary travelers next season."[5]

Carson had established a good relationship with the
Utes. He had known them for more than twenty years in his
employment as a trapper and fur trader and as a guide for John
C. Fremont's expeditions. Having learned to speak the Ute
language, Carson often intervened when they had skirmishes
with encroaching white men. His rapport with the Utes led to
his selection as Ute agent at the Taos Agency in 1854. The
Utes regarded him as a fair and sympathetic man; however,
withholding the government annuities they had received
annually, albeit irregularly, since 1850 made them mad.

The Tabeguache leaders traveled to Abiquiu in October
1859 to council with Carson. He listened to their arguments
that white men settled in their hunting grounds and killed
their game. To maintain peace, Carson finally relented and
delivered their annuities.[6] He recognized the Utes' growing
dependence on government assistance for survival. To prevent

further trouble, he cautioned the chiefs to keep their people away from white settlements.

In response to the meeting with Agent Carson, Ouray and Chipeta, like many other Ute families, avoided their usual fall hunting sites east of the Continental Divide and, as a result, struggled through a difficult winter. By spring many Utes were starving. The supply of meat Chipeta had dried did not last through the cold season. Ouray trapped small game, and the family survived mostly on rabbits and birds. Chipeta stretched the meager food as far as she could and always fed Pahlone first. Sometimes she ate nothing herself. In his annual report to the Commissioner of Indian Affairs Agent Carson noted:

> *The hunting grounds of the Tabeguache being in the section of the country where the whites are in search of gold, their game is becoming scarce; much of it having been killed by the settlers, and a great deal of it driven from the country. Hence it will be absolutely necessary to feed them during the approaching winter months . . .* [7]

Over the years Kit Carson and Ouray encountered each other frequently and developed a strong friendship. In addition to Ute, Carson spoke fluent Spanish, a language both men found comfortable. When they first met, Ouray was a budding leader with a small following of young men, and over the years he rose in stature to a subchief in the Tabeguache band. Carson recognized Ouray as a man with a unique understanding of three cultures — Ute, Spanish, and white American — who had a grasp of the social, political, and military conditions of the time that was far greater than any other Ute's. From his youthful experiences in Mexican Territory, Ouray realized that both Mexico and the United States had far greater numbers of men and weapons than the Utes could ever hope to overpower. He knew the Utes must avoid war with the United States at any cost.

In the spring of 1860 Ouray and a few of his men visited the mining camps at California Gulch (later called Leadville) and saw firsthand the growing settlements and the gaping holes dotting the mountainsides where miners dug for gold. He consulted Kit Carson about the exploding growth of settlers who consumed the game animals on which the Utes depended.

Carson made one important point very clear to Ouray: Although the Utes occupied the lands of their ancestors, the United States recognized title only under its own laws. Until the Utes gained recognition of their territory, the United States would take the position that they had no legal rights. The nomadic Utes, who had no written language, did not understand the concept of private land ownership or land titles. The idea that anyone could own the earth was as absurd to them as owning the air they breathed. Carson suggested the Utes could gain their property rights through a treaty with the United States. Ouray understood. He consulted the powerful Ute chief, Nevava, who refused to treaty with the white government, boasting that the Utes could beat the whites back with sticks and stones.[8] In a bold move for a young subchief, Ouray rode to Denver with Kit Carson to meet the territorial governor and offer to council for peace.

Governor John Evans wrote to the U.S. secretary of interior suggesting that the time was ripe for a new peace initiative with the Utes. Congressman Hiram Bennett recommended that before any treaty discussion took place, a delegation of Ute chiefs and headmen should visit Washington City. They needed, he said, to be "awed by the extent and power of the government."[9]

Plans for a peace council progressed at a snail's pace. Mail service between Denver and Washington was slow, and the newly invented telegraph had not reached the frontier. Meanwhile, many changes took place. A new agency was established at Conejos in 1860 to serve the Tabeguache Utes. Carson recommended Ouray to the new agent, Lafayette Head, as a valuable asset. Head particularly needed a translator so he could communicate with his Ute charges and before long he obtained authorization to pay Ouray five hundred dollars a year for his services.

In the late summer of 1861 Tabeguache families traveled east over the mountains and gathered well north of the communities around Denver City to hunt buffalo. While the men were busy with the hunt and the women with processing the kill, Ouray's young sister, Tsashin, disappeared. Ouray, Quenche, and their distraught father abandoned the hunt to search, but they found no trace of her. Chipeta was devastated by the mysterious loss of the girl who had become like her own sister. Realizing for the first time as a mother how easily a child could disappear, she clung to Pahlone. She carried the heavy toddler on her back while she worked, refusing to leave him with the elderly women who cared for children in a hunting camp.

On the way back to the mountains they met a band of northern Ute warriors who reported several recent battles with a band of Arapahos just north of the area where the Tabeguache were hunting. It was likely that Arapaho scouts had been watching the hunting camp and managed to capture the girl. Chipeta must have cried each time she thought of Tsashin and woke in the night shivering with fear at the thought of being taken captive. The family returned to the mountains in despair.

Colorado became an official territory of the United States that year. Abraham Lincoln was president, and Civil War divided the country. Kit Carson accepted a commission in the Union Army. The Union could not fight the Utes, the Plains Indians and the Confederacy at one time, so the newly appointed commissioner of Indian affairs, William P. Dole, stalled plans for a Ute peace delegation visiting Washington City.

By late 1862 Dole had developed his own grand plan for peace in the Colorado Territory. He announced a peace council with leaders of the Ute, Comanche, Kiowa, and Apache tribes. He instructed the Indian agents to assemble delegations of chiefs in St. Joe, Missouri, and travel with the entire group to Washington City. The folly of this plan was immediately clear to the Indian agents. The Utes and the Plains tribes were hostile foes, hardly prepared to discuss peace with each other, much less endure a cross-country trip in the confines of the same railroad car. After consultation with Agent Head, the Governor notified Secretary Dole that the Utes would come as a separate delegation solely to discuss peace between the Utes and the United States.

By facilitating Ouray's first meeting with Governor Evans, Kit Carson had boosted Ouray's standing as a Ute leader in the eyes of the U.S. government. Ouray became the de facto head of the Ute delegation to the peace talks by filling a budgeted position as interpreter. In addition to Ouray's brother, Quenche, the delegates were Puuwich, Pabusat, Showasheit, Tupuwaat and Tuepuepa.[10] Most of these men, like Ouray, were young. Perhaps the older men were unwilling to leave their mountain homeland and sent instead young men eager for adventure. Or perhaps Ouray and Agent Head selected men who would support Ouray's plan to gain legal title to their lands through a treaty. Whatever the reason for the choice of delegates, the chiefs of the other six Ute bands were not informed of this trip. Only Tabeguache men would accompany Ouray on the great expedition into the unknown world to council with the head chief of the United States.[11]

The prospect of the new adventure thrilled Ouray. He would see places no other Utes had seen. He would council with important chiefs of the United States. The more he talked and planned, the more eager he became to get the trip under way. Chipeta, however, did not share his enthusiasm. She was proud that he would have the honor of representing their people in such an important event and she trusted his judgment; but she feared something dreadful would happen to him.

Despite her fears, Chipeta set to work making new clothing for Ouray. He would wear the finest apparel she could produce. She decorated his leggings, each worn tied to a belt at the waist, with a wide band of lazy stitch beading running the length of the side seams. Chipeta trimmed the Ute-style long shirt that he wore over the leggings with a beaded band down each sleeve. Wide bands of beadwork extended from each shoulder down the front and the back. A long slit in the center front allowed him to pull the shirt over his head and also exposed the pipe-stem bead choker that he wore around his neck. She made his moccasins in the traditional style with pointed toes, two bands of beads around the sides, and a beaded circle on the instep.

Chipeta, Pahlone, and a large congregation of other Tabeguache families remained in winter camp. Agent Head purchased two head of cattle and one hundred head of sheep to feed the families while the men of the delegation were away. Chipeta had Pahlone to absorb her time and attention, and she was camped with her older brother, Sapovanero, and other relatives. She also had the help of her fourteen-year-old brother, McCook. She was safe, but her husband was far away in a foreign country that she could not even imagine. She was afraid he might not return.

The delegation, accompanied by Agent Head, left Conejos for Denver on February 3, 1863. A military escort accompanied the group's wagon as they followed the Platte River along a route that took them thirty days to reach St. Joe, Missouri. From there, the sketchy network of rail lines carried them through Chicago, Detroit, and Buffalo with layovers in each city. They arrived in Washington City on March 28 and remained there until April 27. During that time the Ute delegation concluded an agreement of amity and friendship with the government, which was to be confirmed by a formal council with all the Ute leaders in the fall. Ouray was friendly but firm in stating they wanted their land not presents. He suggested that the United States was already fighting one war and could not expect to win a concurrent war with the Utes.

On the return trip they traveled out of St. Joe with three companies of the First Colorado Cavalry and about two hundred civilians headed for the "Promised Land" of Colorado. Missouri was a hotbed of Civil War guerilla fighting, and military escort was necessary to protect the travelers and their valuables. Typical of people journeying through the West, Agent Head carried uncut sheets of negotiable bills strapped to his back to pay the expenses of the return trip.

As the caravan approached the area of present-day Julesburg, they saw a large gathering of Plains Indians. A few months earlier a band of northern Utes had raided a camp of one of the Plains tribes, taken captives, and left behind a mass of bodies. The Plains Indians had heard some Utes were coming in this caravan and they wanted to "have a talk with them."

The cavalry, riding two abreast, closed around the caravan as they moved through the assembly of Plains Indians. When the caravan did not stop on command, a Plains chief grabbed the bridle of the lead horse. Agent Head jumped from the wagon to intervene. Suddenly the lead horse on the first wagon bolted, or was driven on by a well-placed whip, and the whole caravan raced through the surprised assembly and across the plains. They camped overnight in the protection of a U-shaped curve in the Platte River and the next morning were rescued by additional troops.

The delegation stopped ten days at Camp Weld near Denver to rest and report to the governor that there would be peace with the Utes, even if there were no such hope with the Plains tribes. On the way south they indulged their travel-weary bodies in the hot springs near Colorado City. After crossing the Arkansas River near the remains of Fort Pueblo they took a trail into the mountains where, at last, the Utes could relax.

When the delegation arrived at the military post of Fort Garland they were surprised to find their anxious families waiting for them.[12] Chipeta was so relieved to see Ouray again she rushed forward to greet him, but Pahlone was quicker. Ouray bounded from the wagon, hoisted Pahlone in the air, exclaimed how he had grown, and listened intently to the child's excited chatter. He did not notice Chipeta's short-cropped hair, a sign that she had quite recently mourned the death of a relative.

Chipeta allowed Ouray to enjoy the reunion with his son. Then she led him away, along with Quenche, and gave them the news. Not long after the two brothers left for Washington, their father had died in camp at Conejos.[13] Chipeta related the information simply. She did not want to risk binding their father's spirit to the earth by talking too much about him or calling him by name. The brothers walked together behind the officer's quarters for a short time, then stoically rejoined the celebrating crowd.

The men of the delegation were the center of attention all evening as they told and retold stories of their travels. Later, in the quiet of their teepee Ouray described for Chipeta the places he had seen. Through his eyes Chipeta had a glimpse of the strange world outside her mountain home. Ouray had traveled on a train. It was difficult to describe. It was like a white man's house on wheels that rolled on metal poles with no horses to pull it. The train snorted smoke and steam and traveled almost as fast as a horse could run. As the train carried them eastward Ouray saw wide stretches of grassy prairie and dense forests. There were rivers wider than any he had seen before with boats so large the whole Ute camp could ride on one. He saw a great lake that the white men called "ocean." It was so big Ouray could not see land on the other side.

The cities near the ocean looked nothing like the towns springing up in Colorado. In the east there were brick streets lined with trees and houses of brick and stone or colorfully painted wood. Fine, high-stepping horses pulled flimsy little carts called carriages. Stout horses with wide hooves hauled work wagons. Over and over Ouray interrupted a story to tell Chipeta about another horse he had wanted to bring home. The people, he said, wore strange clothing that looked too tight for comfort, or even for breathing. He slept poorly inside a white man's house, called a hotel, where the air was hot and stale. The food was hard to eat — overcooked and too rich for his stomach. Ouray could not imagine, he said, how the white people could live like that.

His stories occupied many days and were repeated over and over for visitors. He raised his hand high above his head as he described in detail the Great Father Abraham who had presented Ouray with a silver tipped cane.[14] One observation he reserved for Chipeta alone. Though the head chief of the United States had greeted the Ute delegation, he had not participated in their talks as expected. The Great Father Abraham appeared burdened with many worries.

The next day Ouray surprised Chipeta when he emerged from the teepee dressed as a white man. He wore a black Stonewill suit, a white shirt buttoned tight around his neck and bound with a necktie, black boots, and a wide-brimmed black hat. Chipeta smiled politely, struggling to control her desire to laugh at the impractical getup. When she had gained composure, she told Ouray that he looked most handsome but she preferred him in his familiar buckskins.

Ouray explained that, when they reached St. Joe, Missouri, Agent Head had purchased a suit of clothes for each member of the delegation so they would meet eastern standards of dress.[15] Suddenly Chipeta's expression changed. What about the fine suit of clothes she had made for him? Had he not worn them? "The clothes you made," Ouray said, "I wore for the most important meeting with the Great Father Abraham."

One summer afternoon a group of northern Utes rode into camp and delivered a great surprise — Tsashin. They had found

*Although often identified as Chipeta this photo is of Ouray's sister Tsashin or "Susan." Denver Public Library, Western History Department, X-30460*

her walking through the mountains and provided her a horse and an escort to locate Ouray's camp. Tears streamed down Chipeta's face as she ran to embrace the girl who had become a young woman. She sent McCook to find Ouray and Quenche who were off visiting other camps to talk about their experiences with the delegation to Washington City. That evening the whole family gathered to welcome Tsashin home and hear her tales of two years in captivity, her rescue, and the long trek home. The reunion was tinged with sadness, however, that Tsashin's father had not lived to see her safely returned.

Sergeant William Carroll of Company M, First Colorado Cavalry, claimed responsibility for Tsashin's rescue. He reported that she was found in an Arapaho camp on the Platte River near the mouth of the Cache La Poudre River. The Arapahos were about to sacrifice her in vengeance for the loss of a number of their own warriors killed by a band of Utes. Sergeant Carroll with a squad of men rode into the camp in the nick of time.

The sergeant took Tsashin to his home where his wife was able to soothe the frightened girl. Mrs. Carroll soon came to like the bright Tsashin. She taught the girl a little English, made dresses for her, and seemed prepared to make her part of the family. Mrs. Carroll called her Susan. On the Fourth of July, the Carrolls went to a dance some miles down the creek. When they returned, Tsashin was gone. She had taken with her the clothes Mrs. Carroll had made, a piece of meat, and a butcher knife.[16]

Tsashin did not stay long with Ouray and Chipeta. She soon accepted a marriage with a northern Ute called Canella and, contrary to custom, left to begin a new life among her husband's people. Although she no longer saw her family often, whenever a runner left the northern Ute camp to deliver a message to the Tabeguache, Tsashin sent a greeting and her own news.

Ouray and the other men of the delegation spent the summer traveling the mountains to tell the dispersed Ute groups about their experiences in Washington City. They talked about meeting the Great Father and lobbied support for the treaty council to be held at Conejos in October. Agent Head had sent official notices of the council meeting to the agents in charge of other Ute bands. Ouray sent messengers to the chiefs.

In the meantime, the Tabeguache decided they needed a buffalo hunt before the council. Some six hundred Tabeguache traveled to the chosen hunting grounds, setting up camp northeast of Denver City near present-day Fort Lupton.[17] The trip took them right through the heart of the new white settlements and the campsite was on the fringe territory of the same Plains Indians who had so recently confronted the returning delegation — the same Indians who had held Tsashin captive for two years. The Utes camped close enough to taunt their long-time enemies on the plains. Perhaps that was the plan. The invasion of white settlers had the Utes in turmoil, but Ouray had convinced them they could not win a war against the Americans. The aggravated Utes were itching for a fight; and Ouray, like many warriors, relished the danger, the challenge, and the sport of battle. If they could not fight the white intruders, the Plains Indians were a suitable substitute.

Chipeta remained in the main camp where the women processed the meat while all but the old men went out in small groups to set up hunting camps. Ouray took Pahlone and a few men to a location several miles north. There are a variety of tales about what happened next. Some reports say over a hundred Sioux warriors made a surprise attack in the night. In other stories the aggressors were Kiowa, Arapaho or Cheyenne. All agree that Ouray's camp was attacked. In the fracas three or more Utes were killed; half the horses were stolen; and when the dust settled, Pahlone was gone.

Ten years later a newspaper reporter presented yet another account reportedly told by Ouray. With a small hunting party of five men, Ouray and Pahlone camped in Platte Canyon about forty-eight miles from Denver City. Around daybreak the boy wandered away. Ouray set out to find him. Half a mile from camp Arapaho and Cheyenne warriors surrounded him. Single-handedly Ouray fought them for an hour before the other Utes came to his aid. The hand-to-hand battle continued into the late afternoon. The Utes at last routed the attackers and claimed seven scalps, but, while they fought, a Cheyenne brave spirited Pahlone away. [18]

The bottom line in all the tales was that Pahlone disappeared. Chipeta's anguished wails pierced the night when she learned her boy was gone. The women tried to comfort her while Ouray and a group of warriors gave chase. They found no sign of the attackers or Pahlone. It was a dispirited Ouray who faced Chipeta with the news that he had failed to rescue their child.

Hunting ceased as the men rode out again and again in search of Pahlone or any Plains Indians who could be punished for the boy's disappearance. After two days Ouray cancelled the search. He knew they had to return to the safety of the mountains before the Plains Indians assembled a larger attack force. He and Chipeta rode somberly back to the west side of the mountains burdened with a great emptiness. Ouray sent messengers to other Ute bands alerting them to look for the boy if they encountered any of the Plains tribes. He asked Agent Head to contact other agents for help in recovering his son.

Chipeta fastened her mind on Tsashin's miraculous return. Knowing that a lost child could be recovered gave Chipeta hope. For months she rushed from her teepee at the sound of a rider racing into camp. Each time she thought this visitor would bring word of Pahlone or even deliver the boy himself. Each time she was disappointed. Eventually she gained control of her feet, but her heart continued to leap at the thunder of hooves.

Ouray was preoccupied with many meetings in preparation for the impending great council, but Pahlone was never far from his thoughts. More and more he sought solace with Chipeta. He talked to her about issues facing the council, the pros and cons of possible decisions, and the attitudes of each participant. It was unusual for men to discuss such matters with their women, but Chipeta was interested and even encouraged his confidences. They talked during long walks in the forests and late into the night. Chipeta needed this distraction, and she threw her entire attention to understanding

*A typical Ute family from an exhibit at the Ute Museum, Montrose, CO. Colorado Historical Society, F-19670*

the issues. By the time the appointed date arrived, Chipeta understood the need for a treaty better than did most of the men who would attend the council.

Golden aspen leaves shimmered on the mountainsides when the treaty council began on October 1, 1863. The schedule coincided with the distribution of government annuities, a carefully laid plan intended to ensure that many Utes would attend. President Lincoln's personal secretary, John L. Nicolay, led the team of government-appointed commissioners, which included Superintendent of Indian Affairs for New Mexico Territory Michael Stech; Colorado's territorial governor, John L, Evans; and Ute Indian agents Simeon Whitely and Lafayette Head. They arrived accompanied by a contingent of military men and wagons loaded with flour, sugar, coffee, and blankets to distribute to the Indians.

Fifteen hundred of the estimated four thousand Tabeguache Utes arrived at Conejos for the council. Yet the small Capote band sent only one chief, and the similarly sized band of five hundred Mouache sent three chiefs. No representatives of Nevava's two thousand Weeminuche appeared. The Grand River and Uintah bands also declined to make the long journey.[19]

There was an opening ceremony of sorts with introductions of the commissioners and the chiefs and headmen who would participate in the discussions. The soldiers of the escort company gave a demonstration of military weapons. Then for several days the commissioners held council with the chiefs and headmen, followed by private councils among the Utes. Ouray was asked to serve as interpreter for the Utes. With his commanding presence and confident speeches delivered in fluent Spanish, he appeared to the white men present to be the chief spokesman of all the assembled Utes.

Such a gathering of Ute families so seldom seen was usually a special treat for Chipeta. On this occasion, however, the sight of happy children enjoying their games caused her to search for Pahlone's animated face among the group. In the painful awareness of his absence she may have welcomed an opportunity to spend time in the isolation of the menstrual teepee. This special lodging was set away from the heart of the main camp to protect the men from women's monthly cycle of blood that was thought to weaken the power of warriors. As they passed the days waiting for their menstrual cycles to end, the women talked and sewed. Chipeta could lose her sorrow in her beadwork.

On October 7, 1863, the commissioners and the chiefs concluded a treaty. Because only the Tabeguache Utes traditionally used most of the land where settlement and mining were currently taking place, the commissioners elected to negotiate with only the Tabeguache. Besides, they were the only ones present in any great number. The resulting treaty released any Tabeguache claim to that part of their territory east of the Continental Divide. The Tabeguache agreed to allow building of roads, mail stations, and federal military posts on Tabeguache land. The Mouache, who also occupied the land given up, were to go either to New Mexico reservations or combine with the Tabeguache. They granted white

*One of the earliest photographs of Ouray, taken about 1865. He wears his peace medal and sports a cane.*

*Courtesy of Main Street Photography, Montrose, CO*

travelers safe passage through their territory and allowed mining by U.S. citizens.

In return, the United States agreed to give the
Tabeguache Utes ten thousand dollars in household goods and
ten thousand dollars in provisions annually for ten years, five
American stallions, and, as an incentive to take up farming,
750 cattle and 3,500 sheep to be provided over a period of five
years. The government agreed to establish a blacksmith shop
at the agency and employ a blacksmith to repair guns and agricultural equipment. Finally, the government pledged to protect
the Indians in the quiet and peaceable possession of their lands
so long as they conformed to the terms of the treaty.[20]

After the agreement was made the participants smoked
the peace pipe, and nine chiefs made their marks on a treaty
document they could not read. Of the original delegation that
traveled to Washington City in the spring, only Ouray and his
brother Quenche signed the treaty.[21] Nicolay awarded silver
medals to seven chiefs who, he reported, had been the most
cooperative.[22] One by one Nicolay solemnly lifted a medal and
slipped the cord over each chief's head as he announced that
this was a symbol of their perpetual friendship with the government. Whether these were the same seven men who went
to Washington or true chiefs of the Tabeguache is unclear.
Ouray was later photographed wearing the distinctive Lincoln
Peace Medal[23] around his neck while also prominently display-
ing the silver tipped cane the president had presented to him
as head of the delegation.[24]

The stress of the tribal politics and council meetings was
over. The treaty was settled. But Pahlone was still missing.

---

[1] U.S. Census Bureau, 1860 census, <www.npg.org/states/co.htm> viewed
May 6, 2002.

[2] Nicolay, John G., *Special Observations, Report of Secretary of Interior*, 1863,
(Washington, D.C.: Government Printing Office, 1863), 266. The esti-
mated count of Utes supplied by Indian agents included 500 Muache, 800
Capote, 2,000 Weeminuche, 4,000 Tabeguache, and 2,500 Grand River.

[3] Brown, Dee, *Bury My Heart At Wounded Knee*, (New York: Holt, Rinehart
& Winston, 1970), 166.

[4] *Rocky Mountain News,* September 3, 1859.

[5] *Rocky Mountain News,* September 10, 1859.

[6] Dunlay, Tom, *Kit Carson & The Indians,* (Lincoln: University of Nebraska Press, 2000), 215-216.

[7] Ibid., 218.

[8] Roberts, Dan, *A Story of the Centennial State,* (Grand Junction, Colo: Eagle Tail Press, 1973),154.

[9] Viola, Herman, research notes for his book *Diplomats in Buckskin,* Collection of the National Anthropological Archives, Washington, D.C.

[10] Delegation expense records, NARA Record Group 75, Box 2337-C-1863.

[11] Viola, research notes.

[12] Downing, Finis E., "With The Ute Delegation of 1863 — Across The Plains and At Conejjos"; *Colorado Magazine,* (September 1945), 201.

[13] *Denver Daily Times,* October 9, 1873, 2.

[14] Wood, David Jr.,"Chief Ouray and the Washington Hatchet," *Grand Junction Sentinel,* October 6, 1974.

[15] Delegation expense records.

[16] Carroll, Sgt. William C., personal account, *Golden Transcript,* December 17, 1879.

[17] Howbert, Irving, *Indians of the Pikes Peak Region,* (New York: The Knickerbocker Press, 1914), tells the story of the hunting episode and loss of Pahlone.

[18] *Denver Daily Times,* October 9, 1873, 2.

[19] Nicolay, 266, 268-269; Governor Evans, in his report in the same publication, identifies the Mequache (sic) as the non-attending band. However, since during the council meetings Mouache land was ceded and an agreement made for the Mouache to move onto Tabeguache land, it appears that Nicolay more correctly identified the Weeminuche as the absent band.

[20] Kappler, Charles J., *Indian Affairs: Laws and Treaties,* Vol II, (Washington, DC: Government Printing Office, 1904) 856-859.

[21] The nine chiefs who placed their "X" on the treaty were: (meaning of names written by interpreter) Un Cow Rat Gut = Red Color, Sha Wa She Yet = Blue Flower, Colorado [Colorow], U-Ray = Arrow, No Va Vetu Quar Et = One who slides under the snow, Sa Wa Wat Se Wich = Blue River, A Cu Mu Che Ne = Red Wind, Sa Patchi = While Warm, Cinche [Quenche] = Left Hand.

[22] Evans, John, Ex-Officio Commissioner of Indian Affairs for Colorado Territory, *Report of the Secretary of Interior,* (Washington, D.C.: Government Printing Office, 1863), 244.

[23] Belden, Bauman L., *Indian Peace Medals Issued in the United States,* (New Milford, Conn: N. Flayderman & Company, 1966), 36 and Plate 17.

[24] Ibid, 36.

## Chapter 3
# TREATY
# WOES

Confident that they now had title to their land, Ouray, Chipeta, and the rest of the Utes resumed life as usual. Word came now and then that the Plains Indians were aggressively attempting to drive out white settlers by attacking stagecoaches and wagon trains bringing supplies from the East. Because few white men ventured over the Snowy Range (as the Continental Divide was known), the Utes were content to let someone else fight the whites, and so much the better should they succeed.

In early December 1864, Ouray and Chipeta were preparing for a hunting trip when a rider pounded into camp. Leaping from his lathered pony the messenger barely halted for permission to enter the teepee. The breathless man ducked inside and spit out his news. The American army had massacred a large camp of peaceful Cheyenne on the plains at Sand Creek.[1] Ouray pressed for details. As Chipeta heard the gruesome account of the slaughter of women, elderly people and innocent little children, a desire to wail choked in her throat.

More chilling news followed. The leader of the ruthless army unit was a man called Chivington. Ouray and Chipeta

*The Sand Creek Massacre as painted by Robert Lindneaux.*
*Colorado Historical Society, F-40341*

exchanged worried glances. They remembered the somber Colonel Chivington who had so recently accompanied the governor to Conejos for the treaty council. On the first day the governor asked the army to give a demonstration of a small cannon. They set up the artillery in the meadow a good distance from the crowd. Six times as the weapon blasted down stout trees its thunder resounded in the valley and echoed in the ears of the assembled Utes. Chipeta could still see Chivington standing stiffly beside the governor, a satisfied smile curling his lip as he read astonishment and fear in the faces of Utes. She pictured that same smile twisting his mouth as he struck down Cheyenne women and children. Chipeta must have wondered, is this what peace with the white man brings?

Details of the Cheyenne slaughter spread among Ute camps during the winter. Such brutal treatment, even for their Cheyenne enemies, stunned the Utes. Chief Black Kettle of the Cheyenne had made a peace settlement with the governor, which included a promise that his people would be protected by troops at Fort Lyon. Now there were reports that Governor Evans had authorized settlers to shoot renegade Cheyennes on sight.[2] The situation raised many questions for the Utes.

Would a white man know the difference between a Cheyenne and a Ute? Would the governor, who so recently sat in treaty council with the Utes, treat them with any more respect than he had shown the Cheyenne?

The massacre, the problem of the white invaders, and the questionable trustworthiness of the U.S. government generated heated debates during the cold months. Wary families changed their usual spring and summer routes to avoid coming anywhere near white ranches or mining camps. Remaining within the territory defined by their treaty began to seem appealing.

Nature, however, intervened in the best-laid Ute plans. Drought claimed the vegetation that sustained the already dwindling herds of game animals. There simply was not sufficient wild game and vegetation for everyone. The risks of encountering white settlers were forgotten as the Utes struggled to find enough food. To make matters worse, the supplies promised by the government in the new treaty did not appear. Some hungry Utes began to kill ranchers' sheep and cattle.

By early spring of 1865 many Ute bands migrated back to their favorite hunting places on the forbidden eastern slope of the Rockies. Ouray and Chipeta were among a large assembly of Utes who camped on South Fountain Creek near Colorado City in hopes of finding game. Frightened by the presence of one hundred lodges, the town residents protested to the governor that the Utes were in violation of their treaty. Agent Head intervened and responded to the complaints through the *Rocky Mountain News:*

> *I met the Tabeguache on the 5th [of April] at Colorado City and had no trouble whatever, in prevailing upon them to leave and return to their reservation. I found them in a truly destitute condition and issued to them a reasonable amount of flour for the support of their families on the journey home. The current report of their aggressions towards whites in the vicinity of Colorado City was without foundation and to a person familiar with these Indians, no trouble need be apprehended from that quarter. Owing to the*

*difficulties on the plains, these Indians did not receive*
*their presents from the Government last season and are*
*therefore poor and needy.*[3]

Ouray and Chipeta left Fountain Creek with their family and moved to a spring campsite in a high mountain meadow. They were busy catching fish one day when a messenger brought the news that the Great Father Abraham was dead. As the messenger related details of the murder, Chipeta surely cried for Mary Lincoln, a white woman she did not know who lived a world away in distance and culture. Chipeta understood Mary's pain. She and Mary had both lost sons — sweet, lively boys on the verge of revealing glimpses of the men they might become. Now Mary had lost her husband. A shiver crawled up Chipeta's spine at the memory of her own intense fear that Ouray would not return from the trip to Washington. Across the great span of distance and time she held Mary Lincoln in her heart.

In July 1865, a party of Mexicans killed three Utes on Mosca Pass. The governor called for an investigation. Ouray and Chipeta were present at the inquiry in which the investigators determined that the Mexicans shot in self-defense. Ouray had listened to all of the testimony and was satisfied with the fairness of the decision. However, relatives of the three Utes, including the dissident Colorow, disagreed and complained bitterly that Ouray had sided with the Mexicans in the affair. Before this incident was settled, the next one had begun.

On the last day of the investigation, the Ute war chief Shavano left his camp on Indian Creek and rode east. Encountering a Mexican traveler, Shavano whipped the man and took his saddlebags. He continued his one-man campaign of retaliation by stealing five horses from settlers on the Fountain and Arkansas Rivers. Complaints flew to the governor who ordered another investigation. It was a long summer of unrest.

In early autumn Ouray and Chipeta joined several Tabeguache families in a camp along the Huerfano River to hunt deer and harvest piñon nuts. Nearby in the little town of

Badito was the trading post of Don Satillo Piño where the Utes had done business for some years. A young man named Benton Canon, a wide-eyed nineteen-year-old and a new arrival in the west, was employed in Piño's general store. Canon's jovial employer loaded up a wagon with trade goods and insisted that the young man try his hand at trading with Chief Ouray and his band. Despite Canon's protests he was sent on his way with a Mexican interpreter.

Canon stayed with the wagon at the edge of the Ute camp while the interpreter went in with presents for the chief and a request for permission to trade. As he waited Canon recounted every graphic story of wild, savage Indians he had heard since his arrival in Colorado Territory. He recalled the tales of Ouray the fierce warrior and pictured him as "a monster, presumably with horns, eagle feathers and a scalping knife ready for action."[4] Trembling at the ferocious image looming in his mind, Canon looked up to see fifty painted and buckskin clad Indians advancing toward him through a sea of barking and snarling dogs. The dogs frightened the team of oxen and young Canon. He was sure he was about to meet his end.

The terrified young man was dumbfounded when the leader of the group pushed a pretty young woman forward and said, "My squaw" in English. The Mexican interpreter elbowed the speechless Canon and whispered that he should offer a present to the chief's woman. Canon managed to recover his senses enough to find a pair of silver bracelets. The chief nodded his satisfaction and invited the men and their wagon into camp. The interpreter assured Canon that he had, indeed, just met Ouray and Chipeta.

The vigorous trading did not stop until the last goods were sold and Canon's wagon was piled high with more than three hundred animal hides plus beaded bags and moccasins. Ouray invited Canon and the interpreter to his teepee where Chipeta offered them fresh venison stew. To Canon's surprise, he and Ouray carried on a lively discussion about life back east compared with life on the frontier. Chipeta listened to their talk as she roasted piñon nuts, expertly bouncing them in a basket she held over the fire. Ouray brought out tobacco and a pipe, which he lighted and passed to his guests. While they smoked Ouray asked Chipeta to sing, and she obliged without stopping her work. Although the Ute melodies sounded strange to the guests, her sweet voice charmed them. In the sanctuary of the teepee Canon came to know a friendly couple unlike anything stories of savage Indians had led him to expect. Late in the evening Ouray sent two young men to escort their guests and their wagon safely back to Badito. Canon recounted the experience for the rest of his life.[5]

The full Tabeguache band gathered in South Park in mid-October for a buffalo hunt. While there, Agent Lafayette Head arrived with important news — Governor Evans had resigned. Mounting evidence of his role in encouraging the Sand Creek Massacre had led President Andrew Johnson to demand his resignation.[6] Head reported that Alexander Cummings had been named to replace Evans.

Few citizens ever knew that Evans had used the Utes as a bargaining chip in an attempt to forestall his departure from office. Stating that he had the full confidence of the Utes with whom he was in the midst of negotiations, Evans privately asked the secretary of interior to intercede on his behalf with the president. Only his continued personal participation in the capacity of governor, he suggested, could prevent bloody war in Colorado Territory. In his next council with the Utes, he pledged that he would resolve their lingering complaints about the killing of three Utes by Mexicans and also deliver their annuities. He closed his plea with a warning about the danger of thrusting a new man into this volatile situation. "No one," he stated, "can gain the confidence of the Indians in a day."[7]

Evans's manipulations fell on deaf ears in Washington. The new governor, Cummings, accepted the challenge and traveled to South Park to assure that the Utes received their annuities. Cummings arrived with more than food, clothing, and blankets. He delivered seventeen hundred sheep, which had been offered as an incentive in the 1863 treaty but never delivered. Cummings held an impromptu council with the Tabeguache chiefs in which Ouray's services as translator again made him spokesman for the Utes. After all the spring and summer conflicts with settlers, the governor asked the chiefs to reaffirm their 1863 agreement to stay on the west side of the Snowy Range. The chiefs not only agreed but requested that their agency be moved farther west so they would not so frequently come in contact with the white settlements when visiting their agent.

Cummings took a giant step toward winning the Utes confidence in a day or two. He returned to Denver City praising Ouray's good sense and untiring efforts to keep the tribe from difficulty with the whites. Being able to support themselves by raising sheep and living in permanent settlements, the governor noted, was the first step to becoming civilized.[8]

The year that followed, 1866, was a quiet one, and Chipeta enjoyed Ouray's relatively uninterrupted presence. They had time to talk and take the long walks they both enjoyed. Chipeta shared Ouray's optimism that their people were finally coming to accept the benefits of the treaty. They spent part of the summer camped with their family group on the west side of the upper Arkansas River (near present day Salida).

One day three wagons trailing a few cows and a pair of goats came from the north, driving along the opposite side of the river. As the procession passed the Ute camp, Chipeta saw that they were white families. She also observed that each man kept a rifle balanced on his lap while the fearful-eyed women held the children tight and surveyed the Ute camp. Chipeta watched as they continued southward. Twice the wagons halted and one of the men jumped down, walked down to the water's edge, and returned shaking his head and gesturing with his hands. They were searching, Chipeta realized, for a place to ford the river into the broad meadows that lay on the west side. The water was high and swift flowing with runoff from late spring snows that had blanketed the high mountains. Crossing was dangerous even at the two best points. She summoned Ouray from the teepee, and the two mounted their horses and rode downriver after the settlers.

When they were directly across the water from the last wagon, Chipeta saw the driver's hand drop to rest on his rifle. Ouray saw the movement too. Raising his hand in greeting he called out in English that there was a place ahead to cross the river. The driver, his hand still on his rifle, called back to ask how far. Ouray and Chipeta rode ahead and crossed the river. The settlers arrived to find them waiting beside their horses. The lead driver climbed down from the wagon without his gun and walked forward to talk with Ouray. After a few minutes of conversation the man turned toward the wagons and called, "It's alright, Ma." Ouray and Chipeta did more than simply show the settlers the crossing point; they stayed to help them move the wagons and the livestock safely to the other side. It was not the first time, nor the last, that they befriended travelers and settlers.

By late summer Ouray and Chipeta had moved on to Mosca Pass, where they set up camp with enough Ute families to number about one hundred lodges. There had been no rain

*Chief Kaniache, the war chief of the Mouache Utes. Denver Public Library, Western History Department, A. Zeese & Co. Photographer, X-30715*

during the summer, and grasshoppers had stripped much of the low vegetation. The deer and elk looked lean, but Ouray brought home several fat mountain sheep with the thin skins that Chipeta prized for making soft dresses. This pleasant interlude was broken by the arrival of a messenger in early October with word of new trouble. A rebellious Mouache chief called Kaniache and his band of Utes were starving, and they had returned to the forbidden eastern mountains to camp on Raton Pass, near present-day Trinidad, Colorado. Allegations by local settlers that the Utes had stolen horses and corn brought a company of the U.S. Third Cavalry from Fort Stevens. Captain Alexander confronted Kaniache, who insisted his band was on Ute land and when the Utes were hungry they would come and take what they needed. Kaniache and his band moved on to the Purgatoire River, where they stole more livestock. Soon the cavalry was in hot pursuit of the renegades.

Ouray left immediately on a forty-mile ride to Fort Garland to consult Kit Carson. Carson had been assigned in April to command the military post and to keep peace between the Jicarillas, Utes, Plains tribes, and the Hispanic and Anglo settlers. This task was not trivial, yet minimal resources were provided — a garrison of less than eighty men.[9] The army was counting on the power of Carson's personality and the goodwill established in his past tenure as Indian agent. No less a person than General William Tecumseh Sherman stated, with perhaps a touch of envy, "Those redskins think Kit twice as big a man as me. Why his integrity is simply perfect. They know it, and they would believe him and trust him any day before me."[10]

Carson had also received a messenger with news of the trouble with Kaniache. Certain that war with the Utes was imminent, he sent riders to warn area settlers and recruit militia volunteers. His messenger sent to Governor Cummings carried an alert of probable Ute war. Ouray arrived on October 6 to assure Carson that he had no interest in a fight. Although there were young Tabeguache men eager to demonstrate their prowess in battle, Ouray insisted he could control them. A much-relieved Carson suggested the Tabeguache come to the fort and camp nearby. Yet another messenger interrupted their meeting to report that the cavalry continued to pursue Kaniache, who had taken a woman and several children captive and was headed toward Mosca Pass. Both Carson and Ouray saw the makings of a battle if the aggressive cavalrymen, Kaniache's agitated warriors, and Ouray's eager young men collided. Ouray left immediately, accompanied by a sergeant from the camp who could intervene, if needed, with the cavalry.

Chipeta was still on her knees massaging brains into the last of three hides even though darkness had settled on the camp. Ouray roared in, the soldier in tow, barking orders to pack up and prepare to leave at first light. Chipeta knew by his tone that it was best not to ask questions, so she rolled up her hides and started packing. Ouray held a long meeting with the headmen and chiefs, and only late in the night did Chipeta hear the full story of the disaster heading their way.

Before daybreak they extinguished the campfires, pulled down the teepee covers, tied lodge poles over the backs of horses for travois, loaded goods, and set out toward the east. An escort sent by Carson met them part way, and by October 9 the camp was safely established in a familiar spot near the Fort Garland compound.

An isolated military outpost on a windswept plain, the fort sat on a plateau between two rivers at the eastern end of the San Luis Valley. The great hulk of Mount Blanca loomed to the north, and ranges of mountains were visible in every direction. The views were unobstructed. According to one writer, "A quieter, more peaceful, less military post . . . would be hard to find."[11]

The fort was built in the square plaza style of New Mexico with a grassy parade ground surrounded by long, low buildings with thick adobe walls. In addition to the barracks, supply buildings, and stables, the fort included a small hospital and a trading post. The commandant's six-room quarters were centered on the north side of the square with Carson's office facing the parade grounds. The adjoining family area — parlor, kitchen, dining room, and two bedrooms — enclosed a private courtyard.

The Utes camped to the east below the fort among clusters of cottonwood trees lining the Rio Sangre de Christo. As soon as the horses were unloaded, Ouray and most of the men rode up to the fort. The women and children worked together to set up teepees and prepare the camp.

Late in the afternoon, with the teepee organized and food in the cook pot, Chipeta paused to rest and savor her surroundings. The valley's velvety grass had turned a rosy salmon hue in the early chill, and its fragrance sweetened the air. Downy sage covered the low hills, and a blanket of dark green pines wrapped the high slopes. Behind her, the sun filtered through the cottonwoods creating dappled patterns on the teepees and sparkles on the river water. The slightest movement caught her attention, and she tilted back her head to find a golden eagle floating on the breeze. With no perceptible movement of its wings, the great bird coasted in wide circles over the camp. Chipeta returned to her tasks revived by the appearance of this good omen.

Ouray sent a messenger to find Kaniache, telling him to cease marauding among the white settlements and come to Fort Garland. Whether it was Ouray's command or the presence of his trusted friend Kit Carson that made the difference, Kaniache and his band arrived a few days later. Carson, Ouray, and Kaniache counciled, the captives were released unharmed, and the stolen livestock returned. A bloody war was averted.

After restoring the peace with Kaniache and his band, Kit Carson and his family gave a feast for the Utes in the dining hall. During the evening one of the Muache Utes boasted to Carson's daughter that he was wearing shoes taken from a white woman he had killed. The shocked girl refused to serve him any food, and the Ute slapped her with his riding whip.

Carson, the enraged father, rushed the offending Ute to teach him a very physical lesson. Carson's wife, Josepha, intervened. With a firm hand on his arm she stopped her husband in the midst of his blind rage from killing the Indian. She talked quietly to him until he was calm. Carson then recognized that he had been on the verge of undoing the very peace they were celebrating that night.

Josepha Jaramillo Carson came from a respected Spanish family in Santa Fe. She was beautiful, educated, and refined. Although they seemed unlikely friends, Chipeta was welcome female company in the remote outpost of Fort Garland, and Josepha and Chipeta found much to talk about. Chipeta became a frequent visitor during their long stay, and she and Ouray often dined with the family at a table set with Wedgwood china and ivory-handled flatware.

Josepha offered a window into the Spanish culture that had so influenced Ouray's youth. In fact, she became a role model for Chipeta, and it was not just a matter of table manners. A few years later Chipeta intervened to stop Ouray from a vengeful attack, just as she had seen Josepha do at the Fort Garland feast.

Although Chipeta was fifteen years younger than Josepha, the two women had much in common, most prominently a love of children. Josepha had five or six rambunctious offspring by 1866, and her household included an orphaned niece and one or two other children. Chipeta longed for such a brood and enjoyed being in their midst.

It may have been the time spent with the Carson family that spurred Chipeta to take action about her own childless state. Shortly after this period she and Ouray apparently acquired some children in the Ute's loose fashion of adoption by simply accepting a child into the family. They took in a girl named Cooroopits, born about 1864, two boys named Antonio and Atchu, and a girl called Sowanarotance.

Both Josepha Carson and Chipeta married older men who shouldered great responsibilities. Their husbands were close friends and confidants who enjoyed time spent together. The frequent absences of these husbands left the wives in full charge of family affairs. The women also shared great concern for the innocent people whose way of life, and very lives, were threatened by the clash of cultures that erupted in the struggle for power in the Rocky Mountain region.

With such a large gathering of Tabeguache Utes at Fort Garland, Carson requested that Governor Cummings come there to distribute annuities. The governor took the opportunity to convene another council, this time with Carson as translator. In addition to one more plea for the Mouache, Capote, and Weeminuche bands to stay out of the eastern mountains, the governor broached the idea of giving up more land for the use of white settlers.

The Utes balked. Ouray eloquently stated the position of his people:

> *Long time ago, Utes always had plenty. On the prairie, antelope and buffalo, so many Ouray couldn't count. In the mountains, deer and bear everywhere. In the streams, trout, duck, beaver, everything . . . White man came, and now Utes go hungry a heap. Game much go every year — hard to shoot now. Old man often weak for want of food. Squaw and papoose cry. Only strong brave live. White man grow a heap, red man no grow — soon die all.* [12]

Ouray was adamant. The Utes would not give up any more land! There would be no new agreement. The annihilation of the Cheyenne at Sand Creek had further eroded the Utes' trust in the United States government. Ouray's new stand was popular among the Utes and bolstered his leadership.

The winter of 1866-67 was harsh and bitter, one of the worst in memory. A thousand or more hungry Utes camped around Colorado Springs and Denver and went begging for food. The Tabeguache, the only band with a treaty, had their government annuity provisions, which the governor was conscientious in providing. Ouray's decision to make a treaty began to look like a wise one, especially to other bands of Utes who were starving.

Before long a new territorial governor, A. C. Hunt, proposed that another delegation of Ute chiefs travel to Washington (now Washington, District of Columbia) for treaty talks. This time chiefs from all five Ute bands in Colorado Territory would participate. The Ute band in Utah and their agent would also go to Washington for concurrent talks. General confidence increased when the Utes learned that Kit

Carson had been appointed superintendent of Indian affairs for Colorado Territory and would accompany them to Washington.

Chipeta was not happy that Ouray would again make the long trip to the east, but she was no longer consumed with fear. His detailed accounts of his travels made the unknown land of the white man seem less intimidating. She updated his wardrobe with a generously fringed shirt.

The challenges of the past five years that she had shared with Ouray built her self-confidence and her understanding of the issues that confronted her people. Although the adopted children required her attention, she listened carefully to the talk in camp and gathered information for Ouray while she waited for his return.

Agent Head, interpreter William J. Godfrey, and the Colorado Ute chiefs left on January 22, 1868. Since their 1863 trip, the railroad had made its way west to Cheyenne, reducing travel time considerably. The delegation included Ouray's trusted friend, Guero, and Kaniache, Ankatosh, Jose Maria, Piah, Nicaagut, Paant, Suviap, and Pabusat. Kit Carson joined the delegation at St. Louis.

The Capote, Weeminuche, and Mouache bands viewed the trip as an opportunity to get title to their traditional territory with a treaty of their own. The government, however, had plans "to concentrate [three Ute] tribes on one reservation in the Uncompahgre country," [13] as Tabeguache lands were often called.

President Andrew Johnson received the delegation at the White House on February 5 and gave them a tour and a speech. Everyone in Washington treated Ouray as the leader of the delegation without him ever being appointed such by the Utes. The northern and southern chiefs, still rankled by their exclusion from the 1863 delegation, were further aggravated by Ouray's assumed position; but he had become so firmly planted as head chief in the view of the U.S. government that it appeared impossible to dislodge him.

A series of councils followed. At first the Utes balked at government proposals, but the promise of large amounts of annuities resulted in a new treaty agreement signed by all of the Ute chiefs present on March 21, 1868. After the signing, some members of the Ute delegations agreed to pose for Matthew Brady's camera.

In addition to getting the other Ute bands to affirm the 1863 treaty made with the Tabeguache, the 1868 treaty set new boundaries on fifteen million acres of land, recognizing Ute ownership of roughly the western third of Colorado Territory. Unfortunately, none of the boundaries were physical features that the Utes could identify. Survey lines and such technical terms as *longitude* and *latitude* meant nothing to them. The government refused to use rivers or mountain ranges for the boundaries as the Utes had requested. Although they sacrificed more land, the Utes did gain title to a reservation. They also gained two official new agencies — one at White River for the Grand River and Yampa bands and another at Los Piños for the Tabeguache and any of the southern Utes who joined them. Ouray boldly asserted that, since U.S. law now protected Ute land, he expected soldiers to guard their land if necessary. It might have been one of the best treaties ever negotiated with the United States by a Native American tribe.

Ouray and Kit Carson arrived back in Denver on March 25, 1868. Railroad travel to the East was so much improved that the trip from Washington to Cheyenne was made in fewer days than Ouray required to ride the remaining distance to winter camp in the valley of the Uncompahgre River.

*The Ute Delegation to Washington in 1868. Ouray is in the middle of the photo to the right.*
*Colorado Historical Society, Photo by Matthew Brady, 905WPA*

Once more, Ouray entertained Chipeta with stories and observations from his trip. Chipeta shared an "intelligence report" of the people's attitudes to the new treaty and to Ouray's leadership. This time when he made rounds of the Ute camps Chipeta and the children accompanied him. As Ouray discussed the importance of the new treaty terms with the men, Chipeta visited among the women. While they talked of families and friends, Chipeta probably interjected reasons why the treaty would benefit all the Ute families. They were an effective political team.

Chipeta had once waited with longing for messengers who might bring word of Pahlone, but now it seemed that fast-riding couriers brought only bad news. Word came in early June 1868 of the death of the powerful old chief Nevava. The messenger who arrived a few weeks later delivered shocking news. Josepha and Kit Carson were both dead. Josepha had died of complications from the birth of her seventh child, and less than thirty days later Kit had succumbed to a degenerative heart condition. All the Utes mourned the passing of their "Kitty," but the loss of these two friends left a permanent void in the lives of Ouray and Chipeta.

---

[1] At dawn on November 29, 1864, units of the First and Third Colorado Cavalry under command of Col. John M. Chivington attacked a village of 100 Cheyenne and 8 Arapaho lodges housing 500 women, children and elderly. Most of the men had gone hunting. The army opened fire with small arms and four howitzers, ignoring Chief Black Kettle's white flag of peace. Having killed at least 150 Indians, the soldiers roamed the area finishing off survivors, then scalped and desecrated bodies and plundered and burned the village. Black Kettle had recently surrendered at Fort Lyon, reported the location of his village, and believed his people to be under the protection of the military.

[2] Even before the Sand Creek Massacre, in response to the murder of a white family near Denver, allegedly committed by the Cheyenne, Governor Evans issued a proclamation authorizing citizens to kill Indians and seize their property.

[3] *Rocky Mountain News,* April 19, 1865.

[4] Parsons, Eugene, "Benton Canon," *The Trail,* XVI, 2 (July 1923), 16-17. Canon's full account of his trading experience in Ouray's camp.

[5] Ibid.

[6] Seward, W.H. to Governor John Evans, written at request of the President, July 18, 1865, Colorado State Archives, Territorial Governors Collection, Box 19651, FF10, folio 95.

[7] Evans, John to James Harlan, Secretary of Interior, August 1, 1865, Territorial Governors collection, Colorado State Archives, Box 19651, FF10, folio 95.

[8] *Rocky Mountain News*, October 10, 1865.

[9] Dunlay, Tom, *Kit Carson and the Indians* (Lincoln: University of Nebraska Press, 2000), 376.

[10] Guild, Thelma S. and Harvey L. Carter, *Kit Carson - A Pattern for Heroes* (Lincoln: University of Nebraska Press, 1984), 269. General William Tecumseh Sherman visited Fort Garland in mid September 1866 along with Governor Cummings and General James F. Rusling. Sherman held a council with a group of Southern Utes on September 21. Some sources report that Ouray met, and even negotiated with, General Sherman on that occasion. It appears, however, that Ouray was camped on Mosca Pass and did not arrive at Fort Garland until October 6.

[11] Jackson, Helen Hunt, from exhibit Fort Garland Museum and Visitor's Center.

[12] Annual Report of the Commissioner of Indian Affairs, 1868, 642.

[13] *Rocky Mountain News*, January 22, 1868.

Chapter 4
# AN UNEASY TRUCE

In a series of council meetings, forty-seven Ute chiefs signed the treaty of 1868, and Governor Hunt certified that they fully understood its provisions, including those tacked on by the U.S. Senate. President Andrew Johnson signed the treaty into law on November 6, 1868.

The new treaty brought a host of new people and new complications into Chipeta's life. Problems arose immediately that took Ouray away from home. When the official surveyors came to stake out the reservation boundaries, the Utes discovered that many of their good hunting areas had been deeded to the United States. It was also obvious that though the Utes were expected to confine themselves completely to their reservation, prospectors felt free to violate Ute territory. As the men disputed the new boundaries with the agent, Chipeta mourned the loss of favorite childhood camping sites and familiar places where each year she had gathered special foods and medicinal herbs.

In March the *Rocky Mountain News* carried a message from Ouray submitted by Special Agent William J. Godfrey. The entire Tabeguache band planned to go to Denver City during the month of May to trade their "furs and peltries."

They gave this advance notice so white citizens would not be alarmed when they saw a large group of Indians traveling past their settlements. After visiting Denver they planned to meet the northern Utes for a buffalo hunt and would not return to their western reservation until August.

*The first Tabeguache Ute Agency was high in the mountains shown in this* Harper's Weekly *sketch. It was not a place to farm or ranch.*
*P. David Smith Collection*

Preparations began to move the Conejos Agency farther away from white settlements to a site on the Los Pinos Creek. In late summer of 1869 Ouray and Chipeta rode from Conejos with the agent, a work crew, and an assembly of Ute chiefs to visit the new site. When they reached the top of Cochetopa Pass (near present-day Gunnison), the chiefs refused to go any farther. They were barely inside the bounds of their new reservation, but they insisted this was the place where they had agreed to put the agency.

A political compromise saved the day. The nearby creek was renamed the "Los Pinos," and the agency was built on the south side of Cochetopa Pass. The work crew set up a sawmill and began cutting trees for lumber. The Utes watched in horror as their mountainside was cut bare and sawdust and wood pulp floated on the streams.

The Los Pinos Agency soon took shape as a cluster of whitewashed log and adobe buildings arranged around a two-hundred-foot quadrangle with a schoolhouse in the center. The agent's three-room house, built of logs sawed on two sides and chinked with wood chips and mud, claimed the northern end of the square. With a barn and corrals the essentials were in place. Additions in subsequent years included quarters for the staff, shops for the blacksmith and carpenter, a store, and a mill. Construction was slow and sometimes haphazard. Agents reported that sunshine peeked through the log walls and the plank roofs covered with packed earth soon developed leaks.

Chipeta was surprised to learn that the new agency included a house that she and Ouray were expected to occupy. She could not imagine why the white men thought they would want to live in a house. It was two years before they actually moved in and even then the two-room, 585 square-foot house was six weeks from completion.

The transition from teepee to house was difficult. The hard interior surfaces felt uncomfortable, and Chipeta did not know what to do with corners. Fresh-air circulation was limited, and heat from the fireplaces was difficult to regulate. It seemed she was always too warm or too cold inside the house. The agency carpenter built them some benches and offered to make a bed frame. Instead Chipeta lined an area of earthen floor with rushes, spread her woven willow mats and laid out their buffalo robe bedding in the Ute manner of preparing a comfortable teepee. Even with such familiar touches, Ouray and Chipeta missed the teepee. The only part of the house they enjoyed was a small porch where they sat watching hawks and eagles circling above the treetops. They quickly realized that the heavy winter snows at the ten-thousand-foot elevation provided an excuse to abandon the house except during the few warm weather months. Even in summer Ouray and Chipeta took every opportunity to travel away from the agency with their traditional portable home.

In the spring of 1873 the new house burned to the ground due to a defective chimney. The few items Ouray and Chipeta had stored inside were lost along with a few items belonging to Ankatosh, who was staying with them at the time. Chipeta hoped this was the end of living in a house, but the government reimbursed them $400 for their belongings (three saddles, three bridles, one set of double harnesses, one rifle, three pistols, one set of field glasses, and ninety dollars in cash) and quickly built them a new house.

Otto Mears, a general merchant in the nearby town of Saguache, and former Conejos business partner of Agent Head, was appointed the official Ute trader for the agency. He had learned to speak Spanish and Ute while in Conejos and came to know many of the chiefs. He seemed trustworthy to the Utes because he did not treat them in the condescending manner of many white people. Mears made friends with Ouray and Chipeta and often brought his wife along to stay at their house while he conducted business.

*Chief Ouray and Otto Mears posed for the camera in 1868.*
*Denver Public Library, Western History Department, William H. Jackson photographer, WHJ- 10219*

Mears hired Ouray at a good salary to hunt meat for the agency employees. A cook prepared meals for the staff, and Ouray and Chipeta were invited to eat with the rest of the agency residents. Ouray now had a house, a meal ticket, and two good-paying jobs. By white standards he was doing quite well. By Ute standards he was becoming too white.

A new territorial governor, Edward M. McCook, was appointed in 1869. He made no effort to hide his opinion that all Utes were lazy and good for nothing, and he openly complained that one-third of the territory of Colorado was set aside for the exclusive use of savages. In his first meeting with the new governor, Ouray concluded this man was an enemy.

In his capacity as superintendent of Indian affairs for the territory, Governor McCook created a position for his brother-in-law, James B. Thompson, as a Denver-based special agent for those uncooperative Utes who refused to stay in their assigned territory. The governor had great difficulty keeping agents at the often-inaccessible Los Pinos location, and the turnover kept the Utes in turmoil. Lt. Calvin Speer was officially relieved of his command on September 29, 1869 and temporarily replaced by Capt. William H. Merrill. The eccentric Jabez Nelson Trask finally arrived at the agency on May 3, 1871. The fourth agent in three years, Charles Adams, arrived in May 1872. He turned out to be another McCook brother-in-law. Despite his dubious family ties Adams proved to be an honest and trustworthy man.

Adams's wife, Margaret, became the teacher for the agency school. She and Chipeta were often the only women living at Los Pinos, and they became close friends. When the Utes refused to bring their children to the school, Chipeta convinced a few families that learning the words and ways of the white man could benefit the whole band in the future. She recognized that Ouray's knowledge of other languages and customs had empowered him to deal with white leaders. Chipeta delivered her own wards to Margaret Adams's classroom.

The Utes had settled on their reduced territory for only a few years when trespassing prospectors found rich silver deposits in the San Juan Mountains. Reports of hand-sorted silver that assayed as high as thirty thousand dollars per ton created excitement in the eastern slope mining camps and frontier towns. By 1872 illegal mining was actively under way in the San Juans, and hundreds of prospectors attempted to file claims on Ute reservation land. Agent Adams complained to the governor about the intruders but was unable to get military intervention. Expressing the thoughts of many territorial residents, *The Boulder News* declared, "An Indian has no more right to stand in the way of civilization and progress than a wolf and a bear." [1] The white men's lust for gold and silver generated a series of conflicts and councils that occupied Ouray and Chipeta for the better part of three years and affected the rest of their lives.

In his biennial message to the territorial legislature on January 3, 1872, Governor McCook voiced his support for the miners. He officially asked for a new treaty that he hoped would severely reduce the Ute territory or, better yet, remove them from Colorado altogether. The territorial legislature quickly passed a resolution in support of a new treaty effort. President Ulysses S. Grant responded that he would attempt to negotiate with the Utes, but he would not wage war. Pending the outcome of negotiations, he ordered U.S. troops to keep the prospectors out of the San Juans.

During winter camp Chipeta alerted Ouray to rumors circulating among Ute camps that Ouray might consider giving up the San Juans. Already angry about the territory lost in two successive treaties, many Utes concluded Ouray was in conspiracy with government officials. His government house and salary suggested that he had traded Ute land for his own benefit. A few Utes plotted to eliminate him. In a matter of weeks Ouray killed four Utes who made attempts on his life.

The most telling incident, illustrating the depth of suspicion and ill feeling toward Ouray, occurred in early 1872. Five Utes set the plot in motion at the agency blacksmith shop where Ouray was in the habit of stopping each morning. The blacksmith, George Hardman, warned Ouray that some men were waiting in the shop. When Ouray stepped inside, a man lunged at him with an ax. Ouray managed to keep a post

*"An Ominous Meeting"* — *Utes and a San Juan prospector,* Harper's
Weekly, *October 25, 1879.*

P. David Smith Collection

between himself and his attacker. The first swing of the ax
missed his head by inches. The second swing shattered the ax
handle as it struck the post. Ouray lunged at the assailant,
grabbed him by the throat, and pinned him to the ground.
Four other conspirators, who had remained hidden in the
shadows, scrambled out the back door and ran.

As Ouray reached for his knife to finish off the ax-wield-
ing man, a firm hand grasped his arm and Chipeta's voice
commanded him to stop. She talked quietly to him as she
removed the knife from its sheath and tucked it into her belt.
Chipeta's action, so reminiscent of Josefa Carson, saved the life
of her brother, Sapovanero.

Later, when Ouray was calm, Chipeta mediated a truce
between these two men who were both so dear to her. She was
a powerful persuader. Sapovanero asked Ouray's forgiveness
and dedicated himself to supporting Ouray. Eventually he
regained Ouray's trust and was chosen to be the person left in
charge when Ouray was absent from the agency.

The attempts on his life prompted Ouray to hire a Mexican bodyguard who accompanied him everywhere and slept outside his door at night. The stress began to show in Ouray's face, and he complained of sleepless nights and assorted aches and pains. His temper flared more often and more easily. With all the comings and goings of visitors at the agency, and the fear for Ouray's safety, Chipeta treasured the occasional times when she and Ouray could take the children and escape for a hunting trip. During these interludes he relaxed visibly and returned home in a more tolerant frame of mind. Chipeta instructed Sapovanero not to bother them unless it was an absolute emergency.

Although few mentions of the adopted children exist in written records, they must have been a special joy. Chipeta could take delight in watching Ouray, head bent in attentive conversation with the boys, as father and sons strung their bows and cleaned their guns. And she taught the girls to butcher the game that Ouray and the boys brought back to camp and to process the hides. As they worked she described how they would cut the leather to make moccasins and leggings during the winter. These were, no doubt, the times she had dreamed about when she first came to live with Ouray and the baby Pahlone.

It was not unusual to encounter white prospectors on these hunting excursions, and Ouray and Chipeta made them welcome around their campfire. In the spring of 1872, P.C. Sovereign, a prospector who wintered in the area, happened into their camp. Over a dinner of fresh caught trout, Ouray told Sovereign that the Utes did not object to white men mining in the mountains. The problem came when the miners cut the timber to build cabins and frightened away the game. The Utes did not want a fight with the white men, Ouray explained, and hoped there would be no disturbances that might provoke a war.

Sovereign soon made his way to Denver and reported his conversations with Ouray and other chiefs. After expressing the temperance of the Utes, Sovereign went right on to encourage more intrusions into Ute territory by describing in glowing terms the mild winters, good vegetation for grazing, abundant fish and game, and fine mineral resources in the Uncompahgre Valley.

In June 1872, Agent Adams, Ouray, and a few chiefs went to Denver for a meeting at the request of the governor. President Grant had appointed commissioners to negotiate a treaty with the Utes and the governor, a member of the commission, was anxious to get discussions under way. They agreed to hold a council at Los Pinos in two moons, about August 19.

Ute families began to arrive at Los Pinos Agency for the council during the warm days of late summer. Clusters of teepees dotted the meadows and nestled in the trees for several miles. As chiefs arrived Ouray invited them to his home to talk. The house was scorned by some Utes but seen by others as a novelty to be inspected. It was sparsely furnished with blanket-draped benches and a few chairs and stools. Prints from Mrs. Adams's magazines were tacked to the walls; and clothing, Ouray's hunting gear, and Chipeta's beaded buckskin bags hung here and there from pegs.

*Part of the 1872 Ute Denver delegation of Utes and agents posed for the camera.*

*Colorado Historical Society, F-5809*

Chipeta circulated from camp to camp, greeting the women, talking of families and women's things. She also paid careful attention to attitudes toward the coming council. When they were alone, she related to Ouray the opinions she heard in the camps. The Utes were adamant, she said, that they would not give up more land, and they expected Ouray to hold the government to the existing treaty. Chipeta encouraged Ouray to support the will of the people. No more treaties.

Although Ouray trusted Chipeta completely, he was sometimes skeptical of information she gathered from women. One day not long before the council was scheduled to begin, she told him the Weeminuche band was not coming. Ouray did not believe it. Chipeta's skill as an intelligence agent was confirmed when a messenger from the Weeminuche chief arrived a short time later. He wanted nothing more to do with treaties and refused to bring his people to the council.

By the appointed date two thousand Utes gathered at Los Pinos. There was no sign of the U.S. Commissioners. The Utes waited. Ouray and Chipeta spent their days making rounds in the camps encouraging everyone to be patient. They reminded the irritated Utes that the commissioners were city-bred white men unfit to travel over rugged mountain terrain. This tact brought knowing nods, and most Utes agreed to wait. Frustrated with the delay, Agent Adams rode out in search of the missing commissioners.

On the morning of August 26, Chipeta enjoyed her regular visit with Mrs. Adams. While walking home across the agency compound, she looked up to see a procession of soldiers and wagons lumbering down the pass. The commissioners had finally arrived — seven days late.

General Alexander, commander at Fort Garland, and seven soldiers accompanied the commissioners. They set up their white canvas tent behind the agency building and began preliminary meetings with Ouray and key chiefs. The delay had been caused, the commissioners reported, by a search for the Utes' annual annuity goods. The supplies had been shipped July 31, and their whereabouts remained unknown. On top of the commissioners' late arrival, news of the missing annuities started the council off on a bad note.

The commissioners did not tell the Utes that they took the long route to Los Pinos through Pueblo, Fort Garland, and up the San Luis Valley instead of the customary route through Colorado City, Poncha Pass, and Saguache. The short route, in good weather, took five days. The long route required at least eight. In addition, the commissioners spent a day relaxing at Fort Garland and dawdled away the next morning fly-fishing in Sangre de Cristo Creek. Perhaps they hoped that the missing annuity goods would appear during their delay.

On August 27 the Utes staged an opening ceremony to pay their respects to the commissioners. In a light drizzle two hundred chiefs, subchiefs, and headmen, dressed in beaded buckskin, painted men on painted horses, rode down the hill in a line with Ouray in the lead. Chipeta followed behind with the other women and children. Drums, gunfire, and Ute chants accompanied the procession. The parade passed the agency compound, continued into the meadow, then doubled back to halt in front of the agency porch. Ouray dismounted, shook hands with the three commissioners, and formally presented each of the chiefs. Then the Mouache Utes demonstrated a scalp dance to entertain the visitors. The two commissioners who had come west from Maine and Missouri, and perhaps even the governor, were more than a little intimidated by the display of scalps fluttering from long poles. The dance depicted the battle in which the scalps were taken and lamented the braves lost in combat.

With formalities complete, the chiefs gathered inside the agency building for the council. Perhaps Chipeta and Mrs. Adams settled in the adjoining room with their sewing and enjoyed a bit of eavesdropping. The purpose of the council, according to the Colorado press, was to open the southwest portion of the state to settlement by whites. At issue was a strip of land three hundred miles long and two hundred miles wide composed mainly of the San Juan Mountains.

Ouray conducted the meeting. The commissioners sat on chairs; the Utes straddled benches or squatted on the floor.

*Those involved with the 1872 treaty negotiations posed in front of the agency buildings.*

*Colorado Historical Society, F-7045*

Most of the Utes lit their pipes, and the room soon filled with a thick haze. Ouray began by allowing various Ute chiefs to speak at length. He gave the commissioners no opening. Speeches were translated from Ute to Spanish to English by a team of interpreters. Ouray was one of the few men present who spoke all three languages.

Ouray told the commissioners the Utes already had a satisfactory treaty, and they expected the government to protect Ute land from the invasion of miners and settlers. The commissioners could say nothing to sway the chiefs. The council ended in a stalemate.

Throughout their stay at Los Pinos, Governor McCook doted upon the chiefs in an attempt to curry their favor. He boasted to the news reporter who accompanied the commissioners that he longed to tear himself away from the heathenish influences of Denver and live the good life of the Ute.

It was on this occasion that a correspondent for the *Rocky Mountain News* first dubbed Chipeta "Queen of the Utes." But the title was not complimentary. The reporter's account of the council filled the better part of two newspaper columns. Details of the actual council activities were scant. The space was devoted instead to the beauties and challenges of the trip from Denver to Los Pinos and descriptions of the Utes.

Calling the Utes hyenas and vermin, he mocked their clothing, demeanor, and activities. His sarcasm continued in his evaluation of Chipeta.

> *This afternoon the commissioners were waited upon by the queen of the Utes — Madame Ure I suppose she is called — who swept down in all her royal stations, attired in a skirt of buckskin, a pair of moccasins, an old shawl, and a lot of uncombed hair. She was very coquettish in her ways and manifested many of the freaks of the worldly-minded in her fashionable call. Royalty among the Utes has its disadvantages as well as advantages. It gives the chief's family position among the others but it doesn't bring sufficient revenue to keep them in affluent circumstances. Mrs. Ure's household is probably just the same as that of her meanest subject; royalty doesn't change the Ute nature any.* [2]

Ouray, in an effort to lead his people to coexistence with the white culture, had adopted white men's clothing, which he wore much of the time. He was committed to setting an example for the Utes and even somewhat excited by the trappings of Victorian society. Chipeta, however, preferred traditional Ute dress and continued to wear her own elegantly beaded dresses and leggings.

In an editorial denouncing the failure of the treaty talks, the anti-Ute editor of the *Rocky Mountain News,* William Byers, laid the entire "Ute problem" in the lap of former governor, A. C. Hunt. Byers complained that the 1868 treaty, which Hunt negotiated, was written to preclude future reduction of the size of the Ute reservation. In other words, Hunt made an agreement with the Utes that the government was meant to keep. Byers called Hunt's actions "an obstacle to territorial progress." The riches of Colorado, he said, were wasted on a few thousand Utes whose presence in the territory was "an annoyance." [3]

Governor McCook promptly proposed to President Grant that a delegation of Utes travel to Washington where they might, in that more intimidating setting, be enticed to give up the San Juans. Plans were expedited, and by November the trip was under way. Ouray supported this plan. Although he had no interest in giving up land, he needed the often war-ready Ute chiefs to better understand the vastness and power of the U.S. government. With Ouray as principal chief, the delegation included Coho, Tomserick, and Guero of the Tabeguache; Mautchick, Jose Raphael, and Sabeta of the Mouache; and Ignacio of the Weeminuche. They were accom-panied by Agent Adams, Southern Ute Agent Thomas Dolan, Special Agent James B. Thompson, and Otto Mears, Uriah Curtis, and Herman Leuders as interpreters. Mrs. Adams traveled with the delegation and took the opportunity to visit friends and relatives in the East.

The delegation left November 10, 1872, and very nearly crossed paths with another Ute delegation heading home from Washington. Rev. G.W. Dodge, agent at the Uintah reserva-tion, with "disgruntled chiefs" Antero, Tabbecuna, and Wanderodes from Utah, passed through Denver just a few days later. These chiefs complained that game was scarce on their barren reservation and their people needed government annuities in order to survive.

In Washington President and Mrs. Grant received the Colorado chiefs at the White House. A round of talks, tours and entertainments in the great capital city failed to sway the Utes. They returned home January 10, 1873, still firm in their resolve that they had made a deal in 1868, and the government should stick to the agreement.

While Ouray was away Chipeta went to winter camp with her brothers and the rest of the Tabeguache. Antonio and Atchu spent much of their time with McCook while Chipeta and the girls transformed summer-cured hides into dresses, shirts, leggings, and moccasins for the family. As they deco-rated the clothing with beaded patterns, Chipeta told the girls stories of the spiritual animals, the seasons, and the hierarchy of the earth represented by the colors.

Black was the color of winter and the underworld inhab-ited by the snake. The weasel who hunted in the valleys in springtime was red. His powerful color protected the people from snakes and the fearsome underworld. Turquoise (blue/green/grey) represented the wolf who stalked the mountainsides in all seasons. The yellow mountain lion roamed the top of the world where they saw him in summer travels. And white was the color of the sky and the powerful eagle who soared with the spirits. It was also the color of autumn when the people prepared to survive the coming snows.

In late April more than a thousand Utes traveled to Los Pinos and assembled in a village of 150 lodges. Agent Adams sent a letter to the *Rocky Mountain News* informing the people of Colorado of the Ute's peaceful attitude and efforts to remain far from the mining camps. He also reported that Ouray had investigated the murder of a man named Miller the previous fall. Finding that two Utes had killed the man while stealing his mules, Ouray had sent men to track down and kill the offending Utes. Adams called for patience on the part of citizens and moderation by the sensation-mongering press.

Immediately, new correspondence between Colorado Territory and the nation's capital discussed tactics for yet another council. This time the white leaders decided the U.S. government should make an offer to buy the San Juans from the stubborn Utes. Someone, probably Otto Mears, suggested to the commissioner of Indian affairs, Felix Brunot, an unusual bargaining chip. If he could locate Ouray's long lost son, Pahlone, Ouray might be swayed to support the sale.

Brunot made a trip to Cheyenne, Wyoming Territory, in the early summer of 1873, where he met with Ouray and Agent Adams. Brunot first suggested that the government was willing to buy the San Juans for a fair price. Ouray was not interested. Then Brunot brought up Ouray's lost son, Pahlone. He was willing to use the powers of the Indian Commission to locate the boy. Ouray pledged to use his influence with his tribe at a council to be held in mid-August at Los Pinos. Adams described the meeting as "very, very satisfactory," but he advised the commissioner of Indian affairs that the matter should be kept quiet.[4]

Ouray told Chipeta about the government's offer to buy the land and the plans for a new treaty council. He probably did not mention Pahlone. It was too much to hope that the boy would be found after all these years.

Some eighteen hundred Utes set up their camps in the meadows near Los Pinos in preparation for the August 15 council. Again the appointed day arrived, and there was no sign of the commissioners. Ouray and Chipeta faced a much greater challenge this time to keep the people from leaving in disgust.

The commissioners appeared five days late. Brunot himself came to make the purchase offer. Privately, he told Ouray the reason for his late arrival; he had located Pahlone. Brunot had waited several days in Colorado Springs expecting an agent to bring Pahlone, now known as Friday, but the boy refused to come.

The council commenced, and Brunot offered to buy the Ute land for what the U. S. government believed to be a fair price. Ouray spoke for the Utes:

> *We do not want to sell a foot of our land — that is the opinion of all. The Government is obliged by its treaty to take care of our people, and that is all we want. For some time we have seen the whites coming in on our lands; we have not done anything ourselves, but have waited for the Government to fulfill its treaty. We have come here so that you may see that we are not satisfied with this trespassing on our lands; but we do not want to sell any of them.*[5]

The talks continued for four days. In the end Ouray gave orders for his people to avoid the prospectors mining in the San Juans, but announced firmly and finally that the Utes would not give up the land.

Shortly after this council failed Brunot sent word that he had arranged for a delegation of Arapaho to bring Pahlone to Washington. Brunot invited Ouray, with his previous delegation, to come and meet the boy. At this point Ouray must have decided to tell Chipeta.

However he broke the news, Chipeta was overjoyed. No doubt she asked why they needed to go all the way to

Washington when the Arapaho lived just on the other side of the mountains on the flat plains. The agents could arrange a meeting in Denver. They could leave immediately.

Ouray explained that Brunot had made the arrangements and there was new treaty business to discuss. Chipeta wanted to go along. She knew quite well that Margaret Adams had traveled east with the last delegation so a woman could certainly make the trip. It was a rare occasion when Ouray denied a request from his best friend and closest confidant, but his answer was a firm "no."[6] Swallowing her disappointment, and perhaps anger, Chipeta focused her attention on making a beaded shirt and pair of moccasins for Ouray to take as a gift for Pahlone.

To the original 1872 delegation one chief, Tapuche, was added to represent the Capote band.[7] They arrived in Denver the evening of October 5 accompanied by agents Adams and Dolan along with the interpreters, Otto Mears and Herman Leuders. The delegation settled into Denver's Munger House Hotel only to be roused by alarm bells in the night. A westbound train had arrived with reports that a large group of Cheyenne and Arapaho were gathering fifty miles east of town.[8] The city was on all-night alert, and the Utes stayed out of sight in their rooms.

The delegation remained in Denver two nights because of a conference with the governor. Late on the second evening, Otto Mears returned to the hotel and smelled gas in the corridor. Following the odor to the room where four Utes were sleeping, he rushed in to find the lamp blown out and gas filling the room. He threw open the window, roused the groggy Utes, and helped them into the hallway. His actions made him a hero to the chiefs.

During their stay in Denver an unidentified reporter for *The Daily News* scored a rare interview with Ouray. The resulting biographical sketch appeared on October 9. The reporter described Ouray as 5 feet 6 1/2 inches tall, weighing 215 pounds, with a chest girth of 43 inches. He was forty years old. He lived in a two-room adobe house built for him by the government. He and his wife, Chipeta, took meals with the government employees. He stated that he did not drink whiskey and very rarely took a bit of wine. He had given up smoking entirely some years earlier. Ouray reported that he had six hundred sheep that he let out to Mexicans on shares, sixty head of horses, and a few hundred dollars in the bank.[9]

In Washington President Grant received the Utes on October 24.[10] As expected, the commissioners made a new offer to buy the San Juans. This time the Utes were willing to consider a sale — with four conditions. They wanted cash. They would participate in a survey of the land so all parties clearly understood the boundaries. The chiefs wanted a military post built between the reservation and the San Juans, and a new agency to be built in the Southwest corner of Colorado for the Weeminuche, Capote, and Mouache bands. They adamantly refused to give up the Uncompahgre Park (the present-day Ouray to Ridgway valley).

The commissioners agreed to all points except the cash payment. They suggested instead a new system of annuities. Rather than annual gifts chosen by the government, the Utes could make a list of the goods they wanted and Ouray would place the order. After much debate the chiefs agreed.

Then on November 3 the Utes entered a room at the Interior Department and came face to face with their enemies, delegations of Arapaho and Cheyenne chiefs. For the first time Ouray saw the boy called Friday. Commissioner E.P. Smith made a speech about peace between the tribes before addressing the issue of Ouray's lost son. He said Friday was too young when taken to remember his father. Friday asked Ouray where his son was lost, and Ouray said about thirty miles north of Denver. Powder Face, the Arapaho chief, said Friday had been taken in a fight much further north; but there was another boy in the Arapaho camp who was taken near the location Ouray identified. Friday said all he knew was life as an Arapaho, and the Utes were his enemies. Ouray said Friday was not his son. The matter was closed.

Brunot later claimed that everyone at the meeting could see Friday's resemblance to Ouray. No one attempted to check for the childhood scar on the boy's shoulder or to see if he was left-handed. By some accounts, after returning home Friday accepted the possibility that he might be Ouray's lost son but became ill and died before he could visit the Ute camp.

With the issue of the boy out of the way, Commissioner Smith proceeded with his plan to forge peace between the tribes. He told the assembled chiefs that fighting between them must cease. Powder Face said he had warred against the Utes since early youth and admitted that the Arapaho had always been the aggressors. Although he expressed his personal desire for peace, Powder Face refused to speak for the young men back home. Ouray said the Arapaho spoke with two tongues; they would speak peace in Washington but utter their old hatreds at home. The commissioner threatened Powder Face and his people with punishment by military troops if they were found off their reservation fighting the Utes.

Commissioner Smith asked the chiefs to shake hands as personal gestures of peace. Ouray said he would meet the others halfway. Ouray and Powder Face advanced toward each other. Ouray extended his hand, and Powder Face clasped it solemnly. All eyes turned to Stonecalf of the Cheyenne, who still stood with his delegation. After making a speech he walked slowly to Ouray and Powder Face and shook their hands.[11]

Ouray returned home in mid-November, joining Chipeta and the rest of the family in winter camp near the junction of the Uncompahgre and Gunnison rivers. When she heard horses approaching, Chipeta rushed out of the teepee, but her heart sank when she saw that Ouray was alone. His somber face and the weary slump of his shoulders made her stifle the questions burning on her tongue. She helped Ouray unload his travel gear and carry it inside the teepee. When he was settled beside the fire with something to eat, the details of the meeting in Washington at last began to flow. He concluded his account by repeating the words he had spoken in Washington, "Friday is committed to being an Arapaho. He is not my boy."[12] Chipeta swallowed her disappointment and turned her attention to caring for her exhausted mate and the adopted children.

In mid-January a party of twenty-one miners with several wagonloads of gear happened into the Tabeguache camp.
Ouray welcomed the weary white men and Chipeta provided
them a hot meal. Around the campfire that night the miners
related their plans. They had come from Salt Lake City in
Utah Territory to seek their fortunes in the gold fields of the
San Juan Mountains. Ouray advised them of the dangers of
trying to cross the mountains in the heavy winter snows. He
offered the hospitality of his camp until the spring thaw. Some
of the men chose to heed Ouray's advice and remained in
camp. Others divided into groups and struck out into the high
country. One party of six men departed in early February on
the seventy-five mile journey to the Los Pinos Agency. Ouray
gave them ten days provisions and a group of Utes rode out
thirty miles with the men to point them in the right direction.

When Ouray and Chipeta returned to Los Pinos in early
summer, they learned that just one of the six miners had arrived
at the agency. The only survivor, Alferd Packer, had told the
agency staff a gruesome story of the hardships of the trip and
becoming separated from his traveling companions. Packer,
however, looked well fed for the two month ordeal he related.
Packer changed his story several times, later admitting that, as
members of the party died from cold and hunger, the survivors
ate them out of desperation. When the bodies of Packer's com-
panions were found, all in one campsite, some had bullet
wounds. Packer was arrested, tried for the murders of his com-
panions, and sent to the Territorial Prison at Cañon City.[13]

---

[1] Hunt, Inez, and Wanetta W. Draper, To Colorado's Restless Ghosts,
(Golden, Colo: Sage Books, 1960), 315.

[2] Daily News, September 11, 1872.

[3] Rocky Mountain News, September 11, 1872.

[4] Adams to Smith, June 24, 1873, NARA Record Group 75, Colorado
Superintendency, Correspondence Received 1873; Hafen, Ann
Woodbury, "Efforts to Recover the Stolen Son of Chief Ouray," Colorado
Magazine, (March 1939), 55-56 — citing Annual Report of
Commissioner of Indian Affairs, 1873, 112.

[5] Bangert, Buckley, *Journal of the Western Slope,* Vol. 1, No. 2, 1986.

[6] A few sources report that Chipeta accompanied Ouray on this trip. However, she is not mentioned in Colorado or Washington, D.C. newspaper reports or agents' correspondence related to the delegation. Herman Viola, who researched this delegation for his book, *Diplomats in Buckskin,* also made no mention of her in his research notes.

[7] *Rocky Mountain News,* November 11, 1873.

[8] *Denver Daily Times,* October 7, 1873.

[9] Ibid., October 9, 1873, 2.

[10] *Washington Evening Star,* October 24, 1873.

[11] Hafen, "Efforts to Recover the Stolen Son of Chief Ouray," quoting from Indian Treaty Talks and Councils, Packet 1, Office of Indian Affairs, Washington, D.C.; *Denver Daily,* November 4, 1873, 1.

[12] Ibid., 57-62 - from a biography of Brunot by Charles L. Slattery.

[13] "A Colorado Tragedy," *Harper's Weekly,* October 17, 1874, 852.

Chapter 5
# A NEW
# HOME

The first distribution of annuity goods selected by the Tabeguache was scheduled for late summer 1874. Well before the appointed day, Ute families began to set up camp in a broad meadow at the juncture of Cochetopa and Los Pinos Creeks. Chipeta rode the five miles from the agency to the camp daily to greet new arrivals and visit family and old friends.

A few clouds hovered on the mountaintops on the morning of August 19 when Chipeta left for the camp as usual. By the time she returned home, ominous dark clouds stacked one atop another over the western mountain range. After securing her horse in the corral, she paused to assess the impending storm. She could not yet smell the rain.

Inside the house she found Ouray, in the middle of the afternoon, dressed in his best clothes with his peace medals around his neck. When she left that morning Ouray had been lying about the house in a depressed mood and complaining that his back ached. Now he was beaming with excitement.

Visitors came, he told her. Agent Bond, young Bernard Gilpin, and a stranger who arrived last night. They had a long talk. The stranger, a Mr. Jackson, bought a couple of Navajo blankets

*The Ute delegation about 1872 — taken in Colorado before they left or upon their return (Chipeta and Susan did not go on the trip).*
Colorado Historical Society, F-24385

from Ouray. Jackson, Ouray explained, was part of a survey team making maps of Colorado Territory. Jackson was a photographer. This very moment he was setting up a studio on the porch of the agency building. Chipeta must hurry and get dressed, Ouray said. They were going to have their pictures made.

The prospect of posing for a photographer was not welcome. Chipeta was tired from the day's outing, and she had work to do. In addition, there was rumor among the Utes that sitting in front of the black box called a camera could make a person very sick. She knew Ouray had his picture made in Washington several times with no apparent ill effect although she may have wondered about the cause of his recent maladies. Chipeta herself once sat before the camera with Ouray and a group of Utes, possibly in the studio of a Denver photographer. But she was still skeptical. Ouray persisted, and she was pleased by his improved mood. So, she opened the leather trunk he had brought back from his last Washington trip and let him choose what she would wear.

As they left the house, Chipeta checked the progress of the storm. Maybe it would unleash its wind and rain in time to save her from the dreaded camera. But the clouds lingered to the west. Ouray and Chipeta arrived just as the photographer finished a picture of the new agent, the Reverend Henry Bond, and his wife. Pulling his head from under the black cloth that covered the backside of the camera, William Henry Jackson turned to look at his next subjects. He was, for a moment, speechless. That night Jackson recorded his impressions in his diary.

> *Chipeta was that day about the most prepossessing Indian woman I ever saw, and Ouray was immensely proud of her. She evidently had prepared with great care for this event yet at the very last moment was timid about taking her place before the camera; . . .*[1]

Confronted with a circle of observers enjoying the event, Chipeta was hesitant. Mrs. Bond suggested that Chipeta sit down beside her and watch while Ouray's photograph was made. Jackson carefully posed Ouray in a chair then spent a long time with his head under the camera cloth. He emerged to shove a square frame into the side of the camera. He waited. When he pulled the frame from the camera he pronounced the photo complete. Ouray stood up, and it was Chipeta's turn.

Jackson arranged some blankets on top of a crate and invited Chipeta to come and sit. She clung to the porch rail . . .

> *. . . but with the encouragement of her husband and the assistance of Mrs. Bond soon overcame her scruples, and she sat down as full of dimpling smiles as the veriest bride. The doeskin of which her dress was made was almost as white as cotton, and nearly as soft as silk. From every edge and seam hung thick white fringes, twelve or fifteen inches long, with a pretty trimming of*

*bead work and porcupine-quill embroidery. Chipeta's*
*costume must have cost Ouray at least $120.*[2]

Mrs. Bond arranged her dress and shawl (which unfortunately hid the embroidery on her dress). Coached by Mrs.
Bond, Chipeta smiled. As Jackson pulled the square frame of
a completed photo from the camera, he begged to take just one
more photo and popped his head under the black cloth before
Chipeta could respond. A clap of thunder jolted her onto her
feet and brought Jackson's head to attention. He disentangled
himself from the camera cloth just as the storm swept in.
Great splattering raindrops sent everyone scrambling to move
the camera equipment and the materials of the makeshift studio into the agency office. The obliging storm had waited just
long enough for Chipeta's photo to be completed.

The next day Jackson went to the Indian camp and photographed Piah and a few other Utes. Two days later Jackson
set up his camera in the middle of the agency compound and
eagerly awaited the arrival of all the Utes for distribution of
annuities. When the first Utes rode in, the men surrounded

*The Utes at Cochetopa Pass in 1874, waiting for the distribution of*
*their annuities.*
*Colorado Historical Society, W. H. Jackson photographer, 307WPA*

*The W. H.
Jackson photo
of Chipeta in
1874. Note
her ample
supply of
Navajo
jewelry.
Colorado
Historical
Society,
F-40201*

Jackson, covered his camera with a blanket, and kicked at the legs of the tripod. In a complete change of attitude, Piah told Jackson that the Utes would allow no pictures because they caused women, children and ponies to die. The more conservative Utes like Guero and Shavano had prevailed over Ouray's enthusiasm for photographs. Nothing would sway the chiefs.

Jackson was forced to put away his camera and focus in his mind's eye all the photos that might have been that day. He watched sullenly as the women came forward to claim sacks of flour and beans, and the men picked up knives and tools. His frustration peaked when the agent began the release of fat black steers to be chased down by warriors and butchered where they fell.[3] Jackson stomped off to the survey camp and spent the rest of the day packing his camera and gear for an early morning departure. That evening Ouray and Chipeta visited his tent to say goodbye and presented him with a carved

*The W. H. Jackson photo of Ouray in 1874. Jackson noted Ouray usually wore white man's clothing — but not in this photograph. Colorado Historical Society, F-5179*

wooden pipe. They never saw the pictures Jackson made during his brief visit.

Felix Brunot returned to Los Pinos in September for a final council following the survey of the proposed new reservation boundaries. After many difficulties and embarrassing errors, a contract was made to cede a sixty-by-one-hundred-mile area of mineral rich mountain land. The final pot sweetener, quietly added to the agreement by Brunot, was a new financial arrangement for Ouray. His five hundred dollar annual salary as translator was increased to one thousand dollars as head chief of the all the Utes — for ten years or as long as he remained chief and the Utes were at peace. Ouray accepted. He understood far better than most Utes how to effectively use the white man's money to provide for his family.

Three quarters of all the Utes ratified the agreement, and chiefs of all seven tribes placed their marks on the document. The same day Ouray dictated to the agency clerk a conciliatory letter to Felix Brunot, which appeared in the newspaper a short time later.

*Los Pinos Agency*
*September 13, 1874*
*We want you should tell Governor Elbert and the people of the territory, that we are well pleased and perfectly satisfied with everything that has been done. Perhaps some of the people will not like it because we did not wish to sell our valley and farming lands. We think we have good reasons for not doing so. We expect to occupy them ourselves before long for farming and stock raising. About eighty (80) of our tribe are raising corn and wheat now, and we know not how soon we shall all have to depend on ourselves for bread. We do not want to sell our valley and farming land for another reason. We know if we should the whites would go on it right now, build their cabins, drive in their stock, which would of course stray on our lands and then the whites themselves would crowd upon us till there would be trouble. We have many friends among the people in the territory, and want to live at*

*peace and on good terms with them and, we feel it would be much better for all parties for a mountain range to be between us.*

*We are perfectly willing to sell our mountain lands and hope the miners will find heaps of gold and silver, and we have no wish to molest them or make them any trouble. We do not want they should go down into our valleys, however, and kill or scare away our game.*

*We expect there will be much talk among the people, and in the papers, about what we have done, and we hope you will let the people know how we feel about it.*
                    *Truly your friend,*
                    *OURAY* [4]

The protracted negotiations had finally come to an end and life could, at last, return to normal. The strain of constant worry and extensive travel had taken a toll on Ouray. Deep lines creased his once smooth face, and dark circles surrounded his eyes. He needed a good rest, and Chipeta made preparations to take their teepee and steal away to a quiet, remote spot.

As the high country landscape turned golden and rusty red in the autumn chill, Ouray and Chipeta, along with a small family group traveled to Denver. Ouray spent the better part of a week meeting with Agent Bond and the governor discussing details of the new agreement. Meanwhile fifteen hundred Tabeguache gathered east of the city for the fall buffalo hunt. Chipeta set up the teepee in the main hunting camp, and Ouray arrived just in time to begin the hunt. A large herd grazing eighty miles east of the city provided a bountiful supply of winter meat and hides for trade.

With a large contingent of family and followers, Ouray and Chipeta hauled the rewards of the hunt south along the mountain range and set up winter camp at Four Mile Creek west of Cañon City. It was an old, familiar campsite that offered the benefits of nearby hot springs and a growing white community eager for trade. The Utes traded furs for flour at Champion Mills and made enough trips into town that local residents ceased to pay much attention to them.

On one trip between camp and town, a Ute named Tabweah spotted his recently stolen horse tied up at the home of a man called Marksberry. Tabweah removed the saddle and bridle and reclaimed his horse. Seeing Tabweah ride off with the animal he had recently purchased from a man who claimed he bought the horse from the Utes, Marksberry followed him. Marksberry slipped into the Ute grazing area and took back the horse. When Tabweah discovered his mount missing again, he went after Marksberry, shot him dead, and took the horse.

Ouray was called to Cañon City by the sheriff a few days later. When he heard the details of the incident, Ouray promised to investigate and assured the sheriff that, if the Ute was at fault, he would be handed over. *The Cañon City Times* lauded Ouray's approach. "Ouray, in promptly looking into the affair, shows himself to be what he claims, a friend of the white man."[5]

Within the week Ouray delivered Tabweah to the sheriff but did not abandon his loyal constituent. Ouray accompanied Tabweah to Denver for his late February trial where the young warrior was released for lack of evidence.[6]

Agent Bond appeared in winter camp mid-February to discuss possible sites for relocating the agency, which obviously was not working out at such a high altitude. Ouray recommended moving into the Uncompahgre Valley. The Tabeguache had a longtime winter campground in the north end of the valley, which was now accessible by wagon via the new San Juan Toll Road, the Lake Fork of the Gunnison Road, and the Old Salt Lake Road. Ouray sold Bond on the valley when he said it was suitable for year-round living. Bond saw his opportunity to fulfill his mission by settling the Utes and teaching them herding and agriculture. Ouray promised to promote the idea to the other chiefs and deliver their decision when he returned to the agency in May.

Everyone agreed the Uncompahgre Valley was the most desirable spot. At an elevation of 4,200 feet lower than the old agency, the valley was bisected by the Uncompahgre River, was comfortable in all seasons, and offered excellent pasture and farm land.

*Ouray and Chipeta's home near present-day Montrose was a large and substantial structure for the time.*
*Colorado Historical Society, 477B WPA*

In late spring Ouray and Agent Bond set out to select the new location for the agency. They chose a site in the southern part of the valley. Crews set up a sawmill in the nearby mountains, and the agency carpenter, Alonzo Hartman, began framing houses and fencing corrals. Mexican laborers set to work molding 300,000 adobe bricks to enclose the agency buildings. The new location was dubbed "Los Pinos II."

Ouray selected for himself a 160-acre ranch site along the river nine miles north of the agency and hired workers to build an adobe house, outbuildings, a barn, and corrals. Two Mexican workers broke ground to plant crops and helped Chipeta begin a small vegetable garden. Ouray was intent on setting an example of a new way of life for his people. By late summer he and Chipeta moved into their house and abandoned the teepee except for occasional hunting trips. Heavy winter snows in the early months of 1876 caused damaging snow slides in the high mountains, but the spring runoff was a boon to the first plantings of crops in Ouray's new fields.

A few other Utes who were willing to try farming and ranching established farms in the valley. Following Ouray's lead, Chief Shavano built a home south of the agency along Cow Creek.[7] Those Utes unwilling to try farming clung to the nomadic life but set up a winter village near the agency. With this concentration of Tabeguache in the valley, the white people began to refer to them as the Uncompahgre Utes.

The Utes prepared to celebrate the spring bear dance as they had always done at a site in a piñon grove a mile and a half north of the agency. Chipeta rode out every day in late February to greet friends who arrived at the campsite. She spent the days in the comfortable familiarity of well-smoked teepees, cuddling new babies, exchanging stories of the past year's events, and mourning absent faces.

Ouray was tired and grumpy. Complaining that his head and his feet hurt, he said he had no interest in attending the dance. Anxious not to miss a moment of the festivities, Chipeta gathered her best dress and shawl and moved into the teepee of some relatives at the campground.

On the second afternoon Chipeta was stepping and swaying in the middle of the women's line when the dance leader signaled a halt and the musicians stopped playing. Sapovanero stepped into the *avinkwep* and called for all the chiefs to assemble. The curious dancers followed them outside. Across the crowd, Chipeta saw Ouray sitting astride his horse. Beside him were two mounted White River Utes, Piah and Colorow. The Tabeguache chiefs gathered around, and Ouray addressed the assembly. Piah, he told them, had killed the White River medicine man three days earlier. Ouray described the deceased as known to everyone assembled to be a bad Ute. Piah had come to Ouray to ask for protection. The decision, said Ouray, was up to the chiefs. They huddled briefly, and Sapovanero announced their simple, one word answer: "Yes."

The chiefs turned and went back to the dance. Agent Bond, who was a guest at the event along with his wife and some friends, stepped forward to talk to Ouray. The two men agreed to return to the agency and officially enroll Piah with the Tabeguache. While Bond went to collect his horse,

Chipeta pushed forward to stand near Ouray, observing her husband with a worried expression. He assured her he was fine. After a brief exchange she concluded that he was irritated at being dragged out of the house but otherwise well. She waited to watch him ride off with Agent Bond and the two Utes, then returned to the dance.

While she relished the familiar rituals and traditional ways, Chipeta resigned herself to living in a house. She hired a Mexican woman to cook and manage the kitchen, which was located in a separate building with living quarters. Chipeta spread Navajo rugs on the floors, and Mrs. Bond helped select fabric and fashion curtains. Each room had a fireplace or a small iron stove for heat, and oil lamps provided soft light. With Ouray's salary Chipeta was able to buy iron beds, rocking chairs, mirrors, and an elegantly carved bureau. She even acquired a piano. The agency carpenter built a sturdy table that was installed at one end of Ouray's council room. When special guests arrived, it served as a dining room. Chipeta found the china, crystal, and silver they had received as official gifts to be a burden. She stored them away and dragged them out only for white guests. These otherwise unused items were the crowning touch that prompted white visitors to report Ouray and Chipeta were becoming quite "civilized." They even kept a supply of wine and cigars for their guests.

Life in the beautiful valley offered some consolation for the alterations in Chipeta's lifestyle. She enjoyed working in her garden and continued to butcher and preserve meats, gather seasonal foods, and look after Ouray. He dressed in white men's clothing most of the time, so she no longer made his buckskin shirts and leggings. But Chipeta continued to tan fine hides for her own dresses and gifts. She was busy, but missed the close company of other women that she had enjoyed in camp. Often she rode out to Ute homes or camps for a gathering of women determined to process food or animal hides or sew together in the old way. Sometimes friends and relatives raised their teepees in the pasture and stayed awhile. Occasionally white visitors spent a few nights in the house.

Ouray rode to the agency regularly to meet with the agent and often welcomed Tabeguache chiefs and headmen to the farm for councils. He continued to receive periodic messengers from his supporters in the other bands. Occasionally there was a conflict with miners or settlers that required his attention, but he seldom traveled great distances. Ouray supervised the work of the farm laborers and soon had one hundred acres under cultivation. He hired Ute boys to maintain his herd of cattle and care for his horses. His vast herd of sheep grew fat on the rich grass near Del Norte under the watchful eye of old friend, Luis Montoya.

In this gentleman farmer lifestyle Ouray's aching feet became worse, and he complained of back pain, recurring headaches, and frequent fatigue. He fought bouts of depression. Chipeta drew on her store of herbs and tree bark to brew tea to relieve the swelling. The medicine man performed healing rituals to restore his spirit. A doctor who visited the agency suggested Ouray should go to Cañon City to consult a new doctor, J.F. Lewis.[8]

McCook, refusing to let them make the trip alone, accompanied Ouray and Chipeta to Cañon City in the summer of 1876. Traveling again through old familiar territory lifted Ouray's dark mood. They followed the Gunnison River east and crossed the Snowy Ridge at Monarch Pass. The descending trail offered a broad view of the Arkansas Valley where they had so often camped. They found houses and small settlements dotting the landscape and fences divided the land into patchwork parcels. It was no longer the Utes' valley.

They camped in the pasture of the Hutchinson farm near the settlement of Salida. White acquaintances and curious settlers, seeing the teepee, stopped in to visit. Among them were Mr. and Mrs. Nash who recalled Ouray and Chipeta's past kindness to them as they struggled to survive in unfamiliar territory. Mrs. Nash admitted she had been panic stricken when their little procession of wagons rolled along the Arkansas River past the Indian camp on that day ten years past. Now comfortably settled in the valley, she smiled as she thanked Ouray and Chipeta again for leading their wagons across the raging waters. The couple was encouraged to find a few white people who were so friendly to them.

McCook led the way down the winding canyon where the Arkansas River surged over tumbled boulders on its way to the prairie. In Cañon City people on the streets were pleased to see the Utes return. They located Dr. Lewis's office two doors east of the Methodist Episcopal Church. The doctor examined Ouray and diagnosed chronic nephritis, an inflammation of the kidneys. A local druggist filled the prescription scribbled by Dr. Lewis. Chipeta returned home with instructions about Ouray's diet and need for plenty of rest. His condition improved, but he still suffered the dark periods.

Conflicts between the Utes and the white population lessened as most Utes attempted to stay in their diminished western territory. Chipeta enjoyed quiet, uneventful days at the farm. One of the Mexican workers taught her to play the guitar. She was an apt pupil, learning some Spanish tunes that Ouray had known in his youth and developing her own accompaniment for Ute songs. Her voice was a full, round soprano and she delivered her songs with feeling and fire. Her music often soothed Ouray's bad days.

The adopted children were growing up. Antonio and Atchu were young men by this time, perhaps with their own families. Twelve year-old Cooroopits was old enough to help with cooking and household chores. If Sowana was not already married, she was ready to be noticed by the young men at the next spring bear dance. Chipeta must have recognized with mixed pleasure and sadness that she and Ouray would soon be alone on the farm.

The couple made leisurely trips through the valley to soak Ouray's aches and pains in the abundant hot springs. They often stopped to visit ranchers they had befriended over the years. On one early morning ride they paid short visits to a number of ranches. At each stop they were invited to have coffee or even breakfast. When they arrived at the Roberts ranch, accompanied by Ouray's bodyguard and a neighbor, they found the family enjoying a late morning meal. Ouray asked the neighbor to tell the Roberts not to invite them to eat. He was full from being fed at five homes, he said, and if invited it would be an insult to refuse. From time to time Ouray and Chipeta stopped in to have dinner with the staff at Los Pinos Agency where they were the only Utes invited to dine with the agent. Unlike many Utes, they were comfortable in the company of white people and white ways.

Outside the Ute reservation, the attention of white inhabitants was focused on the proposition of statehood. After many meetings and discussions and lobbying and a vote of the white residents of the Territory, President Grant declared Colorado the 38th state of the Union on August 1, 1876. It was the year of the great centennial celebrating the founding of the nation. To the white citizens statehood gave credence to their belief that the people of Colorado should control their own destiny — one which many residents felt did not include the Utes.

The winter of 1877 was exceptionally severe. Snow began to fall in the high country midsummer, and by September the mountain routes were impassable. At the farm Ouray and Chipeta were cut off from their usual communication with Ute bands in the north and south territories. When they did receive reports from the northern White River band, they feared especially for Ouray's sister, Tsashin. The government supplies had not been delivered to the White River agency, and families had received only fifteen pounds of flour in the past year. The people struggled to survive on the limited game found on reduced hunting lands.

An invasion of grasshoppers stripped the bushes and field crops the following summer, increasing the frustrations brought by lingering drought. Ouray said he had not seen grasshoppers in any quantity since the summer of the trouble with Kaniache and his band.

Ouray began to receive frequent messages about trouble with the new agent assigned to the White River agency. Nathan Meeker, a former newspaper man for Horace Greeley, had come west in 1869 as the leader of a New York colony that founded the town of Greeley, Colorado. He had no experience with Indians when he was appointed to the post by the new president, Rutherford B. Hayes.

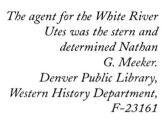

*The agent for the White River Utes was the stern and determined Nathan G. Meeker. Denver Public Library, Western History Department, F-23161*

Meeker arrived at White River with the naíve idea that the Utes were simply waiting for someone to show them how to farm so they could settle down to a life of tilling the soil. First, he moved the agency into the Utes' favorite valley where he fenced the pastures with barbed wire. Meeker insisted the Utes become Christians and send their children to the agency school to be taught by his daughter, Josephine. He forced the proud warriors to do what they considered to be women's work. Although he had no authorization to do so, Meeker cut the Utes' rations if they failed to do as ordered. Every change he made increased the Utes' anger. Finally, he plowed up a long established racetrack in the bottomland and threatened to kill the Utes' ponies. This was the last straw.

Nicaagut and other Ute leaders consulted Ouray about how to get rid of their new agent. Ouray asked the latest Los Pinos agent, Leverett Kelly, to write to Washington about the situation but nothing happened. Nicaagut even rode to Denver and appealed in person to Governor Pitkin, but his pleas fell on deaf ears.

In May 1878 President Hayes appointed another commission to negotiate with the Utes, this time with a proposition to consolidate all the Colorado Ute bands on one reservation along the White River. Any new land selected for settlement of the Utes, he directed, must offer "a sufficient quantity of arable land to enable them to become, by agricultural pursuits, a self-supporting people."[9] The president planned to end the Ute problem once and for all.

The commissioners assembled in Manitou Springs, Colorado, on July 30, 1878. They hired an interpreter and, along with a secretary, set out for Fort Garland. There they acquired a military escort, Second Lieutenant C. A. H. McCauley. The entourage arrived at the southern agency on August 14 and waited a week or more while the chiefs of the Mouache, Weeminuche, and Capote bands assembled for a council. During this time the commissioners devised a strategy to introduce their proposal for a consolidated reservation and then invite the chiefs to accompany them to Los Pinos for one grand council of all the Ute leaders.

The chiefs, however, arrived with their own agenda. They complained that they had intended to sell only the minerals in the Brunot agreement of 1873, not to give up the land. They would not have signed the agreement, they said, had they known that Ouray would profit from the deal with a one thousand dollar salary to be head chief of the Utes. Chief Ignacio still rankled at the idea that Ouray spoke for the entire Ute population. The chiefs complained that their promised agency had not been completed and what construction had been done was "scarcely habitable." The government had not complied with the agreement and had failed to pay them as promised. If the commissioners had not come with money, the chiefs had nothing to discuss.

In fact, the commissioners were authorized to make a payment to the Utes, but the funds had been delayed. With a promise of cash on the way, the chiefs were at least willing to let the commissioners talk. General Hatch, chairman of the commission, laid out the plan for the southern Utes to sell their reservation and join their brothers from the other bands on a new reservation in the far north on White River. There was no discussion. The southern chiefs refused to sell any more land, refused to consider moving to the north, refused to go to Los Pinos for a general council, and demanded that the government pay up on the last agreement.

The commissioners adjourned to their tent in dismay. The interpreter, Albert Pfeiffer, a former Ute agent, suggested an alternative way of gaining the desirable southern Ute land. They could offer to exchange the current reservation for a new location on the headwaters of the Chama, Navajo, Blanco, and San Juan rivers where there was good grass and little encroachment by white settlers. The commissioners, as well as the chiefs, were willing to consider this option. Pfeiffer remained behind to negotiate the exchange after the commissioners distributed presents to the chiefs and left for Los Pinos.

Despite the apparent ill feelings toward Ouray, there were men among the southern bands who kept him informed about the discussions with the commissioners. Although the discomfort of his kidney ailment was compounded by rheumatism, he assembled the Tabeguache chiefs and headmen in his council room to prepare a strategy for dealing with the commissioners.

Ouray's one concession to his stiff joints and declining health was traveling in a horse-drawn buggy. Chipeta often rode alongside on her sorrel mare. This time she was content to watch from the window as he drove through the gate with his bodyguard at the reins to meet with the commissioners.

The August 29 council opened in a positive tone. Whatever the southern Utes chose to do with their land was agreeable, Ouray reported. The commissioners relaxed. Their confidence soon dissolved, however, as Ouray listed the Tabeguache issues. White settlers had moved into Uncompahgre Park, a piece of land the Tabeguache specifically retained under the 1873 agreement. The area contained one of the sacred hot springs that Ouray visited more frequently now to soothe his aching body and weary spirit. Agent W.D. Wheeler had put signs along the reservation boundary line declaring the valley to be Ute territory, but the settlers ignored the signs and began farming the land.

Ouray had instructed his people to leave these intruders alone, but now he demanded that the government remove them.

He had no interest in the commissioners' explanation that this was the only soil where the people of the town of Ouray could grow crops. The commissioners suggested the government would buy the four-square-mile property. Ouray refused, declaring that his people had no land to sell to a government that had not paid for its last purchase. He stated firmly that the Tabeguache were happy with their Uncompahgre Valley and did not want to move north. Realizing they could make no further progress, the commissioners distributed some presents and returned to Fort Garland.

Pfeiffer was waiting for the commissioners with a proposal from the Southern Utes to exchange their land, but only if the government paid them the previous indebtedness. The commissioners sent the proposal to Washington for approval and dispatched the commission secretary, William S. Stickney, and the escort, McCauley, to obtain written release of any interest in the Southern Ute reservation from the White River, Uintah, and Tabeguache bands.

---

[1] Hafen, LeRoy R., and Ann W., Editors, *The Diaries of William Henry Jackson Frontier Photographer*, (Glendale, Calif: The Arther H. Clark Company, 1959), 287-289.

[2] Ibid.

[3] By this time the Agency maintained two cow camps to supply meat for the agency's dining room and beef on the hoof for the Utes. Herman Leuders was employed as chief herder. H.F. Lauter was the herder at the small camp near Los Pinos. The large camp at Gunnison was staffed by James Kelley and Sidney Jocknick (whose memoirs give a picture of life on the western slope in this period).

[4] *Rocky Mountain News*, October 1, 1874.

[5] *Cañon City Times*, January 21, 1875.

[6] Ibid, February 25, 1875.

[7] Jones, William C., and Elizabeth B. Jones, "Archaeology of the Eastern Ute: A Symposium," Colorado Council of Professional Archaeologists, 1998, 173-4.

[8] *Cañon City Times*, January 21, 1875.

[9] Letter from Secretary of Interior transmitting, in compliance with resolution of the Senate of December 8, 1879, concerning the Ute Indians in Colorado (Washington, D,C,: Government Printing Office, 1879), 40-

41; William M. Leeds , Acting Commissioner, Office of Indian Affairs, to Brevet Major General Edward Hatch, June 29, 1878, NARA Record Group 75.

# Chapter 6
# DISASTER STRIKES

In early September Chipeta opened her door to a runner with news of trouble at White River. On September 1 white men had killed a Ute at the Junction Ranch in Middle Park. Two days later a group of White River Utes led by Washington and Piah stole a number of horses from white settlers and shot a man named Elliott at his cabin on Blue Creek. A posse of white men pursued the fleeing Utes. Four miles from the White River Agency, the pursuers came on the peaceful camp of Chief Judge, whose people were fishing and gathering berries. Spying several of the stolen horses, the white men charged the camp. The women and children fled into the bushes. The men jumped onto horses and escaped to the agency, where they raised an alarm that they were under attack. Sixty mounted warriors met the ten white pursuers in the agency compound. Agent Meeker was away but Mr. Post, the agency clerk, intervened.

The white men wanted the stolen horses and the men who killed Elliott. Mr. Post called an impromptu council. Judge said that Chief Washington had arrived at his camp and reported that Piah had killed a white man and fled west with

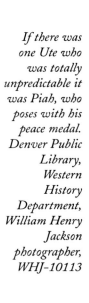

*If there was one Ute who was totally unpredictable it was Piah, who poses with his peace medal. Denver Public Library, Western History Department, William Henry Jackson photographer, WHJ-10113*

his small band of warriors. Washington left a string of horses with Judge and disappeared. Mr. Post said Washington had passed through the agency and reported the killings of the Ute and the white man called Elliott. Chiefs Douglas and Nicaagut had set out for Middle Park to assure the white settlers that this was an isolated incident and that the Utes as a whole wanted peace.

Judge agreed to round up and return the stolen horses. The white posse agreed to take the horses and leave but threatened that any more incidents would bring an army of white men to wipe out all the Utes. They specifically warned that Piah and Washington should not enter white territory.

Ouray listened with growing aggravation that these two Utes could not seem to stay out of trouble. However, the matter appeared to be resolved, and he sent the runner back with a message that he would wait to hear from Piah and Washington. In private he and Chipeta discussed their fears that the reckless Piah and half-crazy Washington could start a war.

On September 18 both Judge and Washington appeared near Hot Sulphur Springs for a meeting with Mr. Stickney, secretary to the commissioners. They were among thirty-four chiefs of the Yampa and Grand River bands (known collectively as the White River Utes) who relinquished any claim to the southern Ute territory. Mr. Stickney authorized distribution of $500 worth of presents to the chiefs. Two days later White River Agent Nathan Meeker purchased from H.E. Peck's general store in Windsor, Colorado, $490 worth of shirts, shoes, socks, belts, fabric and thread, halters and bridles, shovels, pocket knives, crackers, peaches, prunes, canned goods, and sixty pounds of candy for the Utes.

A member of the white posse that pursued the Utes to White River sent a detailed account of the incident to the *Rocky Mountain News.*[1] In addition to the report of murder and horse theft by the Utes, he described vast acres of land given up in the last treaty, which the Utes had burned to make it useless to the white men. A small paragraph noting successful farming under way at White River with plentiful crops of watermelons, corn, cucumbers, squash, tomatoes and potatoes passed virtually unnoticed. Readers around the state, and the nation, saw only vengeful savages ready to wage war on white settlers at any moment.

Tempers had calmed by the time the commissioners met with the southern chiefs in early November to conclude the exchange of reservation land. Each member of the three Southern Ute bands received seventeen silver dollars in payment for past indebtedness from the Brunot Agreement — a total of $15,334 to 902 Utes.[2]

On November 11 twenty-three Tabeguache chiefs gave the final release for the southern land, and three days later William Stickney distributed annuity goods and supplies to seventy-two Tabeguache heads of families. As usual, Ouray and Chipeta did not share in the annuities. They bought what they needed with Ouray's salary and income from the farm. Sapovanero claimed the first distribution. He signed for large quantities of goods, including 2,228 yards of calico fabric, to distribute to families who were not present on distribution day. Most families received calico and red flannel fabrics, needles and thread, flannel undershirts, overshirts, socks, and a little candy.

In their report to the president the commissioners estimated that fifteen hundred Utes lived in Colorado on some ten million acres, and in Utah, five hundred Utes resided on the Uintah reservation. They suggested that the White River and Tabeguache groups seemed amiable to colocating at one agency but none of them wanted to live with the Southern Utes. The commissioners said that the White River and Tabeguache Utes might take part of their payment due from the Brunot agreement in livestock, particularly sheep.

In late December, Ouray, Shavano, Wass, Alhandra, and Galota made a brief trip to Washington. They arrived on January 2, 1879, and negotiated the sale of four square miles of valuable valley farmland to the government for ten thousand dollars. Ouray opposed selling this sacred area that they had fought so hard to keep in the Brunot agreement and thought it foolish to accept another government promise to pay. The other chiefs outvoted him, but his argument proved wise. It was half a century before the Utes received payment.

Shortly after the chiefs returned from Washington, an illegal prospector panning the streams ten miles south of the Los Pinos Agency turned up a few gold nuggets. A city of tents sprang up overnight as miners swarmed to the area. Many Utes clamored to chase the miners out. Ouray said he did not expect that they would find much gold, but the miners could stay as long as they did not build houses. The younger chiefs chafed at what seemed an old man's cowardly approach, but by the end of summer no appreciable amount of gold had been found and the miners disappeared.

William Saunders, a twenty-year-old reporter for the *Ouray Times,* was introduced to Ouray and Chipeta by Dr.

John Lacey, the Los Pinos physician, in September 1879. Although Chipeta had seen thirty-six summers, Saunders mistook her for a much younger woman. He must have fallen a little in love with her because years later her ideal image lingered in his mind when he described her in his memoir.

*She was twenty years old, a straight, slender figure, dressed in buckskin jacket, fringed leggings and moccasins. In the two braids of black hair hanging at the side of her head were laced many little nuggets of yellow gold.³ A light girdle of small hammered silver links, polished until they shone, with pendants of light and dark blue turquoise, circle the jacket.*

*Her skin was the color of deep amber, and she did not have the flat face of the Ute squaw, but her features were regular and well defined, and her nose was straight and finely molded. Her eyes were quick and observant, sparkling with intelligence and good humor, and her whole manner highly animated. Her wrists and hands were small as were her feet. Usually moccasins are clumsy looking. Chipeta's were well shaped . . . they were very plain, without the least ornament. She wore no rings on her fingers and none in her ears, for good reason, for her ears were in perfect harmony with the rest of her beautifully shaped features, and earrings would have disfigured them.*

*Nor was she the servile thing the other Ute women were. She treated chief Ouray and all of us as her equals. Indeed, she was so different from the other Ute women I had seen in camp and about the agency that I sat looking at her intently and wondering from what race this spirited creature had sprung.⁴*

Soon after they met, Saunders and Dr. Lacey accompanied Ouray and Chipeta on a hunting and fishing trip. They all carried Winchester repeating rifles that required cocking the lever under the stock after each shot. To Saunders's amazement, Chipeta handled the difficult gun with the ease of long practice. Chipeta, he later recalled, was the best shot, and Ouray was proud to have her demonstrate her skill.

On his first day of hunting Saunders and Chipeta came to the crest of a hill and he saw movement in the brush down below. He raised his gun poised to fire, but Chipeta put her hand on his gun barrel and warned him to stop. In a few moments Ouray emerged from the underbrush. Chipeta slapped Saunders lightly on the cheek with her fingers, as she might a child, and chided, "Very bad hunter."[5] In the end he had better luck with fishing.

Throughout the spring and summer Ouray had received messages about the increasing tensions at White River. In little more than a year Agent Meeker had made a mess of things with his attempts to domesticate the Utes. As the situation escalated in late summer, level-headed White River chiefs advised white settlers near the reservation to leave. Former Ute Special Agent James B. Thompson, resigned from government service since 1874, had established a large ranch near Hayden,

*The Los Pinos II employees posed with some of the local Utes.*
*Colorado Historical Society, F-7358*

not far from the White River Agency. He and his family had continued a friendly relationship with the Utes, but he avoided being drawn into agency business. When the Ute leaders advised Thompson to get out, he abandoned the ranch and moved his family to Denver.

On the afternoon of October 1, 1879, Chipeta was at home on the farm helping the cook prepare dinner. Ouray and a few friends had gone hunting in the mountains. Late in the day an anxious White River Ute arrived with an urgent message for Ouray. There had been a battle, he reported, between some White River Utes and soldiers. Many were killed. With a sinking heart Chipeta sent one of the hired boys who cared for the livestock to guide the messenger to Ouray's camp.

Years later a number of writers credited Chipeta with riding all night to find Ouray while others made her a heroine who personally rode to White River to stop the fighting. One writer even endowed Chipeta with advance knowledge of the attack which allowed her to spirit away potential white victims.[6] The actual events were described in eyewitness accounts and in testimony before a congressional inquiry panel. Certainly Chipeta played an integral role in the events that followed but not in the way that became part of her legend.

The report delivered by the White River messenger on that autumn night brought Ouray home the next day. Chipeta had already alerted the Uncompahgre chiefs and headmen, and they were assembled at the house ready for a council. Ouray had mixed emotions. It appeared that the White River Utes were provoked. Meeker had made threats that he would call for soldiers to come and take the uncooperative chiefs away to prison. When soldiers were spotted entering the reservation, the Utes believed they were in danger and took the offensive advantage. To make matters worse, some Tabeguache Utes participated in the battle. Ouray had given his all to keep a truce with the white invaders, yet it appeared the Utes would never be allowed to live in peace.

Perhaps, Ouray told the chiefs, it was time to make a stand together and fight to the death. Sitting unnoticed by the door, Chipeta shook her head in disbelief at Ouray's words.

She wanted to argue with him, to quote his past advice for peace at all cost, but she dared not speak in front of the council. She was relieved to hear a few men oppose Ouray, saying they wanted no part of the White River Utes' problems. The heated council went on all night.

By morning Ouray and the headmen agreed they would not support the White River fight. Ouray chose to send Sapovanero to intervene. The chiefs agreed on the message — the White River Utes should stop fighting and no Tabeguache warriors would come to their aid. Ouray asked the Los Pinos agent to send one white man along with Sapovanero as an emissary to stop the soldiers. A young agency employee named Joseph Brady agreed to go. Fifteen trusted Utes were selected to accompany the men as guards. Just as the council broke up to see the riders off on their mission, another messenger arrived.

"They have killed Agent Meeker and all the employees at White River," the frightened envoy reported. "The white women and children have been taken hostage." The assembly was stunned.

Two hundred-fifty White River warriors, entrenched in the hills along the Milk River, held the remnants of three United States cavalry companies barricaded behind overturned wagons and the carcasses of dead mules. Major T.T. Thornburg with a contingent of one hundred sixty men, a thirty-three wagon supply train, and four hundred mules and horses, had left Rawlins, Wyoming on September 24, 1879, in response to Agent Meeker's request for protection at the White River Ute Agency. On September 26, the soldiers were sixty-five miles from the agency and about to enter reservation land. Nickaagut, Colorow, and a small contingent of Utes twice approached Thornburg and advised him not to bring soldiers onto the reservation.

On the morning of September 29 Thornburg ignored the warnings. The Utes attacked. Thornburg and twelve men were killed, forty-two soldiers were wounded, and one hundred fifty or more mules and uncounted horses were shot. Twenty-three Utes were reported killed. On October 1 Captain Dodge and a company of Negro cavalry arrived. They were unable to rout the well-positioned Utes. On October 5 General Merritt arrived from the east with five hundred men. About this time Joseph Brady, the Los Pinos employee, appeared waving a white flag. Unseen by the soldiers, Sapovanero approached Nickaagut and the Utes to deliver Ouray's cease-fighting order. Shooting stopped. General Merritt told Brady to go back where he came from. Some time after Brady left the soldiers realized that their Ute attackers had disappeared. The Utes who had destroyed the agency, twenty-five miles south of the battle scene, retreated into the high mountains with their captives — three white women and two small children.[7]

An army scout had escaped from the fight at Milk River and managed to ride all night and all day to reach a telegraph station at Rawlins, Wyoming. His message reached Governor Pitkin about the same time Ouray received word of the battle. The governor sent telegrams to communities around the state warning that the Utes were off the reservation. Word spread like wildfire and exploded into rumor that two thousand Utes were on the warpath, and Ouray could not control them.

Militia companies organized in every community, collected arms and ammunition, and blockaded streets in anticipation of Indian attack. Rumors of bloody slaughter escalated to gruesome tales of entire towns wiped out by rampaging Utes. Eight days after the massacre at White River, Governor Pitkin sent a special train to Lake City carrying one hundred-fifty Springfield rifles and an equal number of cartridge boxes, ten thousand rounds of ammunition, and other supplies. Lake City was designated a gathering point to supply the southwest with arms. Miners and ranchers gathered food and ammunition and prepared to defend their property. Troops were dispatched from Fort Hayes in Kansas, Forts Clark and Sam Houston in Texas, and Fort Union in New Mexico to protect the terrified white citizens of Colorado. Overnight the state became an armed camp.

Meanwhile, the Tabeguache and the Southern Utes remained close to home, fearful of what might happen next. At Ouray's request, Agent Wilson Stanley sent a message to Southern Ute Agent Henry Page advising him and all the Utes to lend no assistance to the White River Utes. Page later reported that three days after the massacre six White River Utes had appeared at Ignacio attempting to recruit support. There was a council and a war dance, but in the end the Southern Utes had chosen not to join the fight.

In the resulting white panic, several innocent Utes were shot on sight. Among these victims were Ouray's uncle and nephew who were killed while hunting beaver. The conduct of the white citizens compelled Agent Stanley to write to Indian Commissioner Ezra Hayt on October 15th:

> *I hope and trust that the Indian Department in Washington will use every influence to see that the Utes have a fair hearing in this matter . . . I am absolutely disgusted at the conduct of the white people and am not at all surprised that the Indians do occasionally turn upon the traducers and robbers of their rights.*[8]

Two weeks passed and the White River Utes still held five white hostages. Interior Secretary Carl Schurz took action. On October 14 he wired former Ute agent Charles Adams and asked him to rescue the Meeker women and children. There was more to Schurz's choice of Adams than his relationship of trust among the Tabeguache. Prior to his assignment as agent at Los Pinos, Adams had served almost a year as acting agent at White River and established a particularly cooperative relationship with Chief Douglas. Adams was the one man Schurz believed the White River chiefs, the military leaders, and the white citizens would accept as mediator. Adams was by that time a special agent for the post office based in Denver, and Schurz had secured his services on loan. Adams left immediately for Los Pinos.

Arriving at Ouray's farm on October 18, Adams found the chief deeply depressed and looking ill. Chipeta, he later reported, looked like a haggard middle-aged woman instead of the dimpled beauty that he had seen just a year earlier. Both Ouray and Chipeta were relieved to see Adams. Ouray admitted he was so depressed that he had considered taking his own life. The actions of the White River Utes affected the future of all the Utes. Ouray saw no hopeful resolution this time.

Adams, Ouray, and Chipeta talked well into the night, and Ouray at last saw some hope for the situation, if the Meeker hostages were recovered unharmed. Ouray summoned Sapovanero, Shavano, and Young Colorow along with an escort of ten Utes to accompany Adams to White River. An agency employee, Captain Cline, organized men and equipment, a supply wagon, and a buckboard to carry the rescued women and children. Chipeta sent a teepee to shelter the Meeker party.

A messenger rode ahead to tell Chief Douglas that Adams was coming to get the hostages. Two nights later two White River Utes, Coho and Henry Jim, met the rescue party at the Grand River. They reported that the white women and children were safe. The next morning Adams found the captives in a small camp of fifteen lodges on Plateau Creek.

Adams and Sapovanero met in council with Chief Douglas and fifty headmen and warriors. Douglas said he would release the captives if Adams went to White River and persuaded the soldiers to leave. Adams insisted Douglas must first release the women and children. Douglas and his men began to argue among themselves. Aggravated by the delays, Sapovanero announced that if the women were not released, Ouray would come with a company of soldiers and kill Douglas and all his men. As he finished his speech Ouray's sister, Tsashin, burst into the council and demanded that they allow the hostages to leave. She broke the stalemate.

Twenty-three days after being abducted, the white women and children were freed. As they prepared to mount their horses, Tsashin came to say goodbye. She saw that Mrs. Meeker's horse was outfitted with an old torn saddle. Searching through a pile of military saddles recovered from the battle at Milk River, she selected a good one and directed one of the men to put it on Mrs. Meeker's horse. The women later praised Tsashin for her kindness to them, reporting that she had made clothes and moccasins for the children while they were prisoners.

*A* Harper's Weekly *artist drew this scene at the Meeker agency after the "rebellion." Only the smoke house was left standing.*
P. David Smith Collection

Harper's Weekly *(November 11, 1879) captioned this drawing "Major Thornburgh's Last Charge." In fact there was no attack by Thornburgh.*
P. David Smith Collection

The freed captives rode out with Captain Cline who escorted them forty miles to the place where the wagons waited. Charles Adams, with Sapovanero and twenty-five White River Utes (sent along to ensure that Adams lived up to his part of the bargain) rode to the remains of the White River agency. They found General Merritt, who had arrived with reinforcements at the same time Ouray's cease-fire message was delivered. Adams convinced Merritt to withdraw his men. After reporting success to Douglas, Adams left for Los Pinos.

Messengers fairly flew between White River and Los Pinos with reports of each event. The agency overflowed with tense Utes waiting for word of war or peace. William J. Pollock, an Indian Bureau inspector who arrived at Los Pinos in the midst of this suspense, reported to Commissioner Hayt in Washington, "Nervousness apparent here but peace prevails. Saint Peter could not save this country, but for the council of Ouray." [9]

On October 29 Ouray waited at his gate to meet the returning party. Tears streaked Chipeta's face as she ushered the three women into the house like a mother receiving long lost children. She did her best to make them comfortable. After supper she stoked the fires in the stoves and gave them their first good night's sleep in almost a month. The two little children she cuddled and soothed with songs. The next morning Ralph Meeker arrived for a reunion with his mother and sister. He escorted the women and children to his home in Greeley. When they left, Chipeta was still crying over the fear and hardship the women had endured and, no doubt, over the consequences that were sure to come for her own people.

The incident at White River became fodder for a media campaign to rid Colorado of the Utes once and for all. Headlines blared: "The Utes Must Go." [10] The federal government, said the newsmen, must quit coddling Ute savages and make them work or starve to death like a white man — and do it someplace other than in Colorado. Dave Day, notorious editor of the *Solid Muldoon*, opined that the only way "to civilize an Indian is to put him into a wooden overcoat and lay him gently under the sod." [11]

William Saunders visited the Ouray farm and presented the Ute point of view on the Meeker affair in an article that never found a willing publisher. Saunders quoted Ouray:

> *The Utes are not to blame in this. I told you when we were out hunting that I was having trouble restraining my young men. White prospectors and hunters came on the reservation and shot the Utes when they saw them. You know yourselves that this happened. My uncle and my nephew were killed by the soldiers a few days ago, while they were hunting. The soldiers said that they had no right to have rifles. They have to when they hunt.*
>
> *Meeker made the Utes work for his own glory and refused to feed them when they did not work as he wanted them to work. He had no right to do that. The Government in our treaty said nothing about work, but agreed to give us these lands and to give us supplies, blankets and food. They have violated that treaty and my men were angry. They heard that Meeker had sent for the soldiers to punish them for not working and coming to church, they always remember what Chivington did to the Cheyennes, and they tried to prevent the soldiers from getting to the agency by killing them. Then they went crazy and killed Meeker and the other white men, and took the women and the children. They should not have done that.* [12]

Immediately following the release of the prisoners, Secretary Schurz appointed Charles Adams, Ouray, and General Edward Hatch, commander of the New Mexico peacekeeping troops, as commissioners to investigate the Meeker incident. The commissioners set up shop in a former stable at Los Pinos and began their work on November 12, 1879. Ouray sent an order that all White River Utes involved in ambushing the soldiers or taking the hostages should report to Los Pinos and tell their version of the incident. The few Utes who chose to come were armed to the teeth, refused to identify any guilty Utes, and stated that they knew nothing.

While Ouray was busy at the agency, Chipeta had her hands full at home. The chiefs met so often in Ouray's council room that they became residents at the house. In addition, many of the White River Utes who traveled to Los Pinos for the command appearances camped in the fields around the farm. The house became the Ute command center, the place to come for news.

In addition to the frightening situation and the chaos on the farm, Chipeta suffered a growing concern over Ouray's mental and physical health. The implications of the attack on federal troops and the massacre of agency employees, the frustration of being part of the review commission, and fear of what would happen next weighed heavily on Ouray. He was frequently too ill to attend meetings of the commission and, when present, had little to say. He sometimes rejected his seat at the commissioners' table to sit on the floor with the attending Utes. He discarded the white men's clothing and resumed his buckskins. On November 16, Ouray announced:

*I do not want to be a chief. I grow old and tottering. Let some young man with the fire of youth in his veins take my place. I have a farm which I would rather cultivate and watch the seed planted by me grow up to maturity than to be head chief. They all came to me with their troubles. I know everything and have all their burdens to bear. Washington no want me to give up my position, wants me to stay and govern Utes. I want only to be known as Ouray, the friend of the white man.* [13]

Prior to the commission meetings, Adams had gone to Greeley and interviewed the three white women — Arvella and Josephine Meeker and Flora Price. He produced for the other two commissioners a list of twelve Utes the women had identified as their abductors or as involved in the massacre at the agency. The women had reported that they were raped by Douglas, Persune, and Coho, who held them hostage. Nickaagut (also called Jack or Captain Jack by white men), Wahnzitz, Washington, Canella (Johnson), Ebeneezer,

Ahuutupuwit, Serio, Crepah, and Tim Johnson were also implicated. Mrs. Price reported that Tsashin's husband, Johnson, had boasted of killing Major Thornburgh who led the troops.

With the exception of Douglas, Ouray did not believe the men identified would do such things. In the privacy of his home Ouray complained, "These women have told Hatch and Adams tales about the way they were treated by the Utes. I do not believe them. Most of these Utes had their own squaws with them in camp and it would have been impossible for things to have happened as those girls say."[14] As he spoke he paced the room and became increasingly agitated.

Chipeta shook her head in disagreement. "Persune, Douglass, and Jack, very bad Utes," she said. She told him what she had heard among the White River Ute women in the past, including his own sister Tsashin. Ouray shook his head to fight off her words, but he sat down and listened.

The next day Ouray made a suggestion to Adams and Hatch. "No Ute believes he will be treated fairly in Colorado. Interview them in Washington, D.C."[15] The proposal was telegraphed to Secretary Schurz, who quickly approved, and a delegation of Utes was hastily assembled. For the first time Ouray refused to make the trip without Chipeta. The stress of recent events had taken their toll on his health, and he needed her support and council. Quite likely he also suffered some remorse that he had not taken her along to meet Friday, the Arapaho boy who was the grown-up Pahlone, the child she had loved.

As they made preparations to leave, Chipeta called for the medicine man. His ministrations included four small, dark-red pouches filled with of herbs and amulets to bring the company of good spirits during their coming travels. Chipeta sewed these to the front and back shoulder seams of Ouray's best deerskin shirt. The pouches were barely noticeable on the heavily fringed shirt beaded in white, maroon, navy, and gold.[16]

The delegation assembled in the yard of Los Pinos Agency in the early hours of December 29, 1879. Under a clear night sky the temperature hovered at zero. The breath of men and horses surrounded the party like white smoke. Five-day-old snow crunched under stamping hooves. For several days the chiefs had argued that it was foolish to ride into the mountains at this time of year, but General Hatch insisted that the U.S. Army could get through without problem.

Agent Wilson Stanley chose not to travel with the delegation, sending in his place the agency farmer, William H. Berry, as interpreter. Unknown to the delegation, Stanley planned to leave Los Pinos. He had already drafted his resignation. One of his final acts on the last day of December was settling accounts. He wrote a $250 voucher for Ouray's quarterly government salary with a notation that Ouray was unavailable to sign for the funds due to a trip to Washington, D.C.

William H. Berry joined General Hatch, Ouray, and Chipeta to form the lead party. They were followed by Wash, Golata, Jocnick, Sieblo, and Augustine of the Uncompaghre and Nickaagut (Jack), Sowawick, Toppaganta, Alhandra, and Unca Sam of the White River Utes. Lieutenant Taylor with a company of ten soldiers and three wagons brought up the rear. The procession rode out at 5:00 a.m. The soldiers huddled silently in their heavy coats; the Utes, wrapped in blankets and buffalo robes, chanted an east-going song for safe journey.

They followed the Gunnison River, then turned south to the trail over Cochetopa Pass. Intermittent snow swirled about them during the climb up the steep path. As they neared the summit a few days later, they found the route buried in snow six to ten feet deep. Berry and the Indians pushed ahead and succeeded in reaching the cabin where they had planned to stop for the night. But the soldiers struggled to move the teams of horses and heavy wagons. By nightfall they were mired in the snow. General Hatch set the men to work burrowing into a deep snowdrift. With shovels they carved out a cave and huddled together for a cold rest. About three o'clock in the morning, fearing the men would freeze, General Hatch roused them and put them to work shoveling so the wagons could move out at first light. The sun had come and gone when the exhausted company reached the cabin. The men and horses were allowed to rest a day before the journey continued. The 140-mile trip from Los Pinos to Saguache took six days.[17]

Charles Adams and Otto Mears joined the travelers at Saguache. After the exhausting struggle through high-elevation snow, the wagon trip across the broad, flat San Luis Valley seemed easy. The delegation spent the night in Alamosa's Perry House Hotel. Concerned there might be trouble when word spread that the Utes were in town, Adams posted soldiers to stand guard. A number of local people congregated and threatened to hang the Indians, but level-headed citizens tempered the crowds. One angry mob did hang an unfortunate Mexican, an alleged horse thief.

Early the next morning the soldiers accompanied the Utes out of town on the 6:20 a.m. Denver & Rio Grande train. The prospect of her first train ride probably caused Chipeta far more anxiety than crossing a snow-packed mountain pass on horseback in subzero temperatures. She knew the mechanics of rail travel from listening to Ouray's endless tales after his previous trips. But it was still a new and fearsome adventure to actually step inside a big wooden box pulled by the iron horse belching smoke and steam. The clackety-clack of the rails jarred every bone in her body, and the sway of the car as the track curved with the lay of the land made her stomach queasy. The stops in Baldy, Fort Garland, Placer, Sangre de Cristo, Veta Pass, Mule Shoe, Ojo, La Veta, Wahatoga, Walsen's, Cuchara, Huerfano, Graneros, Greenhorn, and San Carlos were too brief to provide any relief.

Right on schedule at 1:45 p.m. the train pulled into the D&RG station in the town of South Pueblo. When the track curved behind the roundhouse Chipeta could see the station house where they would switch to an eastbound train. Passengers began to gather their coats and satchels as the train slowed to a stop. Adams allowed the other travellers to leave the car before he assembled the delegation and led them down the narrow steps into the afternoon sunshine. Chipeta was the last one out of the car, and her legs wobbled as her feet touched the ground. She steadied herself with a hand on Ouray's back.

*The South Pueblo Railroad Station and roundhouse about the time*
*Ouray and Chipeta were mobbed.*
*Courtesy of Pueblo City — County Library District*

With Lieutenant Taylor and his men following, Adams led the delegation across the tracks and into the wood-frame station house. Most of the passengers had already greeted waiting friends and relatives and moved toward the wagons and carriages waiting at the far end of the station. Inside, groups of travelers dressed in their best clothes perched on benches like birds on fence rows. A few men stood at a lunch counter at the far end of the cavernous room, but Adams led the Utes to the back of the station where the spacious dining room was nearly empty. He ordered meals for the group, and they settled back to relax.

Before the food arrived at the table the Utes heard shouting in the station. Lieutenant Taylor and his men rushed out of the dining room to find an angry crowd of local citizens pouring into the station house. Shaking their fists and yelling "hang the red devils," the locals scanned the station for any sign of the Utes. Taylor's men formed a ring around the crowd and managed to drive them back outside.

After a hasty consultation, Adams and Taylor agreed that they should move the Utes onto the outbound train, which could be more easily guarded. The delegation members gathered their satchels and followed Adams into the station house where the waiting passengers sat wide-eyed and silent. The roar of the hostile crowd outside filled the air and rattled the window glass in station house. Huddled among the men of the delegation, Chipeta feared they might not get out of the state of Colorado alive.

Adams, Mears, and Berry formed a shield around the delegation as they emerged from the station house. Lieutenant Taylor and the military escort held the crowd at bay. As the delegation moved toward the tracks, a rock thudded against a nearby railroad car. As if on signal, the crowd surged forward and pelted the Utes with stones and lumps of coal taken from a car parked on the side rail. One man rushed past the soldiers and struck Sowawick over the head with a club. Lieutenant Taylor sprang into the crowd to grab the weapon. The assailant fell backward out of reach, and the crowd turned its attention to the scuffle between the two men. Taking advantage of the momentary diversion, Adams hustled the Utes off to the empty eastbound train. With the delegation out of sight the soldiers and railroad staff dispersed the rabble-rousers. When everything was quiet, the other passengers boarded the train on schedule, furtively peeking at the Utes as they found seats as far away from the delegation as possible. Chipeta trembled in her seat until they pulled out of the station and away from the town.

As the train jostled eastward across the prairie, people gathered along the tracks in small towns to shake their fists and curse the passing Indians. Such hatred from complete strangers must have brought tears to Chipeta's eyes and a knot like a solid rock to her stomach.

Telegraph wires bristled with news of the Utes' advance. By the time they reached Chicago, an abusive mob waited at the Rock Island depot. A strong guard of police and railroad men reinforced the soldiers to break a path to the waiting horse-drawn omnibus. Not to be dissuaded, the crowd ran after the bus. Driving right past the hotel, the driver turned the corner onto the square and the unsuspecting throng followed. Coming around the far side of the square, the driver suddenly urged the horses to a gallop, leaving the pursuers behind. The omnibus came to a halt in front of the hotel. The delegation had just enough time to scramble inside before the mob confronted the guards posted at the door.

The next morning a crowd gathered early at the Baltimore & Ohio station prepared to vent their hatred toward the departing Utes. But the delegation slipped away quietly from another station on a route through Fort Wayne, Indiana. Charles Adams remained in Chicago on business, but two new travelers joined the group. Leverett Kelly, the former Los Pinos agent who was privy to the early complaints about Meeker, came at Ouray's request. S. M. Demmond, travel agent for the Pittsburgh, Fort Wayne and Chicago line, rode along to handle any problems. The eastern part of the trip was quiet.

---

[1] *Rocky Mountain News,* September 22, 1878.

[2] "Ute Indians of Colorado," (Washington, DC: U.S. Government Printing Office, 1879), 44.

[3] Saunders, William, unpublished manuscript in possession of author (Smith). Saunders's description is questionable because no other source describes Chipeta wearing her hair in braids, a style not common to Tabeguache women, or with gold nuggets in her hair.

[4] Ibid, 78-79.

[5] Ibid, 85-86.

[6] Everrett, George G. and Wendell F. Hutchinson, *Under The Angel of Shavano,* (Denver, Colo: Golden Bell Press, 1963), 35.

[7] Dawson, Thomas F. and F.J.V. Skiff, *The Ute War: A History of the White River Massacre,* (Denver, Colo: Tribune Publishing House, 1879).

[8] Stanley, Wilson to Ezra Hayt, October 15, 1879, NARA Record Group 75, Special Case 112.

[9] Ibid, 426.

[10] *Ouray Times,* October 25, 1879.

[11] *Solid Muldoon,* March 21, 1990.

[12] Saunders, 138.

[13] *Denver Tribune,* March 2, 1880.

[14] Saunders, 138.

[15] McClellan, Val J., *This Is Our Land,* Vol II, (Jamestown, Ohio: Western Publishers, 1979), 513-514.

[16] The medicine pouches can be seen in photos of Ouray taken in Washington, D.C., and remain attached to the shirt on display in the Ute Indian Museum, Montrose, Colorado.

[17] *Washington Post,* January 12, 1880.

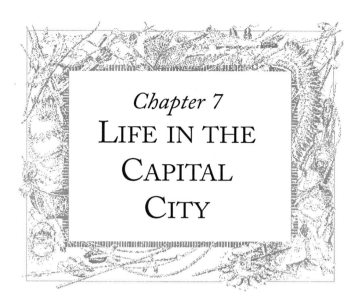

Chapter 7

# LIFE IN THE CAPITAL CITY

The Western Express pulled into the Baltimore and Potomac station right on time at 8:55 a.m. on Sunday, January 11, 1880. Word of the protests and angry crowds in Chicago had reached Washington ahead of the Ute delegation. Fearing more of the same, Secretary of Interior Carl Schurz ordered a detail of metropolitan police to meet the train. But no crowds gathered and the station was quiet.

The *Washington Post* the next day devoted more than a column and a half of front-page space to the arrival of the delegation. The reporter offered a detailed although unflattering description of his first impressions of the Utes.

> *Chipeta and Ouray appeared benevolent . . . while in the others there was a shadow of fierceness and vindictiveness. She is a large squatty woman, about forty-five years old with broad flat features, a large round head and long black hair parted in the center and thrown carelessly at either side, almost concealing her features. Her form was enveloped in the folds of a large black and gray woolen shawl concealing her attires, the only part*

*of which visible was a pair of handsomely worked buck-*
*skin leggings. Arctic rubbers covered her feet, which*
*were encased in buckskin moccasins.*

*Ouray, who is fifty years old, is in appearance*
*very much like his squaw, except that his hair was*
*plaited and rested on his shoulders. He had a dark blan-*
*ket thrown around him concealing a white calico shirt*
*with red figures, and a dark cloth vest, and wore over-*
*shoes and decorated blue flannel leggings. His head was*
*covered with a large broad-brim . . . slouch hat. He car-*
*ried a bundle of wrappings strapped together . . .*

*[The rest of the delegation were] . . . wrapped in*
*blankets, but their costumes could be seen as half-civilized.*
*All wore calico or vari-colored flannel shirts, in which*
*were worked beads, quills and other ornaments. Some*
*were shod in army brogans and with one or two exceptions*
*had on slouch hats. Shells, buttons, and other bright orna-*
*ments were studded in their hair. One fellow carried his*
*blanket on his arm and strapped to his hip was a leather*
*holster containing a large army revolver . . . . The mem-*
*bers of the delegation were mainly chiefs, well advanced in*
*life, and ex-chiefs, but there were several young ones*
*among them. All were lithe and active, with stout,*
*brawny frames and superior muscular development. There*
*was a great similarity in their appearance, nearly all*
*being of medium height and squatty, and bearing evidence*
*of being well-fed men . . .* [1]

Indian Bureau representatives Seward and Andrews met the delegation at the station and immediately handed the interpreter, William H. Berry, a letter from Secretary Schurz instructing him to make no statements to the press. As ordered, Berry politely declined questions posed by the *Washington Post* reporter. However, somewhere between the station platform and the hotel doorway, the relentless news-man coaxed from Berry details of the delegation's travel experiences that made tantalizing Monday morning reading.

*Ouray, Chipeta, and part of the 1880 delegation. This was the only time Chipeta went to Washington, D. C.*

*Colorado Historical Society, F-12058*

Meanwhile, Seward and Andrews assembled the delegation and their few belongings and led them out through the baggage gate. A horse-drawn omnibus waited to take them to the Tremont House hotel. The few travelers milling about in the station stopped to stare at the group, but there were no demonstrations. At this early hour on a damp, cold Sunday morning, the streets of Washington were nearly empty.

The omnibus drove past President's Park on the south grounds of the Executive Mansion (later called the White House). In his role as host, Henry Andrews began a running commentary on each building, park, and monument they passed. Otto Mears translated for the Utes. On their right Andrews pointed out a tall obelisk under construction, a tribute to the first great chief of the United States. The observant Ouray probably mentioned that it took the white men a long time to stack stones as this tower had been partially completed when he made his first trip to Washington as a young man.[2]

Skirting the adjacent open parks of the Agricultural Department and the Smithsonian Institution along B Street NW they had an unobstructed view of the gleaming white Capitol, which dwarfed the rest of the city. Chipeta could not take her eyes off the imposing structure. It was larger than anything she had seen before. She was surprised when Ouray told her that no one lived there.

The little brick Tremont House nestled in the crook of Second and Indiana Streets. Officer Farrar of the Metropolitan Police guarded the front door. Half a dozen curious boys stopped their game of hoops in the street to watch the Indians emerge from the bus. The only other observers were a few regular Tremont House boarders.

Ouray and Chipeta were assigned a private room, and the rest of the Utes shared two rooms. Soon after arrival the Utes were led downstairs to a large basement room under the regular dining room, where they were served breakfast and where they would eat the rest of their meals during their stay. Secretary Shurz requested that they be isolated as much as possible to avoid incidents with other boarders who might share the growing national Ute hatred. Chipeta suffered from the effects of the jolting and swaying of the trains and the emotional stress of the vengeful crowds. She settled into her room, and both she and Ouray received their meal on a tray.

As the Indian Bureau representative assigned to supervise every detail of the Utes stay in the capital, Henry Andrews took a room in the hotel for the duration, along with a parlor that was reserved for delegation business.[3] He quickly became comfortable with his charges and grew to enjoy their company. Likewise, Police Officer Farrar moved into the hotel to manage security. With rooms also allotted to Agent Berry, Leverett Kelly, and Otto Mears, the group took up considerable space.

Late Sunday afternoon, visitors began to arrive. Commissioner of Indian Affairs Mr. Hayt and his chief clerk, E. J. Brooks, came to ensure that the delegation was properly settled. Former White River agent Edward Danforth and his wife also came to call. Having lived peacefully among the Utes at White River for four years, before being replaced by Nathan Meeker, they could not comprehend the tragedy that had taken place.

The delegation spent Monday confined to the Tremont House under Schurz's orders for their protection. Officer Farrar assured that no unauthorized visitors should bother the Utes, although the office was besieged with curious people who read the morning paper and wanted to get a look at the Utes for themselves.

Believing the Utes needed some entertainment, Commissioner Hayt enlisted a group of Italian musicians to present a small concert in the sitting room. Most of the delegation dutifully gathered to hear the music but soon began to talk among themselves. They lit their pipes, and before long the squinting and choking musicians abandoned their carefully planned program. Chipeta remained in her room all day.

At four o'clock in the afternoon Ouray was summoned to meet with Secretary of Interior Carl Schurz. Accompanied by Agent Berry, Otto Mears, and General Adams, he left for the Interior Department offices. It was late in the evening when they returned. Ouray reported that Secretary Schurz wanted to meet with the Ute delegation the next day. However, Schurz refused to include the three White River Utes, Jack, Sowawich, and Unca Sam, in the discussions. Schurz considered the entire White River band ostracized.

Privately, Ouray told Chipeta that as soon as the delegation had departed from Los Pinos, the Tabeguache agent, Wilson Stanley, had submitted his resignation. When informed by Secretary Schurz, Ouray proposed the interpreter, William T. Berry, as his choice for agent. Schurz accepted Ouray's recommendation although the appointment did not become official until June 4, 1880.

The next day, to the further rebuff of the three White River Utes, Chipeta accompanied the rest of the delegation to the meeting with Secretary Schurz, where she was welcomed as a participant. The Interior secretary quickly realized that the key players in the Meeker incident, the Utes named by

Josephine Meeker, were not present to participate in the investigation. He directed Charles Adams to return to Colorado to
round up the implicated Utes. His written directive to Adams,
dated January 23 was brief.

> *Sir, You are to proceed Saturday Jan 24 from
> Washington to Los Pinos, taking with you Jack,
> Sowawick of the White River Utes, and Wash of the
> Uncompahgre Utes and two Indian boys who accompa-
> nied Ouray to Washington and are not to return.*
>
> *xxxxxxxxxxxxxxxxxxxxxxxxxxxxxxxx*
>
> *You will then return to Washington together with
> Jack, Sowawick and Wash, who have promised to
> return with you, and other chiefs whose presence here
> may be desirable for the purpose of further conference
> and negotiation. You are authorized to employ an
> interpreter to be compensated at the rate of $5 per diem
> and necessary traveling expenses.*[4]

The *Washington Post* contended that Secretary Schurz
maintained a policy of "gagging and obstructing the press."
The paper suggested that Schurz and the Indian Bureau were
attempting to prevent exposure of their inept handling of the
Ute situation by examining the Ute delegation in private.[5]

The *Post* also took a stand against the growing anti-Ute
sentiment. Shortly after the delegation arrived the paper issued
a call for rational thinking:

> *There is a strong disposition, in some quarters, to hold a
> whole tribe responsible for the crimes of a few of its
> members. It would be as reasonable and humane to call
> for the hanging of all the citizens of Washington because
> murders and brutal outrages on women have been per-
> petrated here and the authors of these crimes have not
> been given up to justice.*[6]

Colorado Governor Pitkin arrived in Washington on
Monday, January 26. He lost no time in pleading to the media

the case for Ute removal. The governor portrayed the entire Ute population as "uncivilized, savage, roaming nomads" guilty of wanton and unprovoked exploits of destruction, plundering, ravishing women, and murder on a regular basis. By contrast, the late Nathan Meeker, or "Father Meeker," according to the governor was "well known all over the country as a pure and genuine philanthropist." He reported that Meeker had accepted the position as Indian agent not for money but for the benefit of the Indians. His every action had been for their good. The governor complained that the ungrateful White River chiefs showed their appreciation for Meeker's efforts by asking the governor to remove him as agent. The Utes, the governor concluded, could not be civilized.

In relating the feelings of the people of Colorado toward the Utes, the governor revealed the real issue underlying the "Ute problem." The citizens of Colorado, he said, "regard [the Utes] as . . . an impediment to the opening of the best lands in the State . . . the mineral wealth of the unsettled part [the 12,000,000 acre Ute reservation] is exceedingly great." The governor issued a threat that if the government did not remove the Utes from these rich lands, the people would take action themselves. "Two or three mining companies of whites could undoubtedly exterminate the Utes," he boasted. Waving his fist in the air he shouted the rallying cry, "The Utes must go." [7]

On January 28 the *Washington Post* again voiced its exception to the anti-Ute sentiment and to Governor Pitkin's views, calling for a more rational assessment of the situation.

*A tribe of Indians penned up in a reservation without food, while their rations are rotting month after month 175 miles away, are likely enough to get restless and break out . . . . Many of the outrages of which Gen. Pitkin complains were caused by failure to deliver their food when it was needed . . . And bad as these Utes are, they have real, tangible wrongs to complain of. The Government has not kept faith with them. We have agreed for a consideration to give them certain things. The consideration has been paid and the things agreed*

*upon have not been handed over . . . Of course this repu-*
*diation and failure on the part of the Government does*
*not justify murder, but it sufficiently explains the bad*
*temper of the Utes . . . . let us try to deal fairly with*
*those who have committed no crimes. Don't let us cut off*
*the food supply of any more women and children in*
*midwinter, even if their friends have deserved some*
*punishment.* [8]

Back in Colorado the local San Juan pioneers were furious at the pro-Ute stance of the *Post*. David Day of the Ouray
*Solid Muldoon* wrote: "The Utes are highly pleased with
Washington. Well, we are perfectly willing they should stay
there." [9]

A week after Charles Adams and the five Utes departed
for Colorado, Southern Ute Agent Henry Page and his assis-
tant, Will Burns, arrived in Washington with Ignacio,
Buckskin Charley, Ojo Blanco, and Severo. These additions to
the delegation had been sent for to enhance the representation
of the Southern Utes in the negotiations.

As the battle lines were drawn and players descended
upon Washington, Chipeta made productive use of her time.
The weather improved during the last days of January, and she
went on a shopping excursion. Accompanied by Henry
Andrews, she strolled along Pennsylvania Avenue examining
the window displays and the curious costumes of people on the
streets. Ladies with "hourglass figures" created by tightly
cinched corsets walked carefully in long skirts elaborately
draped over bustles. Luxuriously bearded and mustached men
tipped their top hats to the ladies. A few men whizzed past on
the new two-wheeled contraptions called *bicycles*.

At Trunnel, Clark & Company Dry Goods Store she
purchased 8 yards of dress goods, 1 1/2 yards of satin, 2 3/4
yards of cambric, 6 yards of plaid, 3 yards of flannel, 15 yards
of cotton, 2 yards of twill, 4 spools of cotton thread, 3 spools
of silk thread, 2 papers of needles, 1 1/2 dozen buttons, 1 skirt,
3 pair of hose, and 1 pair of gloves. In the custom of many city

women, the items were purchased "on account," but the $27.99 bill was sent to the Indian Bureau rather than her husband.

A few days later Mrs. D.M. Roundtree, a seamstress recommended by the hotelkeeper, was engaged to make clothes for Chipeta. The Indian Bureau outfitted the men of the delegation with suits and Secretary Schurz did not want Chipeta to feel slighted. Between February 1 and March 20, she completed four undergarments, one cashmere dress (which required six days of work), and three additional dresses at a cost of twenty-seven dollars. Clearly these garments did not consume the more than thirty-five yards of fabrics Chipeta purchased on her shopping trip. Chipeta did not intend to sit idle during any more long days in the hotel.

Life in the city was difficult for the Utes. Official meetings came to a halt. Secretary Schurz's orders were very specific that the Utes would be strictly supervised, not allowed to roam about the city, and be protected from encounters with the public. Such confinement was difficult. The food was strange. The tightly closed windows and steam heat made the hotel rooms too warm. The city was full of unusual noises that kept them from sleeping. The damp weather was bone-chilling cold. Used to an active daily life of riding and hunting, the delegation members found themselves bored and weary with little to do but wait.

Under these conditions the Utes suffered a variety of illnesses, and doctors made frequent visits to their rooms. Doctor D.W. Bliss became a familiar face at the Tremont House, making twenty calls to treat the Utes, including two emergency night visits. He saw from two to five members of the delegation on each stop.

Chipeta fared better than the men, or complained less; but she became quite anxious when she learned that the delegation was to receive vaccinations. Ouray experienced this strange procedure on previous trips and described being poked repeatedly with a sharp needle. He survived unharmed except for several days of pain in his arm. Living captive in the white world was difficult enough. Chipeta decided she would not endure the needle. It was Henry Andrews who changed her mind. He described in graphic terms the epidemics that spread like wildfire and randomly claimed the lives of people of all ages. Chipeta recalled strange illnesses that wiped out entire Ute camps. The needle, Andrews explained, poked strong medicine inside the body where it would protect her. On February 4 she lined up with the rest of the delegation and bared her arm to receive a smallpox vaccination.

Lack of regular contact with her Tabeguache family and friends was especially difficult for Chipeta. She had never been so out of touch before. The improved mail and telegraph service, results of the westward growth of white settlements, provided at least intermittent contact with home. Agency Clerk George Sherman sent regular situation reports and news to Ouray. In late January he sent word of the deaths of Tabequacheub and a son of Tomasaraca and suggested that the Utes at the agency were anxious for a letter from Ouray and Chipeta. A February letter informed them of the death of a female relative of Wass. The woman was the widow of Ahgataa, who was killed in the fight at White River. Even Agent Adams sent a letter during his return trip to Colorado with more personal reports than he sent to Secretary Schurz. In closing, Adams told Chipeta to enjoy herself, not worry, and not be sick.

While the Indian Bureau searched for the accused Utes, Congress convened its own hearing committee to review the Meeker incident. The delegation members left in Washington spent day after day attending congressional hearings, sitting stoically through the tedious discussions even though they could not understand most of what was said.

The Utes were well shielded from the press and the public on this trip, but one reporter, Georgie Davis, finagled not only a visit with the delegation but the opportunity to sketch the scene at the Tremont House. Her exclusive account appeared in the April 1880 issue of *Frank Leslie's Newspaper.* Chipeta was the only one who made a favorable impression.

*In four or five little bedrooms at the Tremont House in Washington, fifteen of the Ute delegation are*

*ignominiously huddled together. Each room is so per-*
*vaded and permeated with tobacco smoke that it is dif-*
*ficult to distinguish one representative from another,*
*through the dense cloud.*

*Major Andrews — evidently a favorite of them*
*all — calls them up like so many big children to "Shake*
*hands with the ladies." And this ceremony being duly*
*performed, he wheedingly suggests that the white*
*squaw should take their portraits [referring to a female*
*illustrator for the magazine]. This proposition however*
*meets with extreme disfavor. One or two black-shirted*
*and red-shirted chiefs who are stretched on the bed roll*
*over and bury their face in the pillows with grunts of*
*violent dissent . . . .*

*Ouray and his wife glide in with noiseless moc-*
*casins while I am sketching and exchange some words*
*with the rest, in a mixture of Ute and Spanish. The*
*language and the voice of those Indians are singularly*

*A drawing accompanying the Georgie Davis article. Chipeta is on the*
*left and doesn't seem as "stout" as described by Davis.*
Denver Public Library, Western History Department, X-30709

*musical and the tones of the women have the softest,
plaintive sound, while her [Chipeta's] laugh has a quality of sweetness so rare among her white sisters.*

*She [Chipeta] is a stout and comely squaw, gor-
geous in a red plaid gown and beaded leggings, her fingers loaded with rings, and her wrists with bracelets, a
fashionable white canvas bag hanging from one side of
her belt, and a beaded pouch from the other, which last
she slaps with a burst of merry childish laughter when
Major Andrews points it out as her money purse.*

*The major seemed thoroughly at home with his
charges and thoroughly confident of the attachment and
loyalty to himself. "They are like so many children," he
says, "I would trust myself twenty years among them."
And so as many another man has said, I think to myself,
with a shudder, as I glance around on the swarthy,
stealthy faces.* [10]

A variety of outings were planned for the Utes. Like all
Indian delegations, they were taken on tours intended to
impress them with the benefits of civilized society. Once
exposed to gracious living, the whites were sure they would, no
doubt, burn their teepees and live like white people. Visits to
army and navy bases were standard for Indian delegations, so
that they could see the strength of manpower and the store-
houses of arms and munitions ready to confront anyone who
dared stand in the way of the will of the government.

The first formal evening outing for Ouray and Chipeta
took place in historic Ford's Opera House on January 20. From
Mr. Ford's private box, usually reserved for General Sherman,
they watched a performance of *The Gorgeous Black Crook*, fea-
turing Mademoiselles de Rosa and Brand, one hundred
dancers in the ballet, fifty children, splendid scenery, and special mechanical stage effects. The Great Ronaldo Brothers, the
Young Lightning Caricaturist, and the Wonderful Ulm Sisters
entertained the audience during scene changes. The
*Washington Post* next day noted that Ouray was in full dress —

grave and dignified with the character of a soldier and statesman. Chipeta was not mentioned.[11]

On the evening of January 30 Chipeta and Ouray were
guests at a Literary and Social Entertainment at the Columbia
Commandery No. 2, Knights of Columbus. The evening
included a program of music and readings. Dancing followed
with an opening promenade, several waltzes, lanciers and
quadrilles, and one polka. A "late supper" was served during
the intermission from 10:30 p.m. to 12:30 a.m.[12] Ouray and
Chipeta probably found the evening long, the food odd, and
the dancing strange.

Several times during their stay Chipeta and Ouray had
dinner at the home of Secretary Schurz. He and Ouray had
developed a personal friendship and enjoyed long relaxed talks.
The Schurz home was in elegant contrast to the frontier
houses Chipeta had visited. She was especially attracted to a
cascading crystal chandelier that hung in Schurz's drawing
room. It reminded her of a mountain waterfall shimmering in
the sun. She wanted to know where to find one and how much
it would cost. The drawing room piano was another fascination for Chipeta. Schurz took the time to show her how it was
played and taught her a few simple tunes.

Henry Andrews accompanied Chipeta and Ouray on
several shopping excursions. At Charles Ruppert Toys &
Fancy Goods on Seventh Street they bought gifts for nieces,
nephews, and wards. For Ouray's niece, who had a new baby,
they purchased a baby carriage. They bought Brussels carpets
for their Los Pinos home at Julius Lansbaugh's Carpet House
and browsed the merchandise at A. Saks & Company Tailors
and Benkert & Wilson Boots and Shoes.

Meanwhile, Alejandro, Galota, and Augustine made several trips to the great red sandstone castle that was the
Smithsonian Institution to participate in a study of Indian sign
language conducted by Garrick Mallery. Just as members of
other visiting tribes had done, the three Utes demonstrated
their signs for a standard list of words. Observers wrote
detailed descriptions of the movements and exact positions of
body, head, arms, hands, and fingers for each sign. Back at the

hotel the three Utes entertained the rest of the delegation with accounts of white men with rolled up sleeves asking the Utes to make the sign for bison one more time as they frantically scribbled on pieces of paper. The Utes could not imagine trying to draw sign language. By the end of the year, however, the government printing office issued two illustrated guides to Native American sign language.[13]

Chipeta and Ouray dressed carefully for their appointment with the famous photographer M. W. Brady. On January 29 their interpreter, W. H. Berry, escorted them to the studio at 627 Pennsylvania Avenue, N.W. Brady's enterprise occupied the top three floors of the building above Gilman's Drug Store and the Sweeney, Rittenhouse & Fant Bank. And quite an enterprise it was, with a staff of camera operators, printers, touch up artists, and assorted assistants bustling about.

The spacious second-floor reception room served as a gallery of Brady's work. Photographic portraits were quite fashionable among the well to do, and the exhibit offered a virtual "Who's Who" of Washington elite and eastern society. While waiting their turn before the camera, clients selected their favorite props, backdrops, and poses from the samples displayed.

Ouray used the photographs to introduce Chipeta to people he had met on past visits to the city. Many names were familiar to her from his oft-repeated stories. For the first time Chipeta saw the Great Father Abraham. His long frame folded into a stately chair, as he brought his face close to his son Tad who stood beside him. Father and son appeared unaware of the camera, as they studied an open book balanced on Lincoln's leg. No doubt Chipeta's heart ached as she thought again of Mary Lincoln, who had lost not only this dear son but her husband as well.

Brady's nephew, Levin Handy, ushered the couple up the narrow stairs to the top-floor studio. Assorted props, backdrops, and photographic equipment were scattered about the room. Three rolled-up carpets stood on end, propped against a carved wooded sideboard. On a small table an ornate gold clock, its hands forever set at 11:52, sat beside a stack of leather bound books. Several chairs were shoved helter-skelter

*Matthew Brady's photograph of Chipeta shows her at her finest —*
*dignified, well-dressed, and beautiful.*

Colorado Historical Society

*Ouray and Chipeta made a handsome couple but there were troubled times for the Utes and it showed in their faces.*
*Denver Public Library, Western History Department, Photo by John N. Choate, Carlisle Indian School, X-30600*

into the corner. Chipeta recognized the chair used in Lincoln's portrait and asked to sit in it for her photograph. The particular chair was standard government issue once used in the House of Representatives. Brady had borrowed it in 1859 and never returned it.

Brady himself settled Chipeta in the chair at just the right angle to the camera, positioned her hands, tilted her head, and coaxed a slight Mona Lisa smile. Two images were made of Chipeta that day, one seated and one standing, along with a portrait of Ouray and one of the couple seated side by side. When they left the city, Ouray presented photos to people who had assisted them during their stay.

A few days later Ouray was so ill that he could not get out of bed. Dr. Dexter was called in for the first of several visits that month. This new doctor gave a name to Ouray's recurring troubles — Bright's Disease. He consulted with the cook about a special diet and tried a new medication, which had little effect. Privately he advised Ouray that his condition would continue to deteriorate, and he might not live long.

By Wednesday, February 11 Ouray had recovered enough to join the entire delegation for an overnight trip to the Carlisle Indian School in Pennsylvania. The purpose, of course, was to show them the educational opportunities provided to children from Indian tribes that cooperated with the government. Carl Schurz had approved the concept for the school, which he saw as an effective means of lifestyle modification for the native population. Removed from the influence of their families, the children could be taught academic subjects, social behavior, and occupational skills along with white cultural orientation. The school had opened the previous fall in an abandoned cavalry post. By early 1880 more than one hundred Sioux, Cheyenne, and Kiowa children lived on the grounds.

The boys and girls wore store-bought uniforms and shoes. All signs of the characteristic attire that identified them as belonging to their native family were gone. Everything was orderly. The children marched to and from their classes in straight lines like little soldiers. The children's short-cut hair probably caught Chipeta's attention causing her to think someone very special to all these little ones had died. Mr. Pratt, the school's founder, proudly told her that on arrival the children were given civilized haircuts along with their new clothes.

This school was nothing like the little classroom at Los Pinos Agency. Teachers like Mrs. Adams accepted the children as they were and made an effort to know their families. Chipeta had been an advocate who convinced Ute parents to bring their children to school. She knew firsthand that ability to speak with the white men was a benefit to their people. But this Carlisle school was different. The children seemed somber and without identity. The experience may have turned her into an opponent of Indian boarding schools.

During their visit a local photographer, John N. Choate, was taking pictures of students and asked to photograph the delegation. Individual photos were made before a backdrop of a pillared garden entrance with a shaggy rug on the floor imitating grass. The strain of Ouray's recent illness was evident in the drawn and somber faces of both Ouray and Chipeta that day. Just weeks before, they had appeared relaxed and serene in the Brady photo. In a conciliatory move, Ouray also posed at Carlisle with his longtime nemesis, Chief Ignacio.

The following Wednesday Ouray, Chipeta, and a few others accompanied Captain Blake of the Corcoran Museum on his regular trip to Mount Vernon. The guide who led the tour of George Washington's home showed the Utes the bedstead on which General Washington died. Ouray said, "Oh, no, that is not the one I saw here in 1873." The embarrassed guide admitted that Ouray was right. A different bed had been on display and was recently replaced by the true bed of General Washington that was now on exhibit. Ouray, known for his powers of observation and clear detailed memory, also commented on the different arrangement of furniture in the family rooms and other changes that had taken place since his last visit. Chipeta was probably more taken with the expansive view of the wide Potomac River than with seeing the paraphernalia in one more white man's house.

The group returned to the city to find news from Colorado. "JACK KEEPS HIS WORD," headlined the *Washington Post*. The special dispatch from Los Pinos reported:

*Promptly at the expiration of ten days as prom-
ised, Jack rode up to the agency with three of the twelve
prisoners demanded by the Government, viz: Chief
Douglas, Jim Johnson and Thomas. Jack is very reticent
and declines to say how or in what manner the capture
was effected. Sowawick returned several hours later but
brought no prisoners, and Jack assured Gen. Adams that
owing to the depth of the snow on the mountains and
the scattered location of the camps, he would take at
least three weeks to capture the remaining nine. Chief
Johnson . . . sent his regrets . . . giving as a reason that
he was a medicine man and had a very sick patient
whom he could not leave. Jack insists that the [Meeker]
women were mistaken in the names of certain Indians
who, they testified, were present at the time of the outbreak. Douglas is ill at ease and extremely nervous, and
says but little. Military preparations for the protection
of the prisoners are complete. Gen. Adams will leave
tomorrow with his prisoners for Washington.*[14]

Adams telegraphed Secretary Schurz that he and the
Utes would leave immediately by sleigh for Fort Garland.
"Matters here are perfectly quiet and peaceful," he reported.
"All Indians are expecting a permanent settlement of the trou-
ble and peace."[15]

The trip did not go well. At Lakin, Kansas, the two military escorts unexpectedly departed. Adams hired a fellow
traveler out of Pueblo, Mr. H.F. Lautre, to serve as a guard for
the price of his fare, three dollars per day, meals, and lodging.[16]
Then Chief Douglas became unruly. It took General Adams
and several Utes to restrain him, which only increased his agi-
tation. Adams decided the only option was to deliver Douglas
to the prison at Fort Leavenworth. Adams trusted the Utes
enough that he and Douglas left the train at Kansas City. Jack,
Sowawick, and Wass continued on their way with Shavano,
Veratzatz, Jim Johnson, and Thomas. The incident was unset-
tling, and at Chicago, Wass sent a telegram to Ouray reporting the members of the groups were frightened. They arrived

in Washington on Saturday, February 28 accompanied only by Otto Mears and Mr. Lautre.

Suddenly, the endless days of waiting erupted in a flurry of meetings. The newly arrived Utes told their stories. Schurz and the other Indian Bureau officials listened. Although the Utes had valid grievances, they had murdered quite a number of people. The U.S. government could not overlook such unlawful acts. As punishment, Schurz proposed that the White River Utes would leave Colorado and settle on the Uintah reservation in Utah. The Southern Ute bands would resettle along the LaPlata River near the Colorado and New Mexico state line. The Uncompahgre Utes, as the Tabeguache were ever after known by the government, would vacate their mineral-laden lands and move to a new reservation at the junction of the Grand (later called the Colorado) and the Gunnison Rivers.

The Utes had no room to negotiate. On March 4 the *Washington Post* proclaimed "The Ute Matter Settled." Two days later the Ute delegation signed the agreement drafted by Schurz. He had added a clause allowing the option to locate the Uncompahgres on alternate "unoccupied agricultural land" in western Colorado or northeastern Utah.

The agreement actually called for the Utes to sell their existing lands to the government, which would, in turn, sell the land to miners and settlers. In addition to the benefits due from previous treaties, the Utes as a whole would receive fifty thousand dollars per year. The White River Utes would forfeit their share of this annual payment to the surviving victims of the massacre. Government proceeds from the sale of Ute land would be used to provide annuities for the families of the Meeker massacre victims. The Ute chiefs had agreed to this; however, there was still one major hurdle to overcome. To become effective, three-quarters of all Ute males must ratify the treaty by October 15, 1880.

After signing the treaty the delegation members and government officials assembled for a group photo. Chipeta attended the formal signing and then sat for the photo as a member of the delegation. The group was so large that it was divided into four seatings to accommodate the range of the camera within the limited space of the small studio. The four small group photographs were later assembled into one composite picture.[17] Chipeta was by that time very worried about Ouray's health. She was anxious to put the stresses of the city and negotiations behind them and take Ouray back to the peace and quiet of home.

Signing the treaty was not the end of the Meeker issue. On March 17 Ouray and Chipeta climbed the steps of the massive white Capitol. Their moccasin-clad feet made no sound on the polished marble floors, not that anyone would have noticed in the echoing din of voices that filled the hallways. They entered an elaborately paneled room dominated by a long table at one end. Chipeta watched from the back of the room as Ouray testified before the congressional hearing committee. He spoke in Spanish, and Will Burns interpreted in English. Ouray's testimony clearly supported the White River Utes' story — that Meeker antagonized the Utes, that they attempted to have Meeker removed as agent, and that Jack attempted to stop the troops from coming into the agency. Ouray cited Chipeta as his own source of information about conditions at the White River Agency. Some time before the massacre, she had traveled to White River and observed that the agent was not distributing food and other supplies to the Utes. They were left to barter for provisions, at an inflated price, from an independent store on Bear River.

On March 19 Chipeta took the witness stand before the congressional committee. She spoke only in Ute, and most of her responses amounted to "I know nothing." She followed Ouray's lead in supporting the White River Utes by saying little.[18]

Long after Chipeta's death a number of writers touted her as the darling of the Washington press, the attraction of the season in the illustrated journals, and the rage of eastern society in 1880. They described her outfitted in corsets and silk dresses with high-heeled shoes and fashionable hats as she enjoyed numerous romantic interludes, including the conquest of a handsome young doctor. They reported that the press turned out in force to see her tastefully arrayed in a sealskin sacque, silk dress, and fashionable hat when she appeared before the congressional committee.[19] These creative fantasies of hindsight were far from the truth. In fact, the Washington newspapers barely mentioned Chipeta except to occasionally note that she accompanied Ouray. In the few instances in which she was described, the reporters called her "fat."

With the testimony behind them, the delegation was ready to return home. They faced the daunting task of convincing all seven Ute bands to leave the homelands that had been held by their ancestors for more than five centuries.

---

[1] *Washington Post*, January 12, 1880, 1.

[2] *Red Book Guide to Washington, DC*, 1881, Washington, DC Historical Museum — Construction of the Washington Monument began in 1851 but was abandoned during the Civil War. The capstone finally completed the structure in 1884.

[3] Viola, Herman, personal notes for his 1991 book Diplomats In Buckskin, collection of National Anthropological Archives — (vol 151, pg 471-72, BIA records) letter dated January 10, 1880 from Commissioner E.A. Hayt to H.W. Andrews, clerk in the office of Indian Affairs, "Take charge of the Ute delegation . . . Take them to the Tremont House. Stay with them. Allow no one to interview delegation without presenting an authorization card from Secretary of Interior. No liquor. No visiting immoral places. Each night be sure all are in their rooms and arrange so they can get no visitors or leave during the night."

[4] Delegation Expense Reports, NARA Record Group 75, Box 1880, #1125-1164.

[5] *Washington Post*, January 30, 1880

[6] Ibid.

[7] *Washington Post*, January 27, 1880.

[8] *Washington Post*, January 28, 1880.

[9] Ouray *Solid Muldoon*, January 30, 1880.

[10] Davies, Georgie A., "Illustrated Interview of our lady artist with the Ute Indian Chiefs and prisoners in Washington, D.C." *Frank Leslie's Illustrated Journal*, April 1880.

[11] *Washington Post*, January 20, 1880 and January 23, 1880.

[12] Program for Literary and Social Entertainment, Columbia Commandery No 2 KC, Friday Evening, January 30, 1880, Ouray collection, Colorado Historical Society, Box 1180 FF1.

[13] Smithsonian Bureau of Ethnology, "Introduction to Study of Sign Language Among Native Americans" (Washington, DC: Government Printing Office, 1880), 72 page pamphlet; the more extensive 329 page "A Collection Of Signs, Gestures and Signals of Native Americans" (Washington, DC: Government Printing Office, 1880) identified as participants "Alejandro, Galota and Augustin and other chiefs, members of a delegation of Ute Indians of Colorado who visited Washington D.C. during the early months of the year 1880." The Utes were credited with demonstrating signs for: "above, across, anger, to kill with an arrow, battle, bear, bison, chief, child, corn, dead, deer, god, eat, elk, fire, President of the United States (white man chief), and horse." In 1891 Garrick Mallery produced a pamphlet based on this study titled "Greeting By Gesture," (New York: D. Appleton & Co.) and wrote a feature article for *Popular Science Monthly*, Feb/March 1891 edition.

[14] *Washington Post*, February 18, 1880.

[15] Ibid.

[16] Ibid.

[17] This photo is often credited to Mathew Brady. Brooks Johnson, in his book *An Enduring Interest: The Photographs of Alexander Gardner*, (Norfolk, VA: The Chrysler Museum), 101, attributes this photo to Alexander Gardner. Paula Fleming, Photo Archivist for the National Anthropological Archives and a contributor to the Gardner book, confirms this identification. A 2003 Denver Public Library exhibit of photographs from the Robert G. Lewis collection credits Lewis Emory Walker, Photographer of the Office of the Supervising Architect at the Treasury Department, with this photograph. Mr. Lewis provides documentation supporting this credit.

[18] Testimony in Relation to Ute Outbreak, 46th Congress 2nd Session, House Miscellaneous Documents No 38, 1880, 191.

[19] Johnston, Shirley, "Queen Chipeta", *Journal of the Western Slope*, Vol. 11, No. 1 (1996), 9; Bair, Everett, "Queen of the Utes", True West, (April 1956), 19; Bair, Everett, *This Will Be An Empire*, (New York: Pageant Press, 1959), 24; Sprague, Marshall, *Massacre: The Tragedy At White River*, (Boston: Little Brown & Co., 1957), 310. The description of Chipeta wearing a silk dress and sealskin sacque appeared in the *Montezuma Millrun*, September 30, 1883, in a sarcastic mention Chipeta's and Colorow's attire at a reception for the local school teacher. An August 22, 1887, *Denver Republican* article, "Chipeta's Downfall In Life," appears to be the source of many of the subsequent glorified descriptions of Chipeta as the rage of eastern society.

# Chapter 8
## DEATH OF OURAY

The delegation returned to Los Pinos in late March 1880. Alerted by scouts that the travelers approached, a crowd of Utes gathered to welcome the long-absent chiefs back to the agency and hear about the talks with the Great Father. Seated in one of the wagons, Ouray was visibly tired. He peered out through narrow slits in the puffy skin around his eyes, and his face was drawn and sallow. He remained on the wagon seat and merely nodded to people who greeted him. Sapovanero came forward to exchange a few words with Ouray, then cleared a path so the wagon could drive away. Ouray and Chipeta went home to the farm, leaving the other delegates to tell the people the results of the trip.

At the farm the Mexican workers helped Ouray down from the wagon. He went straight to the house without making his usual trip to the corrals to check on his horses. Chipeta and the Mexican workers unloaded the Washington goods from the wagon to the house. When she finished Ouray was sound asleep. It was late afternoon. Perhaps Chipeta pulled a blanket around her shoulders and slipped outside to turn a slow circle in the yard and absorb the scents of home. The clear, dry air filling her lungs was refreshing after months of Washington's foggy-bottom dampness. The snow-covered mountains to the east shimmered in the sunlight under a cloudless blue sky. A slight breeze ruffled the valley grass, winter bleached to the color of deer hide.

Alone in the solitude of home, Chipeta made a tour of the farm. The spring was likely her first stop; no other water tasted so good. On the way to the barn she noted a new supply of firewood neatly stacked beside the house. Her mare waited at the corral fence to nuzzle her hand and inside the low barn a new spindle-legged foal huddled against its mother. Letting herself out through the back gate, she wandered across the fallow fields. When at last she turned back toward the farm, the adobe buildings glowed golden bronze in the slant rays of the setting sun.

By the time she returned to the house, the sun had disappeared behind the Uncompahgre Range. Leaning against the doorframe she relished the serene comfort of home and watched the western mountains slip into soft gray haze and emerge again as deep blue-purple silhouettes. She loved this place nestled in the valley that had always been her family's

*This drawing of Ouray and Chipeta's house and outbuildings shows how elaborate and "modern" it was for the day.*
*Colorado Historical Society, F-40196*

winter campground. It was not the house but the place she could not think about abandoning.

The next day Ouray appeared rested, and Chipeta lured him outside to see the new foal. One of the Mexican workers piled hay on top of a stack of logs outside the barn and spread blankets over the mound. On this comfortable lounge chair Ouray spent the afternoon surveying his farm and watching his horses mosey about the corral. The fresh air and sunshine revived him. Ouray slowly regained his strength during a month of rest on the farm, but he emerged a changed man. He told Chipeta he wanted no more of white doctors and their gloomy predictions.

In May Ouray and Chipeta began to ride circuit to visit Ute farms and spring camps. While Ouray lobbied for support of the agreement made in Washington, Chipeta visited among the women. She entertained them with stories about the strange ways of white city women. She described their impractical clothing and layers of undergarments. The women gasped as she told of her near-death experience when laced into a corset by the dressmaker. Her demonstrations of what the white folks called dancing drew snickers of laughter. Through her stories the women felt the texture of foreign foods on their tongues, heard the clattering noises of the city, and saw street-lamps so bright that their glow hid the stars in the night sky. Chipeta told them of the endless rounds of talks that occupied the chiefs, and quite likely she mentioned the agreement to move to a permanent homeland on the Grand River, where they would be allowed to live and raise their children in peace.

While Ouray and Chipeta and the other members of the delegation worked diligently to garner support for the new agreement and prevent war with the whites, back in Washington the agreement languished in Congress. In the U.S. Senate, the Honorable Henry M. Teller of Colorado delivered a series of speeches in support of Senate Bill 1509 to ratify the sale of the Ute Reservation in Colorado. But even as he promoted the bill, he proposed a change in implementation of the agreement.

Teller asserted that by their misconduct the Utes had for-feited their treaty rights.[1] He argued that all the Utes, not just the White Rivers, belonged on the Uintah reservation in Utah, which was "sufficient size for five times as many Indians as can ever be congregated on the land . . . . It is well watered, well timbered, easily irrigated and away from mines and mining camps . . . . with 182,400 acres of fine farming land . . . . the most valuable agricultural land in all of Utah . . . . the very best land in the western country."[2]

Senator Nathaniel Hill of Colorado asked what Ouray thought of this Utah land that Senator Teller had introduced into the debate. Teller replied, "I doubt whether Ouray can com-prehend and understand what is intended by this bill . . . "[3]

Senator Hill responded, "Ouray lives in a house on a farm with eighty acres under cultivation. He has as good an eye for farming land as any man I know and I would trust his judgment as soon as any man I know on good location for farming land. Did Ouray choose this [Utah] land?"[4]

Summoning his best evasive skills, Teller responded, "I understand that Ouray dictates this legislation to us, that the interests of 300,000 people in Colorado are left to this rene-gade chief. Gentlemen may talk as they choose of his ability and his devotion to the whites; he is an Indian, with an Indian heart and with Indian blood; and he is working for what he thinks is in the interest of his tribe. He knows his people do not want to be civilized; he is looking to keep his government stipend." Supplanting the Utah land for the land at junction of the Grand [now the Colorado] and Gunnison rivers in the minds of the senators, Teller had the hubris to state, "Ouray and Jack together said they would not go to any other place."[5]

As Congress dawdled, Charles Adams brought the grav-ity of the situation to the attention of the public. His May 26 letter to Secretary Schurz appeared in the *Washington Post*. Because the agreement had not been ratified, Adams said the Utes believed "the government does not intend to act in good faith toward them, and that they expect to be dispossessed of their reservation without remuneration."[6] He went on to say that the Utes did not believe that troops being sent to the reservation would be able to keep out intruders. In fact, they suspected that the government was intentionally stalling until the soldiers were in place and then planned to abandon the agreement and evict the Utes from their land. "They do not understand why a solemn agreement urged upon them . . . which seemed so urgent and was considered as preventing a war two months ago has not been acted upon."[7]

Adams offered an ominous warning: "It will be only a question for them whether to accept the inevitable peacefully or retaliate by the only mode known to them — war in the most cruel and barbarous manner . . . Very few days may change the present status of affairs."[8]

Adams concluded with a plea that his own personal reputation of trustworthiness with the Utes was at stake. He had convinced the Utes to negotiate rather than fight and, along with the Ute chiefs, he had signed his name to the resulting agreement.[9]

The U.S. Army arrived at Los Pinos on May 31, 1880. Colonel Ranald Mackenzie with six companies of cavalry out of Fort Clark, Texas joined nine companies of infantry at Fort Garland. The full complement of fifteen hundred men marched over Cochetopa Pass and descended into the Uncompahgre Valley. They established a supply camp four miles north of the Los Pinos Agency. Over a period of several

*Fort Crawford was located near the Los Pinos II Agency. The whites felt a lot safer with soldiers nearby.*

Colorado Historical Society, F-4497

years they built forty buildings to house men, animals, and supplies at "the Cantonment on the Uncompahgre." The Utes welcomed this military force who would keep eager land-seekers out of the reservation, but the soldiers often had an equally challenging task keeping the restless Utes at bay.

Congress finally approved the agreement with the Utes on June 15, 1880. Six days later Secretary Schurz appointed George W. Manypenny as chairman of a new commission to secure Ute ratification of the agreement and approve the land for Ute resettlement. Alfred B. Meacham, John B. Bowman, John J. Russell, and Otto Mears completed the team. The commission scheduled a great council for all Ute chiefs to begin mid-July at Los Pinos.

These commissioners started off impressively by arriving on schedule. However, the wagon carrying their baggage did not travel with the same speed. They were forced to wear their travel clothes and sleep in borrowed blankets on the floor of the agency for the first two days. Agent Berry escorted them to Ouray's farm where they found the head chief of the Utes barely able to sit up. Chipeta cautioned the men not to tire him too much and hovered nearby to be sure that they followed her instructions.

The meeting with Ouray shattered the commissioners' plans for speedy ratification of the agreement. First, he announced that the Southern Utes were not coming. Ouray said they preferred to have their own council with the commissioners at Ignacio. Second, they would have to wait a few days to begin the council at Los Pinos. The White River Utes were on their way with one hundred lodges. Finally, Ouray told the commissioners he might be unable to participate in the council, and they should make all decisions in consultation with Sapovanero and Shavano.

The initial council convened on July 21, 1880. The commissioners set up a great canvas military tent near the agency building and positioned themselves behind a long table. The White River and Uncompahgre chiefs and headmen assembled on the ground facing the commissioners. Ouray summoned all his strength and willed himself to attend. He explained the actions of the delegation to Washington. Then the agreement was read section by section in both Spanish and Ute. The only issue that raised objections was the government's plan to assign plots of land to individual Utes (allotment in severalty) rather than designate a reservation to the Utes as a whole.[10] A private council of Ute chiefs met late into the night.

The next day the chiefs had many questions for the commissioners, but the discussion was orderly. The Utes wanted to see the land that was to be their reservation and wanted the boundaries established before they signed any agreement. The White River Utes also wanted Chief Douglas released from prison in Kansas.

At the end of the third day's council one Ute stood and denounced the agreement. Ouray replied that the chiefs who went to Washington negotiated the best deal they could under the circumstances. If the complainer didn't like it, he had better join some other tribe.

*Shavano, the Ute War Chief.*
*Colorado Historical Society, F-6375*

The next council was scheduled for July 28. On the appointed day the commissioners gathered in their usual seats behind the long table. No Utes appeared. The commissioners feared the talks had come to an end. Otto Mears became so nervous that he paced about until he looked like he might collapse. The commissioners waited all day.

After supper a few Utes arrived at the agency. The commissioners hurried to their places as more Utes straggled into the meeting place. Sapovanero announced that the chiefs were not satisfied with lands in severalty. They wanted one common reservation.

The commissioners attempted to change their minds. Each in turn made a speech about the benefits of individual ownership of land. The Utes sat stone-faced. Otto Mears rose and made a personal appeal. He reminded the chiefs that they had all known him a long time. He told them individual farms could not be taken away like their reservation land. He told them this was a good treaty. Then he called by name individual Utes he had befriended over the years and asked each one to come forward and sign the agreement. In the silence that followed, no one moved.

At last Sapovanero stood. He walked to the commissioners' table and took up the pen. His action broke the stalemate, and when the council adjourned forty-eight Utes had placed their marks on the official document. Over the next few days most of the holdouts signed. The council concluded, and the Uncompahgre and White River chiefs returned to their homes.

The commissioners prepared to move to the Southern Agency to meet with the Mouache, Capote, and Weeminuche bands. They pleaded for Ouray to accompany them, knowing that his leadership would make the difference in getting the agreement ratified. Although extremely ill, Ouray was determined to go to Igancio. The commissioners left first, taking with them Chipeta's teepee that they would arrange to have set up and ready.

Along with McCook and his wife and a few other men, Ouray and Chipeta left Los Pinos on horseback on August 14. Ouray refused to ride in the carriage or a wagon even though he could not mount his horse without assistance. By the time they arrived at Ignacio on August 18, Ouray was exhausted and had to be lifted from his horse.

The Utes had established their campsites along the river, and the teepee was ready and waiting for them. Chipeta quickly settled Ouray inside, and McCook kept visitors away. After two days of rest and Chipeta's ministrations of herbal tea, Ouray recovered enough to talk with the commissioners. Ouray forced himself to attend the opening of the council meeting but was unable to participate. In a private meeting with Buckskin Charlie, Ouray urged him to convince the Southern Ute Chiefs to ratify their agreement.

The next morning Ouray woke with a severe headache and fever. Chipeta and McCook stayed beside him all day as he moaned and tossed. The medicine man came and ordered an intense fire built in the teepee, then he burned medicinal herbs. Kneeling beside Ouray, he sang a healing chant that began in a feverish high pitch and gradually descended to a deep, solemn tone. He tipped his head back and a gurgle began in his throat. Bending forward he placed his lips on Ouray's chest, and the gurgle seemed to dissipate into the sick man's body. A wailing song rose on the smoke escaping through the vent at the top of the teepee as the medicine man sat back on his heels. Then he positioned himself cross-legged beside Ouray and smoked a pipe.

The medicine man ministered to Ouray through the night beside the raging fire. Chipeta and McCook joined the songs, and, despite the great heat in the teepee, chiefs and other relatives slipped in to add their voices for awhile. The teepee glowed like gold in the darkness and could be seen from all over camp. The people moving about inside cast elongated shadows that appeared as ghostly figures through the translucent teepee covering.

Ouray's condition did not improve and the medicine man continued his work. On August 20 the doctor at the Southern Ute agency visited Ouray. He reported that the chief's condition was grave, and Agent Henry Page sent a messenger to fetch Dr. Lacey, the physician at Los Pinos. The

Utes set up a relay of fresh horses, and the doctor rode the 150 miles straight through. In addition, at the request of the commissioners, Dr. Hopson was called from Animas City to consult on possible treatment. All three physicians concurred that they could do nothing for him. Ouray was dying.

Chipeta remained by Ouray's side while the Ute medicine man carried out his mission to focus Ouray's spirit with the forces of nature. As "one who knows the way," the medicine man encouraged Ouray's spirit to seek its proper path — to return to life or find the way of death.

Ouray slipped into a coma and died on the morning of August 24, 1880. Word of his death ended the day's council proceedings, and the Utes hurried to strike their teepees and move further down the river to re-establish their camps away from the place of death. The commissioners, following white custom, went immediately to Ouray's teepee to pay their respects, but a guard of Utes waved them away.

Inside the teepee, Chipeta functioned in a stupor as she and Haseekep, McCook's wife, washed Ouray's body. They painted him with stripes of red (to protect him from creatures of the underworld) and white (to allow his spirit to soar like the eagles to find the spirits of his ancestors). As they worked, they sang traditional songs to soothe the departing spirit. They wrapped the body in new blankets and rolled it tight in a buffalo robe. Within an hour McCook and Buckskin Charley tied Ouray's body onto his horse.

Buckskin Charley led the horse along the Pine River. Chipeta, still chanting, followed behind, accompanied by Colorow, Naneese, and McCook, who led two more horses. The commissioners tried to join the procession and were again turned away.

Two miles south of Ignacio, Buckskin Charley found a wall of rocks at the head of an arroyo. On a high ledge they laid Ouray's body in a deep natural crevice where some years earlier they had buried a Capote chief, Suvatah. They shoved rocks into the crevice to fill the opening and protect the body. Then they killed Ouray's horses and left them at the base of the wall of rocks.

*Ouray's
successor was
Buckskin
Charlie,
shown here
with his wife,
Ta-wee.*
*Colorado
Historical
Society,
F-5713*

Three hours later the burial party returned to camp. They burned Ouray's teepee with all the possessions inside, which were tainted by death. Chipeta chopped off her hair with a knife and covered her face with a mixture of charcoal and pitch. She did not wash her face again until this widow's paint wore off.

The next morning McCook, Hahseekep, and Chipeta set out for Los Pinos. Agent Berry, who had posted scouts to watch for their return, met them on the road. Knowing the Ute practice of burning the teepee in which someone died, he was concerned that Chipeta might also burn down the house. He reminded her that Ouray worked to set an example for their people and wanted her to continue to live in the house. After a long discussion, Chipeta agreed.

It was a cold and empty dwelling without Ouray. Chipeta was alone for the first time in her adult life. In the custom of her people she gave away all of Ouray's clothes and other possessions. She wrapped the beautiful fringed shirt Ouray wore on his last trip to Washington along with his beaded buckskin tobacco pouch and a powder horn, and asked Agent Berry to mail them for her. He wrote the letter she dictated and sent the package to Carl Schurz. In his memoirs, Schurz recalled this gift and Chipeta's letter:

> *I received from a government agent on the Ute Indian reservation a letter from Ouray's widow Chipeta . . . . In it she told me that . . . I had done much to save Ouray's people from disaster and was, therefore, their best friend. She wished to give a memory of her husband as a present — the things he most valued. A few weeks later I received a box . . . accompanied by a letter from Chipeta giving me the message: If I accepted the present, to keep it while I lived and [then] for my children, it would be regarded by Chipeta and her people as proof of true friendship on my part, and they would esteem that friendship very highly. But if I made a present in return it would be understood by them as signifying that I did not value their friendship much and simply wished to get rid of an obligation and be quits with them.*[11]

Ouray's death was national news and readers across the country followed unfolding events in remote Los Pinos, Colorado. Typical of the interest in Ute affairs, *The Evansville Daily Courier* [Indiana] on September 1 carried a front page report of the selection of Ouray's successor. Four days after Ouray's death the Uncompahgre chiefs met with Agent Berry in the agency office at Los Pinos. Guero, Piah, and Shavano each lobbied to take Ouray's place as head chief. Berry, however, supported Sapovanero, Ouray's right-hand man. Over the past few years, as Ouray's health declined, Sapovanero had assumed greater and more frequent responsibility. He was already chief in fact, if not by title. The chiefs accepted Berry's recommendation. Then they asked who would take care of Chipeta. Berry replied, "The government will take care of Chipeta as long as she lives. Ouray's widow shall never come to want."[12]

Many years later the newsman Saunders related in his memoirs that Chipeta became the overall chief of the Utes for awhile. Perhaps this was his own wishful thinking but he wrote, "Shavano and Sapovanero wanted her to be chief and the others consented, Uncompahgre Utes, White River Utes, and Southern Utes. There were too many jealousies among the sub-chiefs and they were all willing to accept Chipeta."[13]

Although Chipeta did not become the chief, she soon found chiefs and headmen coming to the ranch to consult with her. At first they asked, "What would Ouray say?" about a particular issue. With time, the question changed to, "What do you think about this?" Without benefit of election or title, Chipeta emerged as a wise counselor and a de facto chief.

As Chipeta settled into her new life, things were not going well for the commissioners. After Ouray's death the Southern Utes refused to sign the agreement. Otto Mears settled the matter by paying each chief two dollars for his signature. In October Chairman Manypenny laid a list of problems before Carl Schurz, beginning with Mears's signature buying. Secondly, Manypenny saw a new conflict brewing that might cause the Utes to renege on the agreement. While the commissioners and the Utes were in council at Ignacio, the Gunnison newspaper had announced that the reservation would be opened to settlement by October. When local residents heard that the Utes had ratified the agreement, they swarmed onto the reservation to choose sites and file claims. Manypenny asked the secretary of interior to publicly forbid white trespassers on Ute land.

The Utes were soon to receive a cash settlement due from past treaties. Manypenny reported that gamblers planned to visit the reservation and fleece the Utes of their new wealth. The conscientious Manypenny went on to report that Commissioner Bowman had left to oversee his own extensive

mining interests instead of attending to the business of reset-
tling the Utes. The situation went from bad to worse.

Under the terms of past treaties, roads had been built
across reservation land to service the mining communities
cropping up in the backcountry. The Utes had assured travelers safe passage on these routes. On September 29, 1880, John
Jackson, accompanied by his nephew Andrew Jackson and an
employee named Mannell, left Saguache with a wagonload of
supplies destined for the mining town of Ouray. They made
camp for the night on reservation land. About seven-thirty in
the evening two young Ute men, Johnson Shavano and Henry,
rode into camp and asked for food. The Jacksons and Ute
Henry told different versions of the argument that followed,
but in the end Andrew Jackson shot Johnson Shavano, and the
two Utes galloped off.

The injured Ute, son of Chief Shavano, did not survive
the night. The next morning a furious band of armed Utes
arrived at the agency demanding punishment of the white
murderers. Agent Berry set out with Commissioner
Meacham, two visitors named Charles Holmes and Sam
Hoyt, plus Captain Louis Stelle with fifteen soldiers of the
twenty-third regiment stationed at the Cantonment on the
Uncompahgre. The angry Utes followed.

They found the Jackson party at Cline's ranch, an
authorized stage station on the road through the reservation.
Berry placed Andrew Jackson in the custody of the troops
while he tried to calm the Utes and decide what to do with
Jackson. At last Shavano agreed to take his warriors home. In
return Berry enlisted Cline and the two visitors, Hoyt and
Holmes, to escort Jackson to the jail in Gunnison City to
stand trial for murder. Captain Stelle detailed six soldiers to
accompany them on the sixty-mile trip. Sixteen miles from the
ranch Cline dismissed the guards. A short time later a group
of armed Utes surrounded the travelers and took Jackson.

The story of Jackson's abduction spread like wildfire
through the mining camps and mountain towns. "WAR!" in
big, bold letters leapt from the front page of the *Gunnison
Review*. Rumors about Jackson's fate were embellished with

*Cline's Ranch — the scene of the "Ute Scare."*
Colorado Historical Society, F-44112

each retelling. Absent a body or an eyewitness statement, the Gunnison newspaper reported that the Utes burned Jackson's feet, scalped him alive, then quartered him. A week later the story was more gruesome. The newspaper related that the Utes had cut off Jackson's ears, nose, and arms; pinned him to the ground with stakes through his body; and set him on fire during a six-day marathon of torture.

Panic gripped miners, ranchers, and townspeople. Several hundred people assembled in Gunnison to sign a petition asking the governor to organize two companies of militia. Muster rolls for enlistment circulated at the same time. Western Colorado residents braced for a repeat of the Meeker massacre. On the reservation, troops from the cantonment patrolled the entrance roads, and groups of Utes camped along the well traveled routes. Freighters refused to drive their wagons across the reservation, leaving the far western mining towns cut off from supplies.

Newspapers theorized that Agent Berry and station owner Cline (also an agency employee) had handed Jackson over to the Utes to save their own necks. Warrants were issued for the arrest of Berry and the other white men involved. Berry sent an urgent telegram to Interior Secretary Carl Schurz requesting that the U.S. Attorney General intervene until Berry could get the Utes at Los Pinos under control. Commissioner Meacham notified Schurz that, under the circumstances, it was impossible to attempt the survey of the new reservation.

Rumors spread that a lynching party waited in Gunnison for Berry, Meacham, Cline, Hoyt, and Holmes. Berry and Hoyt surrendered to a U.S. marshall, who escorted them out by the north route through Rawlins, Wyoming, and on to Denver by train. Meacham shaved off his beard and, dressed in a borrowed uniform, rode out in the company of two soldiers from the cantonment to surrender in Denver. Cline and Holmes similarly escaped to turn themselves in to more level-headed lawmen.

*Johnson Shavano and Indian Henry with an unknown white man, probably assigned to guard them.*
*Denver Public Library, Western History Department, Photo by George Mellen, X-30505*

On December 14 a search party found the remains of Jackson a quarter mile from where the Utes had abducted him. Dr. Hoover from Cañon City examined the body and found no evidence of mutilation or torture. Jackson had died from a single bullet wound. Shavano turned over the body of his son, and Dr. Hoover found that he, too, died from one bullet. Despite the factual evidence, the unfounded tales of Ute savagery and torture remained in the minds to the white citizens.

After the state and federal governments wrangled over jurisdiction, a grand jury finally met in May 1881. Holmes and Hoyt were acquitted following three days of testimony, but Cline, Berry, and Meacham were indicted. No trial took place, however, and the men resumed their usual business.

In his annual message to Congress in December 1880, President Rutherford B. Hayes reported:

*An agreement has been made with the Utes by which they surrender their large reservation in Colorado in consideration of an annuity to be paid to them, and agree to settle in severalty on certain lands designated for that purpose, as farmers, holding individual title to their land in fee simple, inalienable for a certain period. In this way a costly Indian war has been avoided which at one time seemed imminent, and for the first time in the history of the country an Indian nation has given up its tribal existence to be settled in severalty and to live as individuals under the common protection of the laws of the country.*

*I . . . hope that Congress will at this session take favorable action on the bill providing for allotment of lands on the different reservations in severalty to the Indians. This measure, together with a vigorous prosecution of our educational efforts, will work the most important and effective advance toward the solution of the Indian problem, in preparing for the gradual merging of our Indian population in the great body of American citizenship.*[14]

McCook, Alhandra, and Colorow went to Washington, D.C., in the spring of 1881. They attended the inauguration of President James Garfield on March 4 and met the newly appointed secretary of interior, Samuel J. Kirkwood. The chiefs asked Kirkwood to reopen talks about the idea of severalty. They wanted one common reservation not individually owned land. Kirkwood was firm. The Utes and the government had to live with the agreement as written. They must "move to the new reservation or go still farther west." [15]

Chipeta was heartbroken and lonely without Ouray but not alone for long. McCook took charge of the farm. Agent Berry stopped in often and helped with anything she asked. Cooroopits and Haseekep visited often. Friends and relatives came and camped in the pasture. Chiefs who sought her advice also told her happenings among the Southern Utes and the White Rivers.

In early May Chipeta paid a visit to Cline's Ranch where traveling military men often stopped. She delivered information for the military commanders that some White River Utes were recruiting support from other surrounding tribes for one final fight against the white men. The Utes were gathering ammunition obtained in Utah Territory. Having delivered her intelligence report, Chipeta emphatically stated that the Uncompahgres were all peaceable and wanted no trouble.

Like most widows, Chipeta discovered there were new routines to learn. She and Ouray had always bought their supplies at the agency store using Ouray's government salary; they never participated in the distribution of rations. But Ouray's income stopped at his death, and before long, Chipeta rode into Los Pinos on her pony for ration day like every other Ute.

Chipeta chatted amiably with the other women while they waited outside the agency to have a hole punched in a ration card in exchange for flour, sugar, and coffee. A new beaded ration purse, the latest practical ornament of Ute women, hung from her belt. She sometimes brought an umbrella from her Washington, D.C., trip to shield herself from the blazing sun. After the women claimed the dry foods, the men lined up for a chance to shoot one of the six fat steers waiting in the corral. As the last animal hit the ground, the men and women rushed in with sharp knives to skin, butcher, and divide the meat in less than twenty minutes. In a separate corral an agency employee shot two steers for the chiefs. Chipeta received a hindquarter of one of these steers as her portion.

A larger than usual crowd descended on Los Pinos for ration day May 29, 1881. The commissioners were meeting at the agency to discuss arrangements for removal to the new land. Otto Mears told the other commissioners that the proposed location on the Grand River did not meet the needs of the Utes. He recommended instead that the Utes be moved to vacant land adjacent to the existing Uintah Ute reservation in Utah.

When the commissioners informed Agent Berry that the Utes would be removed to Utah in August, he replied that he would not attempt removal until the Utes received compensation for their property. He noted that this included Chipeta's farm, which was the most valuable.

In mid-August the commissioners conducted appraisals of Ute properties in preparation for removal. Chipeta's property was described in the August 11 evaluation as "improved farm on Uncompahgre River consisting of fenced cultivated fields, irrigation ditches, hay meadow, story and half residence containing four rooms, four tenement houses, mess house, carriage house, tool house, horse barn, chicken house and three vegetable cellars. Appraised value $5,000." [16]

Six other properties were appraised at values ranging from one thousand dollars for Shavano's farm to two hundred dollars for Billa's hay meadow. Thomas C. McMorris, commissioner, certified the appraisals at a total of $7,700, and the Utes were promised payment when they arrived on their new land.

On August 22 the commissioners met with the Ute chiefs and headmen and announced that they should prepare to leave for Utah in three days. To the surprise of Agent Berry and the commissioners, the Utes refused to leave. The chiefs argued that they had agreed to settle on land at the juncture of the Grand and Gunnison Rivers. They had never agreed to go to Utah.

*The Utes crossing the Colorado River as they left the state for Utah Territory in 1881.*
Colorado Historical Society, F-5458

Three days later in another council Colonel Mackenzie gave the chiefs an ultimatum — they could leave willingly or by force. He emphasized the order by moving six pieces of artillery onto a hill overlooking the Los Pinos Agency. The Utes retired to their own council, and the next day Sapovanero reported that they would go peacefully.

Each Ute family received three weeks' rations of beef, flour, hard bread, and salt for the trip. Agent Berry negotiated from the military cantonment 600 pounds of sugar, 250 pounds of coffee, and 50 pounds of tobacco — rations which had not been issued for the past two months. He distributed these to the chiefs to ensure that they would lead a peaceful removal.

---

[1] Smith, Duane, *Henry M. Teller: Colorado's Grand Old Man*, (Boulder: University Press of Colorado, 2002), 99. It was Senator Teller who lobbied Commissioner of Indian Affairs Edward A. Hayt to recommend the ill-prepared Nathan Meeker for the position of Indian Agent.

[2] Speech of Henry M. Teller of Colorado, April, 1880, Helen Hunt Jackson

collection, HHJ Box 15, Pamphlet 22, Tutt Library, The Colorado College (contains the entire exchange between Senators Teller and Hill).

[3] Ibid.

[4] Ibid.

[5] Ibid.

[6] *Washington Post*, May 26, 1880.

[7] Ibid.

[8] Ibid.

[9] Ibid.

[10] *Boston Herald*, July 26, 1880. Acting Secretary Bell stated, "The scheme of allotment in severalty is so new that it may have startled and dazed the Utes who did not come to Washington last winter when it was incorporated in the agreement concluded by Secretary Schurz and Ouray"; Manypenny to Schurz, July 27, 1880, from unidentified newspaper in Helen Hunt Jackson Collection, Tutt Library, The Colorado College, HHJ Box 6, Folder 23, "Had fourth council yesterday . . . .object to severalty."

[11] Jocknick, Sidney, *Early Days on the Western Slope*, (Montrose, CO: Western Reflections Publishing, 1913, 1998), 230-231.

[12] Meacham to Secretary of Interior, August 26, 1880, NARA Record Group 75, Special Case 112.

[13] Saunders, William, unpublished manuscript in possession of author (Smith), 810.

[14] Hayes, Rutherford B., Annual Message to Congress, December 6, 1880.

[15] *Gunnison Review*, April 2, 1881.

[16] Schedule of Appraisement, August 16, 1881, NARA Record Group 75, Special Case 112, Box 5, Folder 9.

# Chapter 9
# LIFE IN
# UTAH

The hired boys rounded up the cattle and horses. The Mexican workers pulled poles from the barn and tied a travois over one of the horses. Chipeta brought from the house a bundle containing her clothes; a parfleche filled with sewing supplies; blankets, pots, and kettles; and the stores of dried food from the cellar. Slipping a rifle into its sling on her saddle, she took the lead rope for the pack horse in hand and mounted her own mare. Without looking back, Chipeta simply rode away from the farm.[1]

On August 27, 1881, Chipeta joined 1,458 Utes who drove ten thousand sheep and goats, eight thousand ponies, hordes of dogs, and hundreds of wagons out of the Uncompahgre Valley. By some reports she received special dispensation to remain in Colorado, but she chose to go with her people. In response to this mass exodus newspapers around the state proclaimed, "The Utes have gone."

The procession, escorted by Colonel Mackenzie's troops, followed the Gunnison River to its junction with the Grand. When the chiefs had signed their last treaty with the United States, this was the place where they had agreed to live. On the morning of September 7, 1881, they crossed the Grand River on two flatboats built especially for their departure and headed for Utah Territory. Otto Mears, the commissioner who determined that the Grand River site was not suitable for the Utes, rode along with the cavalry escort. Many of the chiefs viewed Mears as a traitor and seethed with anger at the sight of him. Shortly after fording the river, one of the Utes attempted to kill Mears, but several soldiers intervened to save his life.[2]

Without consulting Chipeta, the commissioners arranged to sell the contents of her house, with the understanding that she would have the proceeds. The September 11 sale was badly managed. It was not advertised and known to only a few persons. All the fine gifts Ouray and Chipeta had received in Washington were sold for a pittance. Four Russian leather armchairs brought seventy-five cents a piece, and forty yards of Brussels carpet (worth one hundred dollars) sold for thirteen dollars. Sterling silver dinnerware, two gold cups, and many more personal effects were never offered for sale, causing many people to question what happened to them. Even the *Denver Tribune*, which had campaigned for the Ute removal, questioned the hurried sale. The editors suggested Chipeta might at least be allowed to take a few favorite articles for her new home. White citizens could not imagine she would intentionally leave behind her limited fragments of civilized life. Personal effects and white man's money were unimportant to Chipeta although there is little doubt that she would have preferred to keep the homestead.

At five o'clock on the morning of September 14, 1881, the U.S. Army gave permission to the white land seekers to enter the abandoned Colorado reservation. Within a matter of months all desirable land in the former Ute homeland had been staked, but not until the following year did Congress declare the area to be public land. The Utes, in turn, were on their new reservation for almost four months before it was officially established.

Because of settlers' apprehensions that the Utes would return, the military presence on the Uncompahgre remained. In 1886 the cantonment was officially named Fort Crawford.

The soldiers "protected" the settlers from Indian attack until the last troops departed on December 31, 1890.

The land at the junction of the Gunnison and Grand rivers, deemed unsuitable for the Utes, did not remain unused. In March 1882, George Crawford, president of the Grand Junction Town Company, filed an initial town plan with the Gunnison County clerk. Within three years a community of 850 residents, 70 businesses, 5 churches, a post office, and a newspaper claimed the site.

W.H. Berry accompanied the Uncompahgre to Utah as their agent. The existing Uintah reservation had been established by executive order of President Lincoln in 1861 at the urging of Mormon settlers who had moved into central Utah. The angry Uintah Utes had refused to go to the reservation, and a three-year war ensued. Military intervention and a new chief, Tabby, finally collected the Utes in the northeastern corner of Utah Territory. Not until the arrival of their third agent, J.J. Critchlow, did the Uintah Utes settle into a peaceful existence in the new location between the Uintah and Whiterocks Rivers at the base of the Uintah Mountains.

Colorado's White River Utes were assigned to the existing Uintah reservation, and the Uncompahgre were located on an adjoining two million acres with a separate agency, named in honor of Ouray, located on the banks of the Green River. None of the Utes were pleased with the arrangements and, inevitably, squabbles erupted. Agent Berry reported to the Commissioner of Indian Affairs in January 1882 that his Utes were orderly. He noted that Jack and Colorow were likely to start trouble at any moment, but he believed that the Uncompahgre would not join any White River trouble. Indignant at being forced to live with the Uintahs in this undesirable place, Colorow and a small band of followers simply left the reservation and roamed where they pleased.

The new land was brown and barren in contrast to the lush valleys and forested mountains the Colorado Utes had always known. Scarce grass forced them to move their camps often to find feed for the horses. They were still exploring locations for grazing and hunting when a month of twenty-to-thirty-below-zero temperatures settled upon them. It was a shocking contrast to the moderate climate of the Uncompahgre Valley. One visitor described the new reservation in blunt terms:

> *The bottom [land] lying along the Green River and White River contains all the farming land within the lines of the reservation. There is not a stream outside of the two mentioned that has running water in it two months during the year; the fact is, it is nothing but a desert, and it is an utter impossibility to keep the Indians within the bounds of this reservation, as on three sides it is bounded by mountains where there is plenty of game, grass, and water.*[3]

Recognizing the challenge of keeping the Utes from returning to Colorado, the War Department established a military post near the new Ouray Agency. As if turning the knife in a gaping wound, the government named it Fort Thornburgh, commemorating the late military officer who led

*Otto Mears was a paradoxical man — a good friend and better enemy of the Utes.*
*Colorado Historical Society, F-1073*

his men into the White River reservation and initiated the massacre that drove the Utes out of their homeland. This ill-conceived post was abandoned within a few years.

Otto Mears had received the ten-thousand-dollar contract to build the new Utah agency, which included Chipeta's house, the agent's home, a hospital, and a warehouse. The government had promised Chipeta a new house in Utah that was as well built and furnished as her old one in Colorado. What she received was a small, two-room log cabin that was neither finished nor furnished. There was no drinking or irrigation water. Other agency buildings lingered similarly incomplete, and accusations flew that Mears misappropriated money allocated for agency projects. In October 1881 he narrowly escaped being scalped by some White River Utes and rode all night to get away. Mears resigned as an Indian commissioner the following spring.

Richard Sylvester, disbursing officer for the Ute Commission, spent nine months with the Utes from July 1882 through March 1883. He reported, "They are not well satisfied now as when their reservation was in Colorado, and they constantly talk of their old home in the direction of the rising sun."[4]

Chipeta, like the other women, was bewildered by this foreign land. She had spent her youth building a mental catalog of locations where each edible plant and herb, each source of water, each life-sustaining bit of nature could be found. That cumulative knowledge passed down through the generations was suddenly useless.

Indian agents and others who visited Chipeta in Utah reported that she lived a sparse life in the desert. In spite of these circumstances they reported that she was as big-hearted as ever — offering them food and presents even though they observed that she was living in terrible poverty. Her house was badly constructed and furnished with only a small table and boxes for chairs. However, she covered the table with a clean cloth and served food to her guests. She welcomed the opportunity to talk with visitors and they left convinced that Chipeta was still a strong friend of the white people. Her guests reported that Chipeta yearned for and dreamed of the good times that she and Ouray had shared, which were now only part of the past.

The Utes continued their rituals, such as the Bear Dance, in Utah. A white man named A.C. Moulton spent several years as manager of Hugus and Company Store at the new agency. He recalled that Chipeta "more than once danced me off my feet in the Indian dances while the whole tribe looked on laughing at the 'narawar carnichagut' (storeman) who could not stand up as long as a squaw."[5]

While Chipeta and the Utes struggled to adjust to their new life in a harsh land, they were unaware of shifting attitudes among the white people throughout the nation. New allies used the power of the pen to call attention to the plight of the Indians across the land. The year before he was appointed to the 1880 commission to ratify the treaty and resettle the Utes, George Manypenny had published a book based on his firsthand experience with Indian tribes. His work, titled *Our Indian Wards* attacked the jurisdictional infighting between the army and the Interior Department over control of Indian affairs and laid out the resulting suffering of the

*Chipeta (fifth from right) and other Utes near Bitter Creek in Utah about 1900.*
Denver Public Library, Western History Department, Thomas McKee Photograph, Mc206

Indians.[6] His work did not draw public attention until 1881 when Helen Hunt Jackson shocked the American public with her impassioned publication *A Century of Dishonor*.

An accomplished author before she married wealthy William S. Jackson, president of the Denver & Rio Grande Western Railroad, Helen paid only casual attention to Indian issues in Colorado until during an 1879 visit back East, she attended a speech by the Ponca chief Standing Bear. His description of the mistreatment of his people and the others whose ancestral homelands were ruthlessly stolen away in the lust for land and gold aroused Helen's sympathy. In an age in which women were considered incapable of holding opinions on public affairs, Helen Hunt Jackson became a respected media voice. Her contribution to the Indian cause was her carefully researched book. The text laid bare the government's record of inhumane treatment and broken treaties. She sent a copy of her new book to every member of Congress and initiated a letter-writing campaign to newspapers and influential friends, rallying public opinion on behalf of the Indians. Her work raised public awareness of the plight of the native people and generated pressure on elected representatives to change their attitudes.

President Chester Arthur made Helen a commissioner of the Board of Indian Affairs in 1883. In this capacity, her personal experiences provided material for a new book. *Ramona*, a work of romantic fiction with idyllic Indian characters, was published in the spring of 1884. It found a far greater audience than the previous book and helped to turn the tide of American sympathies toward the Indian population.

Eugene Field initiated new interest in Chipeta's fate with a poem he read at the 1882 Colorado Press Convention.

### CHIPETA

*She is bravest and best of a cursed race,*
*Give her a lodge on the mountainside,*
*And when she is gone on the hill provide,*
*The Queen of the Utes' last resting place.*

*She rode where old Ouray dare not ride,*
*A path through the wilderness rough and wild;*
*She rode to plead for woman and child;*
*She rode in the valleys, dark and chill.*

*O! Such a ride as woman can*
*By the God-like power which in her lies*
*Or inspiration from the skies,*
*Achieve for woman and son of man.*

*They live, and through the country wide,*
*Where'ere they come, where'ere they go*
*Though their heads grow white as wintry snow*
*They will tell of brave Chipeta's ride.*

*She is bravest and best of a cursed race —*
*Give her a lodge on the mountainside*
*And when she is gone on the hill provide*
*The Queen of the Utes' last resting place.*

*But give her a page in history, too*
*Though she be rotting in humble shroud:*
*And write on the whitest of God's white clouds*
*Chipeta's name in eternal blue.*

Field turned the once sarcastic label "Queen of the Utes" into a crown with this poem. His verses tugged at the heart strings of Colorado's white citizens who remembered Ouray and Chipeta at the forefront of peace efforts. People began to speculate about Chipeta's new life, particularly whether she found a new husband. Public interest sparked the news media to address the question, with or without facts. Though some writers proclaimed that no man could ever take the place of Ouray, others reported that Chipeta had found a new mate. In one tale Chipeta married a brave named Commequeuch and joined Colorow's renegade band to be with him. Another writer imagined she married the coarse and portly Colorow himself. Yet another story circulated that Chipeta became a squaw of a dashing brave, called Comanche, culminating a secret romance that began around Ouray's council fires.

The most detailed account of Chipeta's marital state appeared in *The Denver Republican* on April 1, 1883. The story identified Chipeta's new mate as "Too-much-a-gut."

*Toomuchagut is not a celebrated brave . . . quiet, peaceful, friendly . . . admired for his wealth . . . his flock of sheep . . . roam over a thousand hills. Of ponies he also has more than others.*

*Toomuchagut reined up his pony in front of Chipeta's teepee, and made a tender of his sheep, cattle and ponies, together with his heart and hand. Chipeta accepted, and the ties were bound.*

*For some time past Toomuchagut has courted his fair bride. At first she looked down on his advancements, but finally she wilted. She was an Uncompahgre, he a White River Ute. The two tribes have always been at more or less variance, and for this reason the marriage of the two was discountenanced by the two tribes.*

*Toomuchagut had many rivals among the Uncompahgres, too, and jealousy may have added to the discouragement. Chipeta had also had many offers of marriage from the hands of white men. But Chipeta declined them all sternly, but kindly. She has boasted of her prowess in saying 'No' to ardent lovers. It is a well-known fact that six lovers not of her own race have sought her hand within as many months.*

*Chipeta is acknowledged the fairest squaw of her tribe, but it is not conceded that her charms alone brought her admirers; her money and ponies and sheep probably had a great deal to do with it.*

*The Utes have no marriage ceremony, other than the mutual agreement plan. The agreement is considered binding and no Indian has been known to break it.*

*It was quite a little affair. No ceremony was performed, no high dignitary gave away the bride, no silver bordered cords, no minister, and no $250 night shirts.*[7]

All of these writers, building their stories on rumor and fantasy, found scraps of the truth. Sometime after she arrived in Utah, Chipeta took a second husband, a man called Accumooquats. He was not a chief or headman but simply a good man.

The couple reported to the Ouray Agency on June 30, 1885, to be counted with the rest of the 1,255 Uncompahgre Utes in the first government-mandated Indian census. Agent J.F. Gardner listed them on the ledger as household #122. Chipeta gave her age as forty-three; Accummooquats was forty-seven. They had a family, too. Six boys were identified as "wards" in their household. Fifteen-year-old Douascuno and thirteen-year-old Sevito may have been Ute. The Spanish names of the four younger boys — Guadaloupe, Jose La Cross, Francisco, and John Peto — suggest they were Mexican or children of mixed origins. They ranged in age from five to fifteen.

The family had abandoned Chipeta's house for the more comfortable teepee. They spent summers high up along the Book Cliffs and over the line into Colorado grazing sheep and goats. They wintered near Dragon, Utah. Chipeta must have reveled in the teepee full of active boys. The three oldest rode with Accumooquats to hunt and look after the sheep. The younger ones remained in camp to play traditional boys' games and gather around to hear Chipeta sing and tell stories. She watched their eyes grow wide as she described the fearsome Anusacutz trolling about in the night in search of naughty children, just as she had done for her earlier wards.

McCook and Hahseekep camped with Chipeta and Accummooquats. Their two-year-old son, Seagoots, was the image of the little boy, McCook, who once toddled after Chipeta. Sapovanero and Keorarapon, whose children were grown, lived nearby with three young wards. The children made the hard life bearable.

That creative April Fools Day tale of Chipeta and Too-much-a-gut bore one more snipit of truth. Living on the Ouray Agency, with a woman called Tahveeah and three small children, was thirty-eight-year-old Occuptoomuchakut. How

*An unknown woman (perhaps a field matron sent out by the Indian
Bureau) stands by Chipeta's teepee in Utah about 1895.*
Denver Public Library, Western History Department, X-30350

his name, corrupted to Toomuchagut, became linked with
Chipeta's remains a mystery.

In 1886 the Bureau of Indian Affairs consolidated the
Uintah and Ouray agencies under one agent. To keep the
peace between the Colorado and Utah bands of Utes the
bureau requested that a new military base be established
between the two reservations. In late August 1886, General
Crook marched a company of troops across the Ouray reservation. Panic spread among the Utes as runners spread the news
of an invasion of soldiers. No one had bothered to inform the
Utes of plans for a military post. When the troops arrived at
their destination, the juncture of the Uintah and Duchesne
Rivers, they met a contingent of mounted warriors, painted
and armed for battle. The agent arrived just ahead of the
troops, calmed the chiefs, and facilitated a peaceful meeting
with General Crook.

Fort Duchesne was erected at the site of the meeting and
eventually housed 250 soldiers including two companies of
black cavalry. The Indians called them Buffalo Soldiers
because their hair looked like the fur of the great animals.

There are many stories that Chipeta rode with Colorow's wandering band, who refused to stay on the reservation. Although by most accounts, including those of the Indian agent, she settled into a quiet family life on the reservation, her name did surface in 1887 in what came to be called Colorow's War.

The *New York Times* reported the incident, including mention of Chipeta's involvement, and Lieutenant George K. Burnett from Fort Duchesne recorded Chipeta's own account as she related it to him. Events were further documented in letters written by the Ute agent, officers at Fort Duchesne, and officials in Colorado.

In June of 1887 an Uncompahgre Ute named Augustine, who had been living outside the reservation boundaries, was killed near Rangely, Colorado. A party of Utes soon delivered to the agent a witness named Pablo Behil, who identified Adbino Munez as the murderer. A few weeks later a group of Utes stole nineteen horses from the ranch of A.A. Munez near Garfield, Colorado. One was a stallion valued at $350. The thieves gave seven of the horses to the widow of Augustine and divided up the rest among themselves. The stallion ended up on the reservation in the possession of Charley Allhandra.

In the *New York Times* version of the story, Colorow's band of Utes engaged in a horse race with a group of white men. The bet was winner-take-all of the horses raced, but when the Utes won, the white men reneged on the bet. That night the Utes stole the horses from the corral.

On August 6 Enny Colorow (son of Colorow) rode into the agency to collect his annuities. He and a small group of Ute families were grazing their sheep and goats, as they did every summer, on Colorado grass. He reported that his roving father and his band were camped two hundred miles from the reservation on the other side of Meeker, Colorado. Enny returned to his own camp on the Old Rawlins Road near the divide between Coal Creek and Milk Creek, well into the state of Colorado. He found two teepees burned down, supplies stolen or destroyed, and six squaws and eight children missing. Enny rushed back to the reservation for help.

Agent Byrnes immediately saw the gravity of the situation. Chipeta was among the missing women. Byrnes dispatched the agency's chief herder, John McAndrews, and a group of peaceable Utes — Wass, McCook, Wickeree, Charley Shavano, and Mountain Sheep — to return to Colorado with Enny Colorow. He directed them to find the missing Utes and Colorow's band and bring them all back to the reservation. Word of the raid on Enny Colorow's camp circulated on the reservation. Everyone was soon in an uproar that Chipeta might come to harm.

While Enny was away at the reservation, Chipeta, Enny's wife, four other women and the young children were alone in camp. The men, including Accoomooquats and the older boys, were away hunting meat for the winter supply. One morning Garfield County Sheriff Jim Kendall and a posse of 150 cowboys rode into camp searching for the thieves who had stolen the Munez horses. Observing that the women were alone, one of the cowboys pointed at Enny Colorow's wife and leered, "That's my squaw." The other men joined in with lewd gestures and raucous laughter and began to stake verbal claims on various women. The frightened women shoved the children into the teepees while Chipeta stepped forward and told the sheriff they wanted no trouble. She asked the men to leave. Seeing none of the stolen horses in the camp, Sheriff Kendall led his unruly posse away.

When the camp was calm, Chipeta consulted an old acquaintance at a nearby ranch. After hearing about the morning incident, the white rancher advised her to pack up and leave. Kendall's men were up to no good, he said, and might return. Chipeta hurried back to camp, assembled the women and children, gathered a few provisions, and fled. A good distance from the camp, they climbed into an outcropping of rocks on the mountainside. When the group was settled in a hidden spot, Chipeta climbed to a ledge where she could see the abandoned camp. Before long the posse returned. They rummaged through the camp, looted the valuables, then set fire to the teepees.

*Although only a small skirmish involving an over-anxious sheriff, the "Colorow War" was front page on* Harper's Weekly, *September 3, 1887.*
        *Courtesy*
        *P. David*
        *Smith*

As she watched the destruction of the camp, Chipeta considered her options. Accumooquats and the hunting party were far away. Their only hope for protection, Chipeta decided, was to go north to find Colorow's camp. She rallied the little group and led them toward White River. They left behind their large herd of sheep and goats grazing on the hillsides.

Between Milk Creek and Williams Fork, Kendall and his posse reappeared and Chipeta's party scrambled for cover. The two oldest Ute boys fired a few shots, and the posse withdrew. Kendall had his hands full controlling his posse. He managed to convince his cowboys that they had not been assembled to bother with a little band of women and children. He ordered the posse to ride in another direction to continue the search for the horse thieves. Chipeta waited until dark before moving on in search of Colorow's camp.

Meanwhile, in the nearby white communities reports of the original theft of nineteen horses escalated into wild tales of Utes looting and burning on a rampage through Colorado. Residents armed themselves in anticipation of a siege. Townspeople gathered to plan defenses and the frightened citizens of Meeker telegraphed the governor, requesting troops to defend the town. Fifty volunteers from the Aspen Rifles arrived promptly, and three hundred cavalrymen soon followed to protect the four hundred settlers from the anticipated Ute attack.

While the residents of Meeker prepared for war, Charlie Smith, owner of the largest ranch on White River, rode into Glenwood Springs and reported that he had seen the Utes. They wore no war paint and gave no indication that they were preparing for a fight according to Smith. The *New York Times* announced to the nation "grave fears" for Chipeta, the wife of the famous Chief Ouray, who was missing after being attacked by the sheriff's posse that burned her camp.

Chipeta breathed a great sigh of relief when her little group happened upon a small hunting party from Colorow's band who led them to the main camp. The tired women and children were welcomed with blankets and food. Unaware of the storm brewing in the white settlements, a few of Colorow's men rode into Meeker to buy supplies. They returned with the Hughes & Company storekeeper who delivered an ominous message. The citizens of Colorado gave the Utes fifteen days to get out of the state. They wanted the Indians back on the reservation where they belonged.

Colorow paid little attention to the warning until McCook, Enny Colorow, and Wickeree arrived with a message from the agent. All Utes must return to Utah, the message commanded. The situation was critical. McCook prevailed, and the whole camp set about packing.

The next morning the men began driving Colorow's livestock westward. The women and children loaded the supply horses and followed. They camped for the night at the mouth of Wolfe Creek where the agency herder, McAndrews, found them. He came from the town of Meeker and reported that soldiers were on the way. "The citizens mean business," he told the assembled Utes.[8]

At first light McAndrews rode out for the agency to report that Chipeta was safe and Colorow's band was on the way to the reservation. Just after sunrise two companies of soldiers approached the Ute camp. Carrying the written message from Agent Byrnes, McCook and Enny Colorow went out to meet them. The soldiers observed that the Utes were moving westward and allowed them to continue their peaceful return to the reservation.

On the way to the agency McAndrews encountered a contingent of Colorado militia men riding at full gallop. He followed and managed to locate the commander, General Leslie. McAndrews presented a note from Agent Byrnes, which stated that the Utes were peacefully returning to the reservation. Leslie tossed the message on the ground and walked away. The militia men bragged to McAndrews that they intended to follow the Indians at least fifty miles beyond the reservation line. McAndrews left and rode hard to carry the news to Agent Byrnes.

As he passed through the reservation on the way to the agency, McAndrews warned every Ute he met that troops were coming and they might be attacked in their homes. Runners dispersed to spread the word. When Agent Byrnes heard McAndrews's ominous report he requested troops from Fort Duchesne to prevent Major Leslie's men from entering the reservation. Lieutenant Burnett and eleven men of Company B, Ninth Cavalry, accompanied by 125 mounted Utes armed with Winchester rifles, rode out to defend the reservation and protect the Utes who were attempting to return from Colorado.

Colorow's group was by that time beyond Blair's Ranch, thirty miles from the reservation line and eighty-five miles from the agency. They made a long drive west with the livestock in heavy rains and camped that night on what they thought was reservation land. The next morning, August 25, while the Utes were cooking breakfast, the militia opened fire on them. Atchee ran up a bluff and called out in English for the soldiers to stop shooting as there were women and children in camp. He was shot in the thigh. Chipeta and the other women hurried the children out to the west. The men moved downriver to draw the soldiers away. They left behind in the abandoned camp great quantities of jerked deer meat, which was their supply for the coming winter, along with tanned deer hides, blankets, beadwork, and most of the livestock.

While the militia pursued the Utes, Kendall's posse of cowboys rounded up some 600 horses, 37 head of cattle, and 2,300 sheep and goats and drove them off to Rangely. One Ute man and three children were killed and three men seriously wounded in the attempt to reach the reservation.

Chipeta and the rest of the missing Utes arrived at the agency on August 27, escorted by Lieutenant Burnett and company. The reservation was prepared for attack, but the mood changed to celebration when the bedraggled group returned. Accumooquats and the hunting party arrived a short time later having been located by one of the Utes dispatched by Agent Byrnes.

Colorado's Governor Alva Adams sent word for Byrnes to travel to Meeker immediately to discuss the recent situation. The issue of the stolen horses was lost in the arguments over which group had been the aggressors and what happened to the vast number of sheep, cattle, and horses the Utes were forced to abandon as they fled from the pursuing militia. Byrnes defended the Utes as peaceful victims and demanded the return of their stolen livestock. He insisted that the Utes had a right to be in Colorado. There had been an understanding, he said, with the commissioner of Indian Affairs that the Utes could continue to hunt on the land they had once occupied. Byrnes reported that the Indians were on the reservation and quiet. However, he noted that Colorow and Chipeta were "very sore over their losses in ponies, sheep, and goats" taken by the cowboys.[9] Major Leslie refused to return any livestock unless Colorow and his sons, Frank and Ciblro, were turned over to Sheriff Kendall for horse theft. Byrnes refused. It was a standoff. The next day the governor directed that the stolen Ute property be turned over to Agent Byrnes.

On his return to the agency Byrnes held a council with the Ute chiefs. He ordered them all to remain on the reservation. He had been officially notified that any Ute who crossed the Colorado line would be shot on sight. Byrnes agreed to resume annuity payments to Colorow's band, if they stayed out of Colorado, and promised he would make every effort to recover their stolen property. As a result of his efforts, one hundred twenty-five ponies were delivered to the reservation on September 7.

Ten days later the Uintah agent requested a transfer of Colorow's band to the Ouray Agency. He said Colorow was willing to live on the Uncompahgre reservation and the Uintahs preferred for him and his group to do so.

A U.S. Indian inspector named Armstrong arrived in September to investigate the recent incident. In his report of findings he noted that many of the stolen Ute horses had been grazing on public land in Colorado. The Utes had purchased the stock and sheep with proceeds from the sale of hides. Chipeta, the wife of former Chief Ouray, had used money that her husband left her to purchase livestock, and this property was taken or destroyed. Armstrong's sympathetic finding resulted in a November delivery of 450 sheep and goats to the reservation. That was the end of the livestock return.

A year later U.S. Special Indian Agent H. S. Welton visited the Ouray Agency to examine the books, inspect the property, and interview the employees. On October 1 he met in council with thirty chiefs and headmen, including Sapovanero and Colorow, and also Chipeta. Welton observed that the Indians had confidence in Agent Byrnes but they felt deeply wronged in the attacks by the military, destruction of their teepees and supplies, and theft of their livestock. Sapovanero reported that some of the people wanted to go back to Colorado and get even for the sheep and ponies that were stolen from them. He demanded payment for these losses. Colorow, Chipeta, and others asked to go to Washington. The Great Father, they told Welton, would convince the great white council to pay them for their losses, which they estimated at thirty thousand dollars.

Welton, like Special Agent Armstrong, was sympathetic. He recommended in his report to the Commissioner of Indian Affairs that Colorow, Sapovanero, and Chipeta, plus two Indians to be selected by the agent, be sent to Washington during the next session of Congress. He suggested that their personal pleas might garner enough support to pass an appropriations bill.

Agent Byrnes prepared a list of the losses claimed by the Uncompahgre Utes, which Welton attached to his report. Heading the list were Accumooquats and Chipeta with a loss of $2,366.50. Apparently Chipeta and Accumooquats had grazed McCook's herd with their own because McCook and his wife claimed a loss of $3,985.75. There were thirty-two claims totaling $32,050.25.

Welton also suggested that, if irrigation were brought to the land between the Duchesne and the Uintah Rivers, all of

*An 1875 photo of Colorow (front right) and his band — a time when Colorow was a little more dangerous. Colorado Historical Society, F-7051*

the Uncompahgre band would move there for the good land, and the remainder of the reservation could be returned to public domain. The Ute chiefs all stated that they agreed with this plan. They added a request that a schoolhouse be built.

Agent Byrnes added his own letter in support of a new school. He noted that the only school was located at White Rocks and it was overcrowded. No Uncompahgre children attended. Neither did any of them attend the new Indian boarding school in Grand Junction, Colorado. "The People of Colorado have established the east line of this Reservation as a 'dead line' and have notified the Indians that any of them crossing this line into Colorado will be shot," Byrnes stated. "Hence the Indians will not send their children to the Grand Junction school." [10] He reported that the Uncompahgre were eager for their children to be educated.

Welton also included with his report a list, prepared by Agent Byrnes, of Uncompahgre Utes who had "distinguished themselves by good sense, energy and perseverance in the pursuits of civilized life and the promotion of good understanding between the Indians and the Government." [11] The list included rewards to be paid to these Utes.

Heading the list of forty-eight men was Sapovanaro, head chief, with a reward of one hundred dollars for "farming earnestly during the year and raised a good crop of oats, wheat and vegetables. He has good control of the Indians and his advice and councils are wise and earnest." McCook was awarded seventy dollars for maintaining a large herd of fine horses, setting an excellent example, and having a positive influence among the Utes. Accumooquats received forty dollars for his large herd of sheep and goats and good example.

Despite all the investigations, reports, and letters of support, there is no record that the Utes received recompense for their loss of property. Their request to send a delegation to Washington to lobby Congress was apparently ignored.

¹ A few sources report that Chipeta begged to stay, cried, and kissed the ground. However, such behavior seems uncharacteristic for the reserved Ute women and other descriptions of Chipeta's behavior.

² "Fort Crawford — A Symbol of Transition," *Journal of the Western Slope,* Vol. 8, No. 2, (1993), 18.

³ Lloyd, John B., "The Uncompahgre Utes," Master's Thesis, Western State College, 1932, 45.

⁴ *The Denver Republican,* April 2, 1883, 2.

⁵ *Steamboat Pilot,* September 25, 1923.

⁶ Manypenny, George W., *Our Indian Wards,* (Cincinnati: R. Clarke & Co., 1880).

⁷ *The Denver Republican,* April 1, 1883.

⁸ McAndrews to Dole, August 16, 1887, NARA Record Group 75, Box 6, Folder 16.

⁹ Welton, H.S. to Commissioner of Indian Affairs, October 12, 1888, NARA Record Group 75, Box 7, Folder 2.

¹⁰ Ibid.

¹¹ Ibid.

## Chapter 10

# LAND
# GRABS
# CONTINUE

During the intense cold of mid-January 1889, Sapovanero became ill with fever and severe abdominal pain. The agency doctor diagnosed an abscess of the liver. Chipeta moved into the teepee with Keorarapon, and the two women joined the medicine man's rituals. Despite their efforts, Sapovanero, the elder brother whose life Chipeta once saved, Ouray's right-hand man, the chief who led the Uncompahgre into exile, died that same night.

The women washed the body and painted and wrapped it for burial, just as they had done for Ouray. At first light McCook and Accumooquats carried Sapovanero into the nearby hills and buried him. Chipeta and Keorarapon chopped off their hair, and Keorarapon smeared her face with widow's pitch. Then they gathered Sapovanero's belongings and selected items to give to special friends. The remainder they burned.

Charley Shavano succeeded Sapovanero as chief. He had married a daughter of the old Chief Shavano and adopted the name.

Meanwhile, white men were once again invading Ute land in search of treasure. Four years earlier a prospector trespassing on the reservation had noticed wide parallel veins of a glossy black substance cutting across the desert south of Vernal. He slipped out with samples which ended up in the hands of Samuel Gilson of Salt Lake City. The substance resembled solid petroleum. Gilson was sure there was a use for the material, especially after testing proved it to be resistant to acids and moisture. He soon found an application for "gilsonite" as an additive to paint, varnish, and insulating compounds.

With a market available, Gilson faced the problem of extracting the substance from the ground and getting his find out of Utah. Besides being on the Ute reservation, the veins were located a hundred mountainous miles from the nearest railroad. Gilson and partners formed the Gilsonite Manufacturing Company in 1888 and filed claims on the land, even though it was part of the reservation. They began clandestine mining, packing out small quantities of gilsonite on horseback.

The partners sought help in Washington, D.C., where they found an ally in Utah's territorial delegate, Joseph W. Rawlins. He approached the commissioner of Indian affairs about a deal. In October 1889 legal counsel advised the commissioner that the land was allotted in severalty and the president had the power to reduce the reservation without compensating the Indians for unallotted property. The valuable gilsonite mining region was quietly leased to Gilson's company.

The gilsonite mines became a destination for Chipeta. She acquired a new friend in Laura Foster, the camp cook, who saved biscuits for Chipeta's children. Foster said she found Chipeta to be "an intelligent, lovable person, and I never once heard her complain. She was the kindest person I ever knew." [1]

Diphtheria struck the reservation late in 1890, and by January of the new year the agency physician, Howard C. Reaves, proclaimed an epidemic. Accumooquats died about this time, possibly a victim of the disease. As Chipeta mourned her loss, McCook once again stepped in to help with the boys and manage the herd of sheep.

The Utes suffered regular turnover of agents. By the time an agent got to know them and the Utes had determined his trustworthiness, they started all over with a new man. Despite the Utes' request to retain Timothy A. Byrnes as their agent, he was replaced in March 1890 by Robert Waugh.

In July 1891 Chipeta joined two hundred-three Ute chiefs and headmen in signing a petition requesting the secretary of interior to dissolve the consolidated agency shared with the Uintah Utes. The chiefs asked that the Ouray Agency be re-established to serve the Uncompahgre. They wanted their own agent, and not Waugh.

In his annual report for 1892 Agent Waugh reported a total of 1,001 Uncompahgre and 33 White River Utes living on the Ouray Agency. None of the Indians over age twenty could read and none wore "citizen's" dress. Only twenty-five adults used English in ordinary conversation. After ten years in Utah just 230 acres of land were under cultivation raising hay, wheat, oats, corn, potatoes, melons and pumpkins. The Utes grazed 6,550 horses, 35 mules, 10 burros, 425 head of cattle, 2,700 head of sheep, and 1,100 goats and kept 150 domestic fowl.

The requested new school for the Uncompahgre children was completed and opened in March 1893. Only five children enrolled. Enny Colorow and Red Moon, who were opposed to educating Indian children in white man's schools, threatened to burn down the building. The frustrated Agent Waugh asked that four additional companies of soldiers be assigned to Fort Duchesne. He reasoned that the expanded military presence would curb the rabble rousers and command greater respect from the Indians. Then, he suggested, school attendance would increase. Waugh was removed as agent three months after making this recommendation.

James F. Randlett, an officer from Fort Duchesne, became acting agent and made greater progress in "civilizing" the Utes. Two years later he reported forty-five students at the Ouray Boarding School and cultivated land more than doubled to six hundred acres. The resident population had declined by fifty-five persons.

Congress debated Secretary of Interior Hoke Smith's proposal to open unalloted Uncompahgre land to white settlement. Smith devised a plan to put the asphaltum lands up for public auction to the highest bidder rather than include them in lands to be opened for homesteading at $1.25 an acre. Local white citizens were outraged. The *Vernal Express* denounced the plan and the "unlimited gall" of the secretary to bar poor people, including those who had prospected the land, from the benefits of the mineral wealth.

There was great demand in the east for Utah asphaltum, and existing mining leases enhanced the local economy. Payday at the Utah Asphaltum and Varnish Company brought ninety wagons and sleighs and sixty saddle horses to the streets of Vernal. Merchants did a thriving business.

On June 7, 1897, Congress passed an act preparing for the opening of the reservation to white settlement. Yet another commission was appointed, this time to complete allotments. The latest Ute agent, James Jeffries, was named commission chairman. Assignment of initial allotments had been haphazard at best although the chiefs had repeatedly asked about them after they moved to Utah. If allotments were the deal, they wanted the full deal. As it turned out, the Utes waited sixteen years for the deal they never wanted in the first place.

With the prospect of opening the reservation to settlement, the government was suddenly eager to see that each adult Ute received an allotment. The commission proceeded to document individual choices of ground and map the common grazing section that would be set aside for the use of all Utes. The rest of the reservation would revert to public domain. In October Agent Jeffries telegraphed the commissioner of Indian Affairs that the Utes wanted to send a delegation to Washington. They wanted to discuss allotments, and they were willing to pay their own expenses.

A snowstorm blew through the reservation in mid-October as four chiefs — Charley Shavano, McCook, Enny Colorow, and Sam Atchee — departed for Washington, D.C., to discuss the planned redistribution of their lands. The *Vernal Express* reported that Shavano favored allotments. McCook represented "the wishes of those Indians who still adhere to the counsels and advice of Chepeta." He and Shavano were labeled by the newspaper as liberals who would support of the wishes

of the Department of Indian Affairs. Enny Colorow represented a faction who opposed giving up any land. Sam Atchee,
captain of the reservation police force, represented the faction
of Red Moon, who fought any change that might affect the
old, traditional way of life. John McAndrews, a seventeen-year
agency employee and highly esteemed by the Indians, accompanied the delegation as interpreter.

On November 11, 1897, Secretary Bliss and the Ute
delegation concluded their meetings with an assurance
from the chiefs that there would be no trouble regarding
opening the reservation to settlement. The Utes were once
again no match for the government. The chiefs were
treated to opening day of the Benning racetrack before
leaving for home on Monday.[2]

As the talks in Washington ended, a Colorado game
warden found a band of forty Utes hunting deer across
the state line. He shot seven of them, left four dead, and
gathered a posse to pursue the rest. They followed the
hunting party to White River, where they were shocked
to find more than two hundred Utes in the main camp.
The hunt chief refused to leave. He told the game warden that the hunters intended to stay until they had
enough meat for their winter supply.

Posse members quickly spread the news of this
larger than usual congregation of Utes in Colorado.
Local residents feared the Utes would avenge their four
dead comrades by killing innocent ranchers. Troops from
Fort Duchesne left immediately for Colorado to escort
the hunters back to the reservation. This news raised
fears among Utah residents living near the reservation
that the angry Utes would finish their winter hunt by
poaching cattle from local ranches.

The agent set to work assuring locals that the Utes were
back on the reservation and would cause them no trouble. The
owner of S.D. Colton & Company store in Vernal, Utah, saw
opportunity in the uproar and created an advertisement to follow the agent's assurances. His front-page ad in the December
2, 1897, *Vernal Express* announced:

The Indians
have returned to the reservation
and you will now have time
to examine our
FALL AND WINTER GOODS,
DRESS GOODS AND TRIMMINGS
Christmas Goods all on Hand

Mrs. W. H. Beck, wife of the Uintah-Uncompahgre agent, had been away visiting her sister when the incident took place. She vented her feelings to reporters at the Denver railroad station on her way back to Utah. Her son Paul, an officer at Fort Duchesne, had told her in a letter that the killing of the four Utes was "nothing short of murder." He claimed the Colorado game warden was a murderer. Mrs. Beck declared, "As soon as I return to the reservation I am going to write a book on the subject, entitled 'Four Years on a Government Reservation' and in it I am going to endeavor to call attention

*Colorow weighed in at nearly 300 pounds. He could be threatening even in his old age.*

Harper's Weekly, *September 3, 1887*
*P. David Smith Collection*

of the white people to this injustice that is being done to the Indians"³ Any connection may be coincidental, but a month later Captain Beck was removed as Ute agent.

Special Agent Elisha B. Reynolds arrived in December to investigate the four Ute deaths. His findings exonerated the Colorado game warden and determined the Indians were the aggressors.

Ships and land were the main topics of conversation among both whites and Utes in the spring of 1898. White residents were up in arms over an attack that sank a ship called the *Maine* in far-off Havana harbor. They waved the daily newspaper as they recited predictions of imminent war. Chipeta and the few chiefs who had been to Washington were the only Utes who had ever seen a ship.

Repeatedly, Chipeta described the boats that were larger than any building on the reservation and that floated on water so vast that you could not see the other shore. She sounded like an authority as she described tall masts laced with rigging, wooden decks lined with cannons, and spaces underneath where sailors lived. The ship she described was twenty years out of date, but her moccasin-clad feet had once walked its deck during a tour of the Washington Naval Yard. By late April most of the troops were withdrawn from Fort Duchesne to support the Spanish-American War.

Land was a topic of much greater importance to the Utes. The opening of the Uncompahgre reservation to white settlement was scheduled to begin on April 1. The *Vernal Express* predicted the greatest land rush ever. "[D]espite outward appearance of aridness and barren waste, the practiced eye of western farmers and miners will discern beneath the unpropitious exterior a mine of wealth. They will be on the ground early and ride hard to gain their end. May there be enough land for all." [4] The Utes feared further infringement on their way of life; white residents worried that big companies would gobble up all the valuable asphaltum land.

On February 1 the agent reported to the commissioner of Indian Affairs that 232 Uncompahgres had received allotments. He noted that Chipeta, McCook, Enny Colorow, and Atchee were some of the most influential members of the band. Chipeta's 160-acre allotment was recorded on White River. McCook held 160 acres on Bitter Creek, where he and Chipeta and the family had lived part of each year since they arrived in Utah.

The agent proceeded to call the commissioner's attention to unpaid debts due to the Utes. He noted that by the 1880 agreement the Uncompahgre, White River, and Southern Utes ceded some 8 million acres of Colorado land to the government. The land was to be sold for cash and the proceeds deposited in an account with the U. S. Treasury. The Utes were promised that the interest on these funds would be paid annually with their annuity money. The agent could find no such account, and none of the Utes had received payment in the past eighteen years.

Despite Uncompahgre protests and unpaid debts, the reservation opened for settlement in 1898. Ironically, the land was so barren that many white homesteaders soon gave up; and the Utes argued that the settlers got the best land!

In November the commissioner of Indian affairs sent a letter to the Ute delegation who had visited Washington a year earlier. At long last he sent answers to questions the chiefs had posed. Regarding hunting rights in Colorado, he reported that the U.S. Supreme Court had determined that the admission of a state into the union annulled such treaty rights. Therefore, the Utes could legally be held by the officials of the state of Colorado for violating game laws. He reiterated the old song that as soon as they cultivated the soil and engaged in raising cattle, the Utes would no longer need to leave the boundaries of the reservation.

The Episcopal Church sent Reverend Milton Hersey to serve as missionary among the Utes and rector of the Church of the Holy Spirit at Randlett, Utah. The little white clapboard church, along with a small parsonage and hospital, huddled at the base of a sandstone cliff that towered eight hundred feet in the air. Three or four houses were scattered some distance away, but it hardly looked like a village.

Hersey and his young wife, Ruby, a teacher and former matron at the Colorado Indian School, came from a mission with the Mojave Indians, where they had met and married two years earlier. Reverend Hersey was an affable and hearty man, who made every effort to visit the nearby towns and camps to make friends with the Utes. He was always ready to help someone in need and thought nothing of saddling his horse to ride thirty-five miles to Vernal or forty miles to Theodore to comfort someone who was ill or dying. Often Mrs. Hersey cared for elderly Utes in her home. Through this care and attention Hersey developed a congregation of Utes who huddled on the back pews or sat on the floor during Sunday services.

Chipeta appreciated the kind reverend and his wife and was one of the first Utes to allow Hersey to baptize her. Years earlier she and Ouray had been baptized in the Methodist church at the prompting of another missionary.[5] Religion for the Utes was a personal experience, a part of everyday life focused on harmony with the spirits of the natural world, and belief in an afterlife. Christian rituals were compatible and social without infringing on traditional beliefs.

Reverend Hersey recognized that winters were long and confining for the Utes. He saw an opportune time to plan something special to benefit the Utes and strengthen the role of the church in their lives. Writing to friends at Grace Church in Chicago and several churches in northern Minnesota, Hersey asked for donated gifts. Several months later a crate arrived filled with children's toys, sacks of hard candy, packets of needles, spools of thread, and boxes of pipe tobacco. Mrs. Hersey sorted the treasures into boxes labeled for men and women and for boys and girls by age groups. Soon another delivery arrived, and another. By late December the small parsonage overflowed with presents.

Reverend Hersey announced that there would be a special service for the Utes on Sunday evening — with presents. News of the event spread by word of mouth, and on Sunday evening Utes came on ponies and in wagons and crudely formed sleighs. Chipeta must have joined the other blanket-wrapped women who filled the front pews along with the children. The men, appearing disinterested, lined the back rows. Boxes of gifts filled the steps and platform of the altar, but even the Ute children appeared not to notice.

Reverend Hersey, dressed in his black cassock, mounted the pulpit and read the Christmas story from the Bible. The Utes sat expressionless. Then Hersey came down to stand

*Chipeta in Utah about 1900 using the traditional Ute wickiup, which was very cool in the summer.*
*Denver Public Library, Western History Department, Thomas McKee Photograph, MC-324*

amid the gifts. He explained that the presents came from Christian friends in other churches who wanted the Utes to share in the glorious love of God expressed by Christmas. One by one he called each Ute forward to receive a gift selected by Mrs. Hersey, along with a word of blessing from the reverend. It was a quiet and unemotional ritual. Each Ute took his or her gift and filed out of the church.

The event became an annual affair known as "Mr. Hersey's Christmas."[6] The date was flexible, depending on the arrival of the big boxes from the East, which came by train to Dragon and by wagon for the final sixty-seven miles to Randlett. Each year the invitation spread by word of mouth, and the Utes appeared.

Reverend Hersey later added an Easter event with foot races and athletic contests that attracted as many as 250 Uncompahgre Utes. Prizes include dress patterns for women and tobacco for men. The timing of this springtime event was carefully planned with the hope of discouraging participation in the Bear Dance.

Hersey had his competition for the souls of the Utes. Not long after he arrived in the Uintah Valley, the Ghost Dance religion swept through the western tribes. Inspired by the mystic vision of a Paiute Indian, proponents promised that an Indian messiah would come and cleanse the land of whites and nonbelieving Indians. The grass would grow again on the prairies, the buffalo would return, dead ancestors would reappear, and the Indians would live the free happy life of days gone by. It was an attractive antidote to the collective despair that had settled over the people as reservation life eroded their traditional lifestyle and culture.

Ghost dancers wore loose-fitting muslin or deerskin shirts decorated with spiritual symbols, which they believed were impervious to white men's bullets. As the ghost dancing spread, military men grew concerned that a secret society was forming to plot a major Indian uprising. They issued orders on many reservations forbidding the dance and officers confiscated ghost dance shirts when they could find them. Ghost dancing was short lived, but other new rituals followed.

The Utes imported the Sun Dance from the Shoshone Indians. Though they insisted the dance had no religious significance, the Utes believed it offered health benefits. The ritual took place inside a circular brush enclosure similar to that used in the Bear Dance. The enclosure was open at one end for musicians and spectators. Around the inside, rough partitions created semiprivate booths where participants rested between rounds of dancing. A pole set into the ground in the center of the circle was the focal point of activity. Dancers blew shrill whistles as they stepped around the pole in time to the vocal rhythm of the musicians. Sometimes dancers dipped eagle feathers into the dirt at the base of the pole and sprinkled themselves with the earth dust.

The dance lasted three or four days with participants forgoing food and water for the duration. Each dancer sought spiritual commitment, and collectively they performed for the well-being of the entire tribe. The Ghost Dance might not have attracted Chipeta, but she and McCook often packed up the whole family and traveled to White Rocks to attend the Sun Dance.

By the turn of the new century Indians had become exotic attractions recruited for rodeos, fairs, and parades. Just as they had imported the Sun Dance, the Utes adopted the feather-bedecked war-bonnets from the Plains Indians. It was the costume white audiences seemed to expect.

Chipeta became a celebrity in Colorado, not only welcomed in her old haunts but invited as an honored guest. With a small entourage of relatives she traveled often to Grand Junction, Delta, Montrose, and Durango — even though Native Americans were officially prohibited from leaving their reservations until 1912.

In Grand Junction one day she happened into the mercantile business of an old acquaintance. It was a customer in the store who told the proprietor, Benton Canon, that the old woman swathed in a blanket was the famous Chipeta. Canon did not recognize in her aging face the young woman who had once so captivated him on his visit to the Ute camp. After his clerking days for Don Satillo Piño in the little town of Badito, Canon had moved to the bustling town of Grand Junction in 1886 to seek his fortune. Canon and Chipeta enjoyed a good laugh recalling his first trading venture with the Utes.

Wherever Chipeta went, local dignitaries took her riding in their new motor cars to show off the improvements made to her old stomping grounds. She smiled through tours and banquets, accepted gifts that she could not use, and said how much she was impressed. Chipeta returned home to tell her friends there were too many people, too many houses, and too many fences. Their beautiful homeland was a sad place, she reported.

In Denver a grand state capitol was under construction, and plans called for stained-glass portraits of sixteen Colorado pioneers to encircle the dome. Ouray was a unanimous choice of the selection committee. He was joined by Kit Carson and Governors Gilpin and Evans. It is doubtful that Chipeta ever saw his completed portrait.

Chipeta's name began to appear in print more frequently in stories and poems that romanticized Indian life.

## CHIPETA COMES BACK
### E.N. Holden

Chipeta comes back to her old time dwelling
The old, old Chipeta that we knew of yore.
We see her stand by the wigwam door
With her great eyes and her bosom swelling
She makes as though our friendship welcoming.
She fain would lie where she lived before;
Chipeta has come back to her old time dwelling,
The old, old Chipeta that we knew of yore.
Ah, who shall keep us from over-telling
Of kind, unforgotten Chipeta's dwelling
In this great Uncompahgre valley floor
E'en as we doubt in our hearts once more
With a rush of tears to our eyelids swelling,
As Chipeta comes back to her old time dwelling.

In January 1901, Stephen Stridiron of Yampa, Colorado, registered at Denver's St. Elmo Hotel, where he regaled other guests with his tale of a boyhood spent in Chipeta's teepee. Claiming also to be a grandson of Daniel Boone, Stridiron said that his parents had several children and allowed a childless neighbor couple to adopt him. A few years later his new family took him west. In 1860, four-year-old Stridiron was with his adoptive parents and a group of men driving cattle to the new mining camps in the Rockies. While camped near the mountains south of Colorado Springs, he was stolen away in the night by a stealthy band of Utes.

Stridiron claimed that he was given to Ouray and Chipeta and raised along with their own son, Julian, who became chief after Ouray's death. The two boys were near the same age and grew up together as brothers. To prevent discovery of this white child in her teepee, Chipeta kept Stridiron's skin painted with a dark stain. When stolen, Stridiron wore a small locket around his neck that contained a daguerreotype portrait of himself taken before his family left Kentucky. Chipeta strung the locket with beads and other trinkets on a necklace that he continued to wear as he grew. Schooled by Ouray in the ways of Ute men, at age fifteen Stridiron and Julian joined the Ute warriors in battles against the Arapaho and Cheyenne.

When he was about seventeen (in roughly 1873), Stridiron was lent to the U.S. Army as a scout and guide for General Crook. The general washed the dye from his skin and recognized him as a stolen white child. It was the locket photo so carefully preserved by Chipeta that led to a reunion with his natural mother. Stridiron reported that he remained with General Cook's unit for some years before becoming a prospector, and by the time of his stay at the St. Elmo, a respectable married man. When the story appeared in the *The Denver Times,* the storyteller disappeared.[7]

Though the facts of Stridiron's tale appear far fetched, the story illustrates the western settlers' fascination with Chipeta and the way the events of her life evolved into legend. Stridiron was not the only person who built a story around a few bits of information, or misinformation, about Chipeta.

By 1902 the outside world was invading the reservation at an alarming pace. Demand in the East for gilsonite exceeded the mines' production rates. The greatest barrier was transportation. The Gilson Asphaltum Company began construction of a railroad over the 8,473 foot divide between the Green and Colorado river drainages. The fifty-three mile narrow guage line from Mack, Colorado, to Dragon, Utah, was completed in 1905. Telephone service arrived the same year, connecting Dragon and Vernal, Utah, with the world. It was a development of little consequence to Chipeta and a device that she never used.

Chipeta's wards grew to young adults and left home one by one. But Chipeta was not forsaken. Her faithful brother saw that she was treated as a member of his family. By 1904, according to the agent's records, McCook's family included a new wife, Sahpiuke, and her mother, Tahsahwats. Sixty-one-

*Chipeta in 1902, she holds pine pitch baskets, which were water tight and were used by the nomadic Utes instead of pottery.*
        *Courtesy of Main Street Photography*

year-old Chipeta was listed in the agent's records as McCook's sister and "Old Chief Ouray's widow." Two of the children adopted by Ouray and Chipeta were still with the family. Cooroopits, age 41, was with the family along with husband Namran, known as Tom Patterson, and their three children: PooWoon (Jimmy McCook), Arrahtats (Albert McCook), and Nettie Colorow. The father of the two boys was listed as dead. There was also three-year-old granddaughter Mamie McCook, daughter of Jimmy McCook. She often appeared cuddled beside Chipeta in photographs of the period. Antonio, age forty-nine and single, was also present although misidentified by the agent as McCook's brother rather than Chipeta's adopted son.

John Peto, youngest of Chipeta's wards, was often nearby. He appeared in the agent's 1905 register book as #524, John

Chipeta, living in Colorado. McCook and Chipeta were listed as contacts. John received his allotment close to Chipeta's property. In 1906 they both appeared on a list of landowners to receive compensation for right-of-way in construction of the Uintah Toll Road. John Peto (J.P. Chipeta) and Chipeta each received $1.25/acre for use of less than three acres of land.[8]

Congress extinguished Ute title to the unalloted portions of the Uintah reservation in 1905 and opened the land to white settlement. This opening generated greater excitement than had the offer of Uncompahgre lands seven years earlier. People came from all over the country ready to homestead. Claims offices were established in Vernal, Price, and Provo, Utah, and Grand Junction, Colorado. Private homes in Grand Junction turned into boarding houses to accommodate the visitors flocking to town. Land seekers

*Chipeta in 1905. Colorado Historical Society, F-40197*

drew lots for the order in which they could file claims on soon to be chosen sites. However, many left in disgust after they got a look at the land. The sale did generate some six hundred thousand dollars in proceeds, which funded twenty-two irrigation projects, diverting streams into eighty thousand acres of once arid land that had been part of the Unitah reservation for more than forty years. White farmers reaped the benefits of the irrigation projects.

Utes in growing numbers began to petition to sell allotment lands, which were to have been held in trust for twenty-five years. Each petition required an assessment of the land by the agency farmer. Typical reports by William E. Endicott, the agency farmer, stated, "Lessee has tried every available means to get a crop to grow on his land, but cannot because of the excessive amount of alkali present." Or "This allotment is worthless for agricultural purposes." [9] By 1906 the Utes occupied very few of the original allotments. Many families roamed

*Chipeta and other Utes in Montrose, CO. Thomas McKee took many photographs of her — this one in his studio. Courtesy Walker Art Studio*

*Chipeta in 1907 as photographed by Thomas McKee. Although labeled with different dates the photos on pages 191, 196, 199 and 204 may have been taken at the same time.*

*Colorado Historical Society, F-1696*

in sections of Willow Creek, White River, and other localities extremely remote from the agency.

"Indian trouble of gigantic proportion is brewing," the *Vernal Express* announced on May 26, 1906. Disillusioned by allotments and general conditions on the reservation, Chief Red Cap and some four hundred followers packed up and left. They announced that they were going to South Dakota to live with the Sioux on their Cheyenne River Reservation. Wyoming ranchers feared trouble as the disgruntled Utes passed through, so the Ute agent rode along. On arrival the Sioux were generous in giving their visitors clothes, teepees, and money, but the Utes soon found that life on the Sioux reservation was not the paradise they envisioned. The Cheyenne River agent listed the 175 White Rivers, 145 Uncompahgres, and 50 Uintahs as "prisoners of war." In the fall the government supplied wagons, horses, and mules, and by October most Utes had returned to Utah under escort of federal troops.

While disgruntled Utes wandered and complained, Chipeta, McCook, and the family made do and raised their herd of cattle, sheep, and goats. Sidney Jocknick, one of the cowboys at the old Los Pinos Agency, later wrote in his autobiography:

> *Today it is easy to see how harsh has been the [Ute] tribe's punishment. Their superb lands have been taken from them and they are herded on a barren reservation where there is a scarcity of water and where successful farming is impossible. When they try to escape from their miserable surroundings they are called "marauders" and are herded back under military guard after suffering all the tortures that can come through insufficient protection against the weather and insufficient food. As for Chipeta, the brave and womanly, she has not been given the page in history of which Field wrote, but is suffering, old and feeble with her broken and despairing tribe. If there are any Utes left who took part in the Meeker massacre, it would appear that they have been made to pay the penalty many times over.*[10]

[1] Look, Al, *The Ute's Last Stand,* (Denver, CO: Golden Bell Press, 1972), 7.

[2] *Vernal Express,* November 11, 1897.

[3] *Vernal Express,* November 25, 1897; *Salt Lake Herald,* November 25, 1897.

[4] *Vernal Express,* January 6, 1898.

[5] Ouray and Chipeta's membership certificates from the Methodist Church were among items auctioned when contents of the Colorado farm were sold.

[6] Ford, Grant M., "An Indian Christmas," *The Spirit of Missions,* (Domestic and Foreign Missionary Society, May, 1907), Vol CXXII, No. 5, 368.

[7] *The Denver Times,* January 13, 1901; the 1900 census includes one Sinclare Stridiron, born August 1857 in Kentucky, living in Breckenridge, Summit County, Colorado, with his wife Annie (V16, ED152, S7, L23).

[8] Schedule of Appraisement Right-of-Way Over Allotted and Tribal Lands of Uintah Toll Road, June 29, 1906, NARA, Record Group 75, Box 9, Folder 11. In 1890 Commissioner of Indian Affairs Thomas J. Morgan

directed that Indians must adopt the white custom of family names when allotments were made. He prohibited translation of Indian names into English except when Indian names were too difficult for whites to pronounce. Then Indian names could be shortened. He also authorized the assignment of a Christian given name to precede the Indian name as a surname. This plan was revived and enforced in 1902 under President Theodore Roosevelt. [Francis Paul Prucha, *The Great Father: The United States Government and the American Indians,* Vol II, (Lincoln: University of Nebraska Press, 1984), 673-676].

[9] Petitions to Sell Original Allotment Land, 1915-1916, NARA Record Group 75.

[10] Jocknick, Sidney, *Early Days on the Western Slope of Colorado,* (Montrose, CO: Western Reflections Publishing, 1913, 1998), 195-6.

# Chapter 11
# RETURN TO COLORADO

The president of the United States, William Howard Taft, visited Colorado in late September 1909. After stops in Denver and Glenwood Springs, his private train steamed into the Grand Junction station early on the afternoon of September 23. An open touring car and driver waited to take him to the fair grounds. Chipeta and a few Ute chiefs were among the twelve thousand people gathered to hear his brief speech. Afterward, specially invited guests, including Chipeta, stepped onto the platform to meet the president. She appeared like a shriveled and shrouded gnome as the three-hundred-pound Taft tilted forward and enveloped her hand in both of his. The jovial Taft did most of the talking, perhaps acknowledging Ouray's diplomatic peace efforts to his famous widow. When Taft learned that the group of invited guests was scheduled to accompany him to Montrose for the opening of the Gunnison Tunnel, he insisted that Chipeta ride to the railroad station in his car.

Late that same afternoon a few thousand people assembled on both sides of a deep ravine in the hills outside Montrose. Chipeta stood quietly among the crowd surveying familiar territory. In the distance a light haze settled over the mesas and mountain ranges, tinted bronze by the sinking sun. No signs of the white man's settlements were visible from this remote location. She turned to see black smoke curling up the ravine. A double-header train climbed the winding rails toward the six-thousand-foot elevation, where a gaping hole, the mouth of the new tunnel, was chiseled into the rock wall. The white men were redefining her homeland.

The president mounted a wooden platform from which he peered 150 feet down into the tunnel. He spoke briefly of the great feat of engineering that was about to deliver water to "this incomparable valley with the unpronounceable name — the Uncompahgre."[1] Then he pressed a button that signaled workmen several miles away to knock out the bulkhead that held back the water. All eyes were on the great hole in the mountain, waiting. When the first stream tumbled from the opening, the cheers of the crowd echoed in the ravine. The tunnel delivered Gunnison River water 5.8 miles through a hole in the mountains to irrigate the Uncompahgre Valley.[2]

*Chipeta participated in this Montrose parade in 1909 at the opening of the Gunnison Tunnel.*
*Denver Public Library, Western History Department, Thomas McKee Photograph, F-40122*

*Chipeta and an unknown Ute man in 1907.*
*Denver Public Library, Western History Department, Thomas McKee*
*Photograph, Z-1480*

Life was not any better on the Utah reservation. The Utes once again had a new agent in 1910. Designated as "acting agent," Captain H. J. Brees was also the officer in charge of Fort Duchesne. He was already familiar with his Ute charges and made a great effort to listen to their concerns. In early December he met in council with Uncompahgre leaders at Ouray, Utah. As was often the case, Chipeta sat among the chiefs. Brees opened the floor to the Utes.

McCook spoke first. He complained that sheep belonging to white ranchers were grazing on his allotment. He said the previous agent had promised to collect grazing fees, but he had seen no money. Sam Atchee, Witchits, and Joseph Arrive reported similar problems. They also asked when a requested irrigation ditch would be dug to serve new allotments on bottomland farms.

Then Chipeta spoke:

*We did not know this part of the country before we came here from Colorado; we moved through four places to here. Where the state is surveyed is just through the mountains. I have heard about this. There were two Indians, head men, who I heard from about this country. After that they built the Agency at Ouray. They call it "White Water" now. Today, up at White Water we are without an agency. I do not know anything about this country down this way. They told me I would have a good house to live in and a good living. They have never done it. These sheep they have been coming along through the allotments. These sheep men tell their herders that this land does not belong to the Indians. That is all I have to say.*[3]

Chief Charlie Shavano summed up the problems of too many white men's sheep and too little water. The new agent said he would attempt to collect grazing fees. He also suggested that the Utes protect their livestock by branding them.

Chipeta was one of the few Utes who followed Captain Brees's advice. Her animals soon displayed the Flying Ute brand — a waved line with a T in the middle and wings on both ends.[4]

Less than a year later Captain Brees and most of the troops marched out of Fort Duchesne headed for Boise Barracks, Idaho. Sixteen men remained behind. Locals speculated that the fort might become the terminal point for an extension of the Uintah Railroad from Dragon. The *Vernal Express* reported that the fort would have closed years earlier but for the pleas of locals to keep it open to control the Indians. However, "now that conditions have changed and the Indian problem is practically settled," the *Express* saw no urgent need for an armed protection force.[5] By November the *Express* announced that the Whiterocks Indian School would move to Fort Duchesne as soon as it was abandoned by the remaining soldiers. Commissioner of Indian Affairs Robert G. Valentine made an inspection of the fort and the reservation in November 1911, and the fort closed the following year.

In the summer of 1911 Chipeta, accompanied by her niece, an adopted grandchild, and two young men mounted their horses and rode out on an annual visit to Colorado. They stopped in Montrose for the Fourth of July celebration. During the festivities Montrose District Judge Bell called Chipeta to the bandstand and made a speech. He said of Chipeta, "She was ever humane, discreet, motherly and merciful in all her tendencies and became not only popular with the Indians but so popular with the whites during her residence on the Western Slope that she was always pointed to as the ideal of the white women."[6] Judge Bell presented her a purse filled with silver coins, a gift from an anonymous citizen.

For the first time in more than thirty years Chipeta stopped in the town named for her mate near one of his favorite hunting spots. William Rathmell, secretary of the Commercial Club of Ouray, organized a reception and a breakfast party for the Ute visitors at the Beaumont Hotel. The town offered a band concert, special entertainments, and a handsome silver donation to "the Queen of the Utes, who saved the white women by her daring and heroic actions . . . in 1879."[7] Hale and hearty for her advancing years, Chipeta wore fabric dresses most of the time, and a plaid shawl replaced her usual blanket. But her

*Chipeta was given an automobile ride in Ouray, CO. She was also taken to a motion picture.*

*Colorado Historical Society, F-44107*

feet still sported traditional moccasins. Many old timers were present who remembered her well. Dr. Crosley took Chipeta and her party for a tour of the town by automobile, stopping along the way to chat with curious citizens.

After being wined and dined in the town of Ouray, Chipeta and her relatives left for Ignacio to visit Buckskin Charley. They had barely set foot on the Southern Ute reservation when Agent Werner presented Buckskin Charley an invitation from Colorado Springs for a group of Utes to participate in a parade. Buckskin Charley declined since he had a guest, but Chipeta broke in to say she would like to go. Plans were quickly made. Teepees and horses were loaded on a D&RG train, and by July 30 the Utes were encamped in South Cheyenne Canyon. Chipeta knew this spot from years of buffalo hunts.

The Utes rode in a grand parade of pioneers that marked the fortieth anniversary of the city's founding, attended a wild west show in Roswell Park, and demonstrated Ute dances at night. Chipeta's presence was an added bonus for the city and made front-page news. After some coaxing she posed for the camera of Joseph Langer of *The Denver Post*. Her loose dark hair was lightly streaked with gray, and she still wore vermillion on her face.

All the publicity surrounding her visit caused local citizens to notice that Chipeta still lived in a teepee and held out her hand for coins when someone asked to take her photograph. People began to discuss the shame of her hard life. A group of citizens established a fund and invited public contributions to provide a better future for Chipeta. "A woman who has done as much as she has for the state; a woman, who as the wife of Ouray, was instrumental in saving of Colorado from a most horrible massacre at the time of the Meeker affair, should not be allowed to go in actual need and privation," read the committee's appeal.[8] They expressed hope that with these new resources Chipeta might return to live in Colorado

At the end of August, Chipeta, Buckskin Charley, and a contingent of Southern Utes returned to Colorado Springs for the inauguration of a new event. The city fathers created a festival in hopes of bolstering the depressed economy with tourists' dollars. They called it Shan Kive (reported to mean "Heap Big Fun") and advertised it as a commemoration of the Utes' visits to the area in autumns past.

The white residents believed the Utes had made annual pilgrimages to worship their god "Manitou" at the mineral springs now known by that name.[9] The beads and trinkets found in the springs convinced them this had been the mystical site of secret pagan rituals. Certainly the Utes had frequented the spring, like the white people who followed them, to soothe their bodies in the hot mineral waters. The Utes believed the breath of spirits caused the water to bubble and provide healing medicine. They left customary gifts for the spirits of the waters and, perhaps, chose a nearby site for the ritual dance seeking good fortune in the buffalo hunt that brought them to this place on the brink of the plains.

*Chipeta in 1911 at the Garden of the Gods. Note the laundry on the bushes.*

*Denver Public Library, Western History Department, X-30456*

*Another Thomas McKee photo of Chipeta. This is the photo that Chipeta probably sent to Cato Sells with her thank you letter for the shawl. Courtesy Walker Art Studio*

The occasion offered Chipeta a very special reunion with her old friend Margaret Adams. They had not seen each other since their days together at the Los Pinos Agency on Cochetopa Pass. Both were widows. Charles Adams had died in an 1895 fire in Denver's Gumry Hotel shortly after he and Margaret returned from service with the U.S. diplomatic mission to Bolivia. The two women sat side by side on the vine-covered porch of Mrs. Adams little rented house at 822 West Huerfano Street. They talked of old times, then simply sat holding hands, each lost in her own memories.

After their visit Margaret Adams reported that Chipeta lived on a barren bit of Utah land where even an experienced farmer could not make a living, much less an old woman. The government had placed her there to make a living or starve. Winter was coming on and Mrs. Adams appealed for improvements to make Chipeta's little house more comfortable.

Shan Kive began with a parade that stretched two miles to the edge of town. Spectators lined the route and gathered at the reviewing stand on Kiowa Street. Grand Marshall Charles H. Ferrin, in the Shan Kive uniform of white riding breeches and blue coat with a red, white, and yellow sash, led the parade. The fifty-piece Midland Band followed, setting the marching pace. The Utes, dressed and painted as if for a hunt, waved to the crowd from horseback. Chipeta and Margaret Adams rode in the back seat of an open touring car. They were followed by costumed cowboys and cowgirls, volunteer firemen, hose carts, water wagons, and the brand-new city fire truck. Local organizations displayed themed floats and city officials waved from crepe-papered automobiles. Gladiators and chariot racers costumed for the Roman Circus brought up the rear.

Northwest of the city, the grand park of towering red rock formations known as the Garden of the Gods became the Shan Kive grounds for a few days. An arena hosted bronco-busting contests and the Roman Circus. Visitors wandered through the Indian camp to gawk at real Indians dressed in buckskin and living in teepees. They ate picnic lunches on the grass and delighted in watching the cowboys practice rope twirling. At night the grounds glowed with thousands of electric lights. The bark of ticket sellers mingled with the music of three bands and the shrieks and laughter of the crowd. Games of skill and chance challenged the talents, and the pocketbooks, of all ages. Now and then, boys shot fireworks that lit up the night sky and sprinkled to earth like twinkling stars.

The climax of Shan Kive was a masked ball. The intersection of Kiowa and Tejon streets was closed to accommodate the event. As opening entertainment the Utes presented a moon dance and competed with Pueblo Indians from New Mexico for Indian dance prizes. A grand march of masked and costumed citizens was followed by a quadrille on horseback. Then the street was cleared for waltzing, which soon gave way to the latest ragtime music enjoyed by the younger crowd.

Shan Kive continued for two more years. On August 27, 1912, some seven thousands spectators attended the Ute dances

*Utes at the Garden of the Gods performing the "Moon Dance."*
*Denver Public Library, Western History Department, H. S. Poley*
*Photograph, P-1307*

in the Garden of the Gods during Shan Kive. A newspaper reporter with little understanding of the purpose or ritual of Indian dances attempted to interpret the activity for his readers.

> *In a riot of color, with their gay blankets and many hued feathers, and to the tune of the weird music handed down from generation to generation, the band of 75 Ute Indians . . . gave their dances . . . in the Garden of the Gods, historic stamping ground of their forefathers. The Indians danced upon a platform high up on the side of the southern Gateway rock of the Garden, so that everybody had a clear view of their interesting gyrations.*
>
> *The famous sun dance, a sacred dance with the Utes, was the feature of the program. And the Indians proved to the palefaces that the worship of their gods*

*was not all in vain. The sun dance started under unfa-
vorable conditions, so far as the red men were concerned.
The sun was behind a heavy bank of clouds, and every
indication pointed to rain. The Utes began their dance,
using the short, jerky, bumpy step peculiar to all Indian
dances. Accompanied by tomtoms and singing, the
braves and squaws danced for perhaps five minutes,
and just as the dance ended the sun broke through the
clouds and shone brightly for quite a while . . ."*[10]

In the final year of Shan Kive, Pathe Weekly Moving
Pictures sent cameramen to record the events for the entertainment of audiences in moving picture houses across the
country. Chipeta stepped out of her teepee for her motion picture debut on September 3, 1913.

That year the Utes camped at Adams Crossing between
Colorado Springs and Manitou Springs. Games and conces-
sions separated the Indian camp from the cowboy camp.
Thousands of people took the five-cent trolley ride or arrived
in buggies and Model-Ts to see the Indian dances. The
Colorado Springs *Free Press* reported that thirty thousand people watched the Shan Kive parade that included fifty Utes,
three hundred cowboys, seven hundred pioneers, several
prairie schooners, and floats depicting the progress of civilization. Although it appeared successful, Shan Kive became a victim of excessive expenses and the disapproval of the Indian
Bureau. The festival was not repeated.

One year on their return trip to Utah from Shan Kive,
the Utes camped along the Gunnison River near Delta,
Colorado. Most of the young people went into town, where
they attracted the particular attention of a local man named
Newton Castle. He approached the group to ask about
Chipeta. When he learned that she was resting in the camp
near the river, he packed his wife and several children into the
car and drove out to see her.

Castle knew Chipeta from his trade business with the Utes
when they first settled on the Utah reservation in the 1880s. Her
pronunciation of his named sounded like "Caswop," which

Castle found charming. Chipeta always wanted news of her old homeplace. Once she asked him about the Uncompahgre Valley, "Does it have heap wickiup?" He described for her the growing towns and sprawling ranches. "Too, too much fence," she said and wanted to hear no more.[11] Castle had not seen Chipeta in many years.

At the Ute camp Castle was pleased to be welcomed again as "Caswop" by a beaming Chipeta. The Castles took her back to their home, along with her ten-year-old great-niece, for an overnight visit. The Utes planned to continue their journey toward Utah the following day, so the Castles delivered their guests to the camp early the next morning. Castle rigged a small wire cage and gave Chipeta a few chickens to eat on the journey home. The Castle family waited until the Utes left camp. As they watched Chipeta ride away on her horse with only a blanket for a saddle, they thought they had seen and heard the last of the old Indian woman.

The following spring Mrs. Castle was interrupted in the midst of housecleaning by a knock at her door. She found three young squaws on the doorstep. They told her they had

*Chipeta at Red Mountain — on her way to Durango about 1901. She was still riding a horse!*

*Colorado Historical Society, F-40200*

come to bring a report on the chickens along with Chipeta's thanks. She had carried the birds all the way back to Utah, where they were still producing eggs and offspring.

Chipeta discovered that travel by train was easier on her aging body than long hours on the back of a horse. She and McCook became friends with W.A. Banks, the agent for the Uintah Railway at Dragon, Utah. McCook, a straightforward businessman who was very careful in making deals, struck a bargain with Banks to supply cut firewood to the small store at the station. After each delivery the two men enjoyed swapping stories. McCook reminisced about trips with his parents onto the plains to hunt buffalo in the area where Denver was built.

Chipeta often visited the store with McCook, and Banks was struck by her large hands that showed the abuse of hard work. After they became familiar friends, Chipeta sometimes brought presents. She made a pair of moccasins for Banks, and on another occasion presented a beaded purse for his wife.

*Chipeta loved children. Here she is holding Jim McCook's baby about 1912.*

*Thomas McKee Photograph. Photo courtesy of Main Street Photography*

One day Chipeta arrived at the station carrying a beautiful Navajo blanket. Several people who were waiting for the train wanted to buy the blanket, but Chipeta insisted she brought it for Banks. Realizing that this was more likely a business proposition rather than a gift, Banks asked the price. Chipeta said, "Twenty dollars." Banks made no attempt to bargain and handed over the cash. The blanket became the focal point of Banks family stories about their days among the Utes at the little station in Utah. Years later Banks still said he got his money's worth.[12]

On visits to the town of Ouray, Utah, Chipeta often stopped in at Matt Curry's trading post. One day a white man known as Buckskin Shirt came toward her, pushing along in front of him a small boy. The man introduced his nephew, George Emery Stewart. He said the boy wanted to meet her. Chipeta bent her face down close to the boy's and stroked his cheek. She spoke to him in English, and the poor boy looked like he might cry. Reverting to Ute, Chipeta commented to herself about the "poor little frightened boy." She was astonished when young George responded in Ute. He said he was not frightened. Chipeta smiled and said he spoke good Ute. George's father was a mining prospector, and the family lived near Ouray. George had picked up the language from Ute playmates.

After that first meeting, George went out of his way to speak to Chipeta whenever he saw her in town. She always smiled and greeted him in Ute with "Hello, frightened boy." He was pleased that she remembered him, but he hated that moniker. One day George got up the courage to tell Chipeta that he hoped she would not always call him "frightened boy." She smiled, nodded in understanding, and thought for a moment. Then she gave him a new name — "Uviev." Chipeta said the word referred to a turkey and George walked like one. George was thrilled with his new name, especially since it was bestowed by Chipeta. From that day on he was known as Uviev among his Ute friends.[13]

Chipeta paid another visit to the town of Ouray, Colorado, in August of 1913 on one of her annual trips through Colorado. She was traveling south with nine adults, a little girl, and a baby. The whole group was fed and lodged once more in the Beaumont Hotel at the expense of the Commercial Club. William Rathmell and a few delegates from the club joined the Utes for supper. Chipeta was quiet and somewhat sullen through the meal but ate heartily of the great quantities of beef, potatoes, beans, bread, and pudding. She left the talking to Mountain Sheep. After supper Rathmell could see that Chipeta looked uncomfortable and concluded that the large meal she consumed had given her a stomachache. He brought her a glass of brandy, which, he claimed, not only eased the pain, but "thawed" her out. She became quite sociable and answered questions from her hosts.

In return for his hospitality, Chipeta presented Judge Rathmell one of her small beaded buckskin bags. He boasted afterward that Chipeta also made him an honorary Ute. The next day the city band played for her in front of the hotel, and the whole Ute group saw a picture show. The movie included a short film of a wild west show and some bronco busting. Before they left town a photographer captured Chipeta and company on the steps of the Elks Club.

Trips through Colorado typically included stops at some of the hot springs Chipeta and Ouray had frequented. With age she developed rheumatism, and a long soak in the warm water eased her pain and renewed her vigor. A favorite spring was located on the Orvis ranch near Ridgway. Mrs. Orvis had originally homesteaded the ranch when it was still in the Ute reservation and knew Chipeta well. The two women always enjoyed a visit even though Chipeta repeatedly told Mrs. Orvis that all the land between the hot springs and Ignacio was Ute land and that she didn't like the encroachment of the whites.

In September 1914, Chipeta and McCook took the train to Glenwood Springs, where a health resort monopolized another "boiling waters" they had once enjoyed. At the invitation of hotelier Elmer Lucas, they mingled amiably with visitors from many states in the courtyard of the beautiful Hotel Colorado. They even posed for photos with guests including General Grenville Mellon Dodge, chief engineer of the Union

*Chipeta with Grenville Dodge and Chief McCook at Hotel Colorado. Denver Public Library, Western History Department, Kirivan Photograph, X-30547*

Pacific Railroad. At the pools Chipeta told fellow bathers, "Me here long time ago. Boiling waters make me well then; make me well now again."[14]

The change from the nomadic life to the more sedentary life of the reservation created a variety of new health problems for most Indian tribes. The Bureau of Indian Affairs established a field matron program in 1890 to improve health conditions on the reservations. The matrons were dispatched to the various reservations to give instructions in sanitation and hygiene, provide emergency nursing services, and prescribe medication for minor illnesses. They reported unsanitary living conditions, poor nutrition, and widespread disease of horrific proportions among the Indians. In 1909 a medical supervisor for the Indian service was appointed, and the government began to conduct health surveys of the Indian population. The 1909 Trachoma Survey was the first major study conducted in response to reports of unusually high incidents of blindness among Indians. The study confirmed a widespread trachoma epidemic and also found unusually high concentrations of other infectious diseases, such as tuberculosis.

In January 1914 the *Vernal Express* reported that trachoma was spreading on the Uintah-Ouray reservation. Miss Lucretia Rose, an expert in trachoma and a supervising nurse of the Indian service, was sent to Utah for a year to oversee treatment. Trachoma resembled conjunctivitis with symptoms of excess tearing, sensitivity to light, pain, swollen eyelids, and crusty buildup in the eyes. The swollen upper lids often turned inward causing the eyelashes to scratch the cornea. These scratches became infected and resulted in scar tissue, which could become so extensive that it caused blindness. Transmitted by direct contact with an infected person and by flies or gnats, the disease was preventable with adequate diet, proper sanitation, and education.

Miss Edith Richardson, a Uintah Ute and granddaughter of Chief Tintic, became a nurse and spent fifty years working in the hospital at Fort Duchesne. She described the

*Chipeta, Buckskin Charlie, Ta-wee, and children about 1911.*
*Denver Public Library, Western History Department, H. S. Poley*
*Photograph, P-108*

hospital as crude, lacking proper sanitation, and having only one ward and one doctor for everyone. She recalled that Chipeta came to the hospital nearly blind with trachoma and was treated by Dr. Lloyd. Even during treatment for such a painful condition, Nurse Richardson described Chipeta as warm, friendly and cultured.

Chipeta made a friend in Mrs. W. G. King, a nurse at the gilsonite mines near Dragon, Utah. Mrs. King recalled that Chipeta was one of the first Indians to come to her home and once came to have the nurse look at her eyes. Although years later Mrs. King said the visit followed cataract surgery, it is more likely at that time that she treated Chipeta for trachoma.

> *One day Chipeta came in to see me about her eyes. I telephoned to her doctor [probably Dr. Lloyd at Fort Duchesne], and he gave me instructions for treatments. Hot packs were to be put on her eyes, and he sent medicine to be dropped into them. I explained she must have treatment for a long period of time in order to get relief and to have improved eyesight. The Indians were very cooperative. They moved down from their camp on Bitter Creek, and made camp up on "Vack Creek," a short way from Dragon. At last the eye treatments for Chipeta were over and her eyes were improved. Our Indians moved back to Bitter Creek where the summer Indian camps were.*[15]

In late 1913 a Denver newspaper announced the death of Buckskin Charlie at Ignacio. Just as word of this great loss began to spread on the Utah reservation, a letter came to McCook from the allegedly deceased Southern Ute chief.

> *John McCook:*
> *Dear Brother: I did not die yet. I am a live yet. I thing the Denver newspapers tell lie about me — but just my brother, Old Chief Ignacio die on December 9, 1913 at Navajo Springs Agency.*

> *We are feel sorry for him: he was visitor us about two weeks ago; he was no sic then. I wish you tell all rest your people about old Chief Ignacio die. Rest Ute all well.*
>
> *I am well since my sister last see me, Chipeta. There is nothing new here: its very cold here now, but not of snow. I think this all I know. If any happen I will always write to you. Goodbye, I am your brother.*
>
> *Buckskin Charlie*[16]

The letter was reproduced in the *Vernal Express*, probably at the suggestion of the agent. Buckskin Charlie's use of the endearing terms "sister" and "brother" caused some people to mistakenly conclude that Charlie, Chipeta, and McCook were of the same immediate family.

Another one of Chipeta's friends, Mary Boulter, ran a railroad boardinghouse and store just over the state line in Atchee, Colorado. Chipeta bought or bartered supplies from the store, and Mary often fed her lunch and invited her to spend the night. Chipeta returned this kindness with hand-made gifts.[17]

Mary's fourteen-year-old son, Eddy, ran the store. Many of the Utes came in groups to shop. They sat or squatted on the floor in front of the counter surveying the merchandise. After awhile one man got up, pointed at an item and asked, "How much?" Eddy told the price, the Ute said, "Gimme," and handed over the money. The buyer took the item and sat down. Then another Ute rose, pointed out an item, asked the price, made the purchase, and sat down. Sometimes they traded beaded purses, hatbands, and watch fobs for their goods. The selection procedure went on one item at a time until everyone bought what he or she needed. Then the Utes loaded their pack horses and rode away.

The Utes' marathon shopping events tried young Eddy's patience. One afternoon the floor of the grocery was packed with Ute shoppers when Chipeta arrived. She tiptoed through the crowd and into the boardinghouse to visit Mary. Darkness settled in by the time the shoppers departed and Eddy closed the store. Just as Eddy entered the dining room, Chipeta stood up and announced it was time for her to go home. Worried about the elderly woman riding off alone in the night, Mary insisted Chipeta sleep in the guest room. Chipeta agreed but said she would go out to look after her horse.

"Eddy will feed your horse," Mary said. Chipeta insisted on going out to check on her horse so Mary told Eddy to go along. After the aggravating afternoon with the Ute shopping party, Eddy did not want to talk to another Ute. However, he knew better than to argue with his mother. Eddy and Chipeta picked their way in silence down the rutted quarter mile path to the corral. Chipeta fed and watered her horse and secured it for the night while Eddy watched. Then she said, "Little boy, stay here," and disappeared into the brush. Eddy stood with head down, hands jammed into his pockets, and shuffled his feet in embarrassment as he heard the sounds of Chipeta urinating in the bushes.[18] She never appreciated outhouses.

Jewell D. Martin became the new Ute Agent in late 1912. His tenure was battered by a variety of problems that drew media attention and created rumbles all the way to Washington, D.C.

In the winter of 1913-14 a group of Utes led by Red Cap began to complain of hunger. A delegation of chiefs visited Agent Martin and asked that all 1,185 Indians on the reservation be placed on ration rolls. Martin explained that there were 420 elderly and disabled Utes receiving rations and there was not enough money to provide that for everyone. He said there might be others in need but likely they had either shared their rations with young and able-bodied idlers or they lived in outlying districts and had been unable to get to the agency for their rations.

Not satisfied with the agent's response, the Indians went outside the reservation to plead their case. They sent to the Uintah County Commissioners a petition signed by 122 Utes appealing for aid. The Indians declared that they were hungry and could get nothing to eat. The commissioners scheduled a meeting with Agent Martin.[19]

The *Vernal Express* picked up the story as front-page news. One local man interviewed by the paper reported an

Indian family reduced from eight members to two during a recent epidemic of grippe. They could have been saved, he said, with proper care and food. Agent Martin was interviewed by telephone and reported just what he told Red Cap's group.

In February the secretary of interior received a letter signed by thirty white residents of the Uintah Basin requesting that a commission investigate conditions of the Utes. The citizens reported many Utes were facing starvation. They asked that the investigator tour the whole reservation rather than confining an inquiry to the agency office at Fort Duchesne. Either the Utes or the white citizens also contacted Utah Senator Reed Smoot, who began his own inquiry.

Whatever the outcome in terms of aid to the Ute, the matter was handled quietly. However, the following autumn, after politely looking the other way for thirty years while the Utes continued to hunt in Colorado, the commissioner of Indian affairs forbade the Utes from entering Colorado to acquire their winter meat supply. Despite years of complaints and open hostility from Colorado residents, the Utes had never given up the practice and continued to claim hunting rights from the 1872 treaty. The sudden restriction on hunting simply exacerbated the Utes' complaints of hunger and mal-treatment by the agent and the government.

In May 1914, Agent Martin attempted to abolish the Sun Dance. He contended that the dance conflicted with farming season and took the Utes away from their intended work. Martin so strongly argued his case about the evils of the Sun Dance to the Bureau of Indian Affairs that a U.S. mar-shall arrived at the reservation with an official order from the attorney general to cease the dancing. Only ten Utes actually danced that year, but there were three hundred observers. The intrusion of a white lawman into Ute life fueled the Utes' dis-trust of their agent but did not end the Sun Dance practice.

Martin fielded another controversy, not of his making, when the government began issuing annuity payments by checks instead of cash. The older Utes could not read and did not understand the value of a check. They wanted cash, which they understood. Another unpopular change in annuities was the elimination of ongoing payments to the relatives of deceased Utes. In the past, for example, a mother whose child died had continued to receive the child's annuity portion. The changes created controversy and complaints that endured for several years.

---

[1] Look, Al, *Bits of Colorado History*, (Denver: Golden Bell Press, 1977).

[2] Directory of Colorado State Register Properties <www.coloradohistory-oahp.org/1503directory/cty43.htm> Viewed April 9, 2001; *New York Times*, September 24, 1909.

[3] Transcript of December 3, 1910 council between Captain H.J. Brees, Acting Agent, and Uncompahgre leaders, NARA Record Group 75, Box 10, Folder 7, pages 3 & 4.

[4] Mesinger, Maggie, interview with Mark Fry, Farmer, Fruita, Colorado, from *Farm '99*, <www.kentart.com/Mark%20Fry/> viewed March 16, 2002 . One of Chipeta's branding irons is on display in the Ute Museum at Montrose.

[5] *Vernal Express*, September 16, 1911.

[6] *Ouray Plaindealer*, July 7, 1911.

[7] *The Durango Democrat*, July 12, 1911; Denver Times, July 16, 1911.

[8] *Colorado Springs Gazette*, August 5, 1911,

[9] Manitou is an eastern Algonquin term, not a Ute word.

[10] *Colorado Springs Gazette*, August 28, 1912; <www.geocities.com/Heartland/Trails/8119/shankive.html> viewed January 18, 2002.

[11] Castle, Mrs. Newton, "Chipeta, Famous Ute Chieftain's Wife, Was Friend to Pioneers," *Vernal Express*, December 11, 1941.

[12] Banks, W. A., oral history, Doris Duke Collection, Interview #64, Marriott Library, University of Utah.

[13] Gardner, MaryEllen Stewart, *Tales From Indian Country by George Emery Stewart, Jr.*, (Orem, Utah: SunRise Publishing, 1997) ix and 17.

[14] *Commonweal News Bulletin*, September 25, 1914 - item #47:25 of the Dawson Collection, Colorado Historical Society.

[15] King, Mrs. W.G., "Our Ute Indians," *Colorado Magazine*, Vol. XXXVII, No. 2, (April 1960).

[16] *Vernal Express*, January 30, 1914.

[17] A beaded pouch given by Chipeta to Mary Boulter about 1913 is part of the collection of the Ute Indian Museum at Montrose.

[18] Boulter, Edmund, transcript of June 14, 1884 oral interview pg 6-10, Fort Collins Public Library.

[19] *Vernal Express*, January 30, 1914.

# Chapter 12
# THE LAST YEARS

Jewell D. Martin left the Uintah-Ouray Agency after three years, but he did not forget Chipeta. From his new assignment at the Fort Belknap Indian School in Montana he wrote to Commissioner of Indian Affairs Cato Sells in March 1916 about Chipeta's destitute condition. Ouray's vital role in settling the Meeker affair was, Martin said, "worth a thousand times more than the services rendered by scores of men who are recognized today by our Government and are receiving at its hands, liberal pensions."[1] Martin reported that Chipeta left an attractive home in Colorado and the government promised her a good home in Utah; the new home was tiny, poorly built, and unfurnished. He pleaded for Sells to take the initiative to provide Chipeta some "creature comforts" in her remaining days.

Upon receiving Martin's impassioned letter, Sells sought the advice of Albert H. Kneale, the superintendent at the Uintah & Ouray School at Fort Duchesne. Kneale replied in late April with an eight-page letter. He reported that the previous summer he had spent two nights at Chipeta's ranch and had several "very interesting talks" with her since his arrival at the agency. He felt that he knew her well.

"Chipeta," Kneale said, "to all outward appearances is not different from the ordinary Indian woman of this tribe, and the casual observer would see nothing in her to cause him to look a second time. It is only when one becomes rather intimately acquainted with her that he realizes that she is in reality a superior woman."[2]

A week prior to writing the letter Kneale had met Chipeta on a visit to the town of Ouray, Utah. During their conversation Kneale raised the idea of some compensation from the government to make her more comfortable.

Chipeta replied, "I am an old woman. My brother McCook is an old man, We will soon be dead. This matter . . . is cold. It has been dead a long time, and there is no occasion to try to revive it."[3]

Kneale pressed Chipeta to confirm the stories he had heard about her removal to Utah. She told him:

> *You have heard the truth. I did have a good home. I was told by the representatives of the Government that if I came to this country I would be given a home better than the home I was abandoning. My people were made the same promise that they would be given good lands and the water would be placed on their lands. None of these promises have been kept. I and my people were located for the most part on White River and in the bottoms of the lower Duchesne, and these lands are desert lands today. The Government has made no effort to place water on them. Believing the promises of the representatives of the Government, that they would put water on these lands, I built for myself a house on my allotment and sat down there waiting for the water, but the water did not come. This was many years ago, and the water has not been placed there yet and it appears that there is no prospect of its being placed there soon."*[4]

Chipeta went on to relate the plight of the Uncompahgre who received allotments in the bottom lands

*Chipeta with Hazel Eagan — 1916. She still enjoyed children of all ages and races.*
Denver Public Library, Western History Department, X-30458

of the lower Duchesne River. They irrigated their lands and built good homes. Then canals were constructed up river that diverted the water, and the people were forced to abandon their land. She concluded that the people in Washington had forgotten the Uncompahgres.

Kneale asked if she had the necessities of life. Chipeta replied, "I am as well provided as are the other members of my tribe. I desire nothing. I am not better than they and what is good enough for them is good enough for me."

"Could the government do anything for you?" was Kneale's final inquiry.

"No. I expect to die very soon," Chipeta said.[5]

In his letter to Cato Sells, Kneale confirmed the truth of Chipeta's statements. He said the house Chipeta built on her allotment was long ago deserted and falling into decay. She and her brother McCook spent the greater part of the year in the mountains on Bitter Creek, where they grazed sheep and cattle. He described them as careful and thoughtful people.

Water rights were filed in 1905 on some three thousand acres of bottom lands, but the government never built the promised irrigation ditch. The Indians dug a small ditch and began farming. Off the reservation a canal was built upstream that diverted the water and left this ditch dry most of the year. Some work was started on a larger ditch, known as the Henry Jim Ditch, but it was never finished. The Indians gave up on farming, and the bottom lands reverted to desert.

Kneale reported that he had repeatedly advised the government to complete the ditch, but his advice was ignored. The Unitah Railroad Company was prepared to buy the allotted bottom lands and was confident that irrigation ditches could be constructed for no more than ten dollars per acre. The government engineers had estimated a much higher price, which had caused the project to be abandoned. The water rights filings would expire in 1919.

Kneale concluded, "The greatest monument that we could erect to the memory of Chief Ouray or to Chipeta his widow would be to redeem the pledges of the Government and place water on the Utes' allotments." Water for the allotments of her people was all Chipeta wanted. Kneale enclosed a petition signed by 150 adult Utes requesting that the Henry Jim Ditch be completed.[6]

Commissioner Sells quickly quashed the idea of completing the irrigation ditch. The estimated cost of forty thousand dollars was too much to risk on the uncertainty of sufficient water. They would wait for court adjudication of water rights. Sells did, however, propose to buy Chipeta some furniture for her house.[7]

Kneale replied on May 31 that many of the Indians, including Chipeta, were "houseless" and lived in wickiups or tents. He noted that Chipeta had two residences.

Her summer place in the foothills of the Book Cliff Mountains had several log structures. She and her family went there with their herds as soon as the spring snow melted and stayed until the fall snow drove them out. They wintered near Dragon, Utah, where they "hibernated" in tents and wickiups.

They had no need, he said, for chairs, tables, or beds. The only article of furniture they required was a trunk to keep valuables.

About the nicest thing the government could do for Chipeta, Kneale advised, would be to send her twice a year a nice Indian robe. The robe should be selected by someone who knew her tastes, and he recommended Mr. Curry of the Curry Mercantile Company at Ouray, Utah. Mr. Kneale was adamant that the chosen robe should be sent to Washington and then mailed to Chipeta by the commissioner of Indian affairs, or better yet, the president of the United States along with a personal letter. Such a robe would cost fifteen to twenty dollars.

Chipeta had received many expensive presents over the years which were of no use to her, Kneale reported. She was once presented a trunk full of silk dresses that were not suitable for her lifestyle; she gave them away. In a cellar on Bitter Creek Kneale found remnants of a beautiful set of china tableware, which Chipeta did not use. She preferred the more durable enamelware. Chipeta was, he said, an Indian of the old school who wore a blanket, painted her face, and ate and slept on the ground. She had not adopted any of the customs of the white man and did not desire to do so. Kneale concluded his long letter, "I do believe it would be a mighty fine thing to present her . . . an Indian robe twice a year." [8]

On June 16, 1916, Kneale was authorized to arrange for Mr. Curry to select a robe, not to exceed twenty-five dollars in cost, and forward it to the office in Washington. The expense was to be paid from the account "Interest on Confederated Band of Utes 4% Fund" (the Utes' own money). The authorization was specifically limited to one robe, one time only. [9]

The robe, or blanket, began its journey to Washington on September 19. It was shipped back to Utah on October 3 via Wells-Fargo Express. The accompanying letter from Cato Sells read:

*Chipeta,*

*My friend:*
*I have read with great interest of the valuable services rendered to the whites by Chief Ouray and yourself at the*

*time of the Indian troubles many years ago. I understand that your husband did everything in his power to stop the fighting and that you both made every arrangement for the comfort and welfare of the captives. It is good to know that these unfortunate conditions no longer exist but that the Indians now live side by side with the white man in peace and friendship.*

*To show that the Government has not forgotten what you did at that time and as a slight token of its appreciation, I am sending you, through our good friend Superintendent Kneale, an Indian robe or shawl, with the request that he have it delivered to you with this letter. I hope you will like the shawl.*

*With best wishes,*
*Your friend,*
*Cato Sells, Commissioner* [10]

The day after Christmas Agent T.M. McKee wrote a letter to Sells at Chipeta's request:

*My Friend, Your beautiful shawl received, and was appreciated very much. In token of shawl received am sending you a saddle blanket also picture of myself.*

*I am in good health considering my age and hope to live much longer to show my friendship and appreciation to all the kind white people. I am also glad that there is no more trouble existing between the Indians and white people, and hope that this state of affairs exists through the rest of my life time.*

*Under separate cover you will find the saddle blanket, and hope that same is appreciated as much as the shawl was. With best wishes I am always, your friend, Chipeta..* [11]

Chipeta signed the typewritten letter with her thumbprint. McKee wrote her name beneath her mark and signed as witness. The accompanying photo captured Chipeta sitting on the ground in front of her teepee wearing a bold plaid shawl — perhaps the very gift sent by Commissioner Sells.

Although Sells spent the better part of 1916 determining what he could do for Chipeta, life in Utah went on. The members of the Hayden, Colorado, Camp Fire Girls named their summer camp in honor of Chipeta. The *Vernal Express* speculated that Chipeta might be named honorary president of the organization. In late June the newspaper ran a story about Chipeta's life under a headline that she was celebrating her 101st birthday.[12] Perhaps it was the headline that caused the story to be widely copied by other newspapers. Chipeta's name was in the news across the country. She was, however, unaware of the attention as she and McCook with twenty Utes were visiting the Southern Utes in Ignacio. She was actually about seventy-three years old.

In Ouray, Colorado, pioneers Martha and Ernest Ripley published a book recalling their early experiences in the West, including stories of how Chipeta had befriended settlers. On the flyleaf of a copy of the new book Mrs. Ripley wrote a thank-you note to Chipeta for her past kindnesses and mailed the book to the agent in Utah. Her accompanying note asked that an interpreter read the inscription to Chipeta along with certain marked passages in which other people fondly recalled the Ute woman. The agent replied to tell Mrs. Ripley that tears had rolled down Chipeta's face as she listened to the words of appreciation. He reported that Chipeta meekly said she was glad if she had ever been of help to the whites.

World War I was underway in Europe, and the United States began to gear up for inevitable participation. The nation's first military draft was held on June 5, 1917. All the shops in Vernal closed for the event, and many business people served as volunteer registrars. Families proudly accompanied their young men into town to signup. Three days later the *Vernal Express* reported that seven hundred young men of the county had registered for military service. Agent Kneale reported sixty-six Indians of military age on the reservation. However, they did not come to town to register. In the paternalistic government approach to Indians, the agency clerk completed their registration cards for them and sent the cards to the county clerk.

Superintendent Kneale reminded the Utes that some of their own young men would serve in this war. He told them every person in the United States had an obligation to support the government in the war effort and the Red Cross in its work of mercy. Mrs. L.W. Curry of the Red Cross visited the agency and met personally with Charley Mack, chief of the Uintahs, and Charlie Chavanaux, chief of the Uncompahgres, to explain the work of the organization. As a result, 450 Utes joined the Red Cross at ten dollars per person. The Uintah Chapter of the Red Cross promptly claimed the greatest number of Indian members in the United States.

On Decoration Day 1918, the Utes arranged a fund-raising event for the Red Cross. The Ute horse race, Indian dance demonstrations, and a sale of Indian fancy work and baked goods generated $435 for the cause. In October Superintendent Kneale announced that the Utes continued to support the war effort by purchasing war bonds. They had subscribed fifty-thousand dollars to the Fourth Liberty loans campaign.

Spanish influenza, which had already attacked thirty to forty percent of the population of Europe, raged across the United States in 1918. Schools were closed, and emergency hospitals were set up. People pressed for quarantines on all public gatherings. By the end of the year the epidemic found the reservation, claiming the lives of sixty-two Utes, including Chipeta's Bitter Creek neighbor, Atchee.

Claude Taylor, who lived forty-one years along Bitter Creek on a ranch three miles from Chipeta, recalled that "pret-near all the old Indians died from the flu. Most died because they stayed home rather than let the white men take care of them." [13]

Taylor remembered Chipeta as good hearted and very hospitable. He recalled a particular occasion when she invited him to dinner. He arrived to find Chipeta in the yard "graining" deer hides (scraping away the fur) with a butcher knife. When Taylor appeared, she stopped work and settled near the fire to peel potatoes for the meal. Taylor sat down to visit with her and saw that she cut the potatoes with the same knife she

*Chipeta — totally blind — as taken by Thomas McKee.*
*Colorado Historical Society, F-40198*

had been using to scrape deer hides. She had not stopped to clean the knife. She fried the potatoes, rolled them in tortillas, and presented Taylor his dinner on a metal plate. He thanked her, stood up, and walked some distance away with his food. Unable to escape the thought of fur and other bits of the deer in his potatoes, he fed it all to one of Chipeta's dogs.

The decennial federal census of the entire U.S. population included the Utes for the first time in 1920. McCook bundled the family into a wagon and drove to Duchesne in mid-January to be enumerated by Jasper W. Elliott. Chipeta was recorded as head of household number 378, and Mr. Elliott noted that she owned her house free and clear. Her age was seventy-seven. The census identified place of birth for each person recorded and place of birth for his or her mother and father. Elliott either lacked a translator or assumed that all Utes and their ancestors had been born in Utah, and that is how he listed Chipeta and every other Ute who had relocated from Colorado.

Chipeta was still in good physical condition for her advancing years, but her eyes caused her great problems. Her vision was so poor that McCook stretched a rope from her teepee to the brush so that she would not lose her way while doing chores or relieving herself. Neither the medicine man nor the reservation doctors had been able to improve Chipeta's diminished vision. So McCook decided to try one last resort.

On September 6, 1921, Chipeta squatted on the platform of the railroad station in Dragon, Utah. The morning was warm, but the breeze raised goosebumps on her skin. She tilted back her head and slowly inhaled. It smelled like autumn — buffalo hunting season. With her shawl snug about her shoulders Chipeta closed her eyes and perhaps daydreamed.

She thought of long-gone days of buffalo hunts. Her pulse surged with excitement as she pulled from her memory's storehouse mental images of painted warriors brandishing spears and arrows, riding out on painted ponies in swirls of dust, accompanied by whoops and shouts. The pungent odor of sagebrush mingled in her memory with dust, sweat, fresh blood, and musky beasts. She touched her fingers together, recalling the sticky slickness of blood and fat from freshly butchered meat. Wetting her lips with her tongue, she could almost taste roasted buffalo hump, the first reward of a successful hunt. The clank and clatter of the arriving train broke her reverie. As she struggled to her feet, she wondered if there were any buffalo left.

Carrying one small cloth valise, Chipeta stepped aboard the eight o'clock morning train. She had made this trip many times, often accompanied by McCook. It was a scenic but hair-raising sixty-three mile ride. The narrow gauge line with rails just three feet apart was all steep grade and hairpin turns so tight the engineer boasted he could reach out and shake hands with the conductor in the caboose. The cars jerked and tugged their way to the 8,437 foot elevation atop Baxter Pass and then descended two thousand feet in just six miles.

For Chipeta it was a tedious journey because her eyes were now clouded by cataracts that reduced the scenery to a blur of beige and sage and rusty earth red. She arrived in Mack,

Colorado, at 1:30 p.m. and caught the Denver & Rio Grande Western train into Grand Junction. Waiting for her at the station was William Weiser, president of Grand Valley National Bank, who drove her the few blocks to St. Mary's Hospital.

Weiser was a Grand Junction pioneer. He had arrived as a teenager in 1895 when the town was struggling and the Utes often returned to the area to hunt. He knew of Chipeta from her frequent visits to the town over the years. As a young attorney and later district attorney for Mesa County, he was often involved in the aftermath of conflicts between entrenched settlers and the exiled Utes.

Settling the estate of an elderly client, probably in 1916 or later, required Weiser to visit the man's remote sheep ranch on the western border with Utah. He remained three months paying bills and liquidating property. During that time he met and visited with Chipeta and McCook, who summered their herd nearby in the high meadows.

Weiser observed McCook's wife setting separate bowls of colored beads beside Chipeta so she could decorate a miniature cradle board. Her sight was so poor that she could no longer distinguish the colors. Weiser suggested to McCook that a doctor in Grand Junction might be able to repair Chipeta's eyes. When McCook argued that city doctors were too expensive, Weiser said he would help. Sometime later McCook sent word through Mr. Banks, the railroad man, to ask if Weiser's offer of assistance for Chipeta was still good.

Weiser arranged a consultation with Dr. Guy Cary, who convinced Chipeta to undergo cataract surgery. Cary had studied eye, ear, nose, and throat diseases at Harvard Medical School before establishing his practice in Grand Junction in 1917. He offered to perform the operation at no charge. Weiser agreed to cover hospital expenses.

Chipeta was admitted to the hospital Saturday afternoon, September 6, 1921. Her name was entered in the hospital register as "Chipeta (Indian)." Further details of patient number 1682 were written in columns across two pages of the wide ledger: age 78; born Colorado; resident of Dragon, Utah; widow; no occupation; no religion.

Chipeta's stay was lengthy compared with other patients. Cataract surgery was performed on one eye at a time. Typical patients stayed a week or less and went home to recover. Some returned months later to repeat the procedure on the other eye. To protect the delicate stitches while the eye healed, the patient spent several days lying flat on the bed with the head immobilized by tightly packed sandbags. Cataract surgery, or any other surgery for that matter, was not frequently performed in those days. During the seven weeks of Chipeta's hospitalization, Dr. Cary, the only eye surgeon in town, operated on the eyes of only three other patients.

St. Mary's Hospital was located at Eleventh Street and Colorado Avenue, near the edge of town. A row of stately homes lined Main Street a block to the north, so the hospital had purchased the entire block south of the facility to assure that the growing town would not encroach on fresh air and sunshine for the patients. The original rambling 1896 wooden structure stood in striking contrast to the "new wing" next door — a stately three-story brick building added in 1912. A modern kitchen, cafeteria, examining rooms, and surgery were located at ground level. Twenty patients were accommodated in private rooms on the upper floors. An electric elevator, reputed to be the first in the town, moved staff and patients up and down between levels. Hidden away in windowless, locked rooms in the basement were patients being treated for "mental defects" under a contract with the county.

The Sisters of Charity of Leavenworth, Kansas, managed the hospital and operated a nursing school across the street. On the east side of the grounds, the sisters worked a garden, which supplied the hospital and school with fresh vegetables and winter canned goods. They also kept cows, goats, and chickens in the backyard to provide milk and eggs for the patients and the sisters.

Chipeta requested to stay on one of the long wooden porches attached to the south side of the new building rather than one of the regular rooms. A waist-high wall of wooden slats enclosed the porch where those patients who were able to move about enjoyed fresh air and reprieve from the confines of their rooms. The hospital installed a bed and chair for Chipeta and a folding screen for privacy.

Before the sun rose each morning Chipeta heard the sisters singing in the chapel of the old hospital building. The familiar noises of grazing livestock and the clucking and scratching of chickens below her room were comforting. In the afternoon she enjoyed the excited voices of children at play in the yard of Emerson School a few blocks west on Ute Avenue. She relished the feel of sunshine, the smell of rain when a storm passed, and the breeze that carried the faint scent of juniper and pine from the high mountains.

Chipeta's aerie provided a panoramic view of the Uncompahgre Plateau, Grand Mesa to the east, and the junction of the Gunnison and Grand rivers to the west. Perhaps it was as well that Chipeta's failed eyesight prevented her from seeing the expanding sprawl of homes and businesses claiming the land that had been promised to her people as their reservation. Although the newspapers made no mention of her hospitalization, word of mouth drew local people to the hospital yard in hopes of catching a glimpse the legendary figure.

Chipeta was a favorite of the sisters and student nurses. They brought her special treats, indulged her, and checked often to see that she had plenty of blankets when nights turned chilly. Even the hospital administrator, Sister Mary Celestine, stopped by periodically to visit her celebrated patient.

Young Emma Nagel entered the hospital to give birth to her first child while Chipeta was in residence. She remembered the small Indian woman wandering the hallways at all hours of the day and night. Chipeta insisted on visiting each new baby. No doubt more than one mother was wary of the elderly woman wrapped in a plaid blanket, who shuffled into the room, arms fairly quivering to hold the newborn infant. The accompanying nurse reassured the mothers that this was a famous and harmless visitor, while Chipeta cooed strange words to little ones that she could barely see.

Chipeta's surgery failed, possibly because the nurses found it impossible to keep her still. She was discharged from the

hospital on October 24, 1921, and returned home with limited vision in one eye and only light and shadow in the other.

Diminished eyesight never kept Chipeta from traveling. By 1921 her annual income was $320 collected in quarterly annuity installments that had replaced the ration system. She continued her annual visits to the Grand Junction area where she often stayed at the Park Hotel in Fruita. Accompanied by her faithful brother, McCook, she made her final visit in September 1923.[14]

Chipeta died of chronic gastritis on August 16, 1924, at Bitter Creek.[15] She was eighty-one years old. She outlived her beloved Ouray by forty-four years. In the traditional manner of Ute burial, McCook wrapped her in a blanket and carried her into the hills. He laid her body against the wall of an arroyo and with his fists caved the sandy soil on top of her.

*Chipeta's faithful companion, who took care of her even after death — Jim McCook by T. M. McKee. Photo courtesy of Main Street Photography*

1 Martin, Jewel D. to Cato Sells, March 10, 1916, University of Utah Library, Manuscript Collections, Box 12, Folder 6.

2 Kneale, Albert H. to Cato Sells, April 24, 1916, University of Utah Library, Manuscript Collection, Box 12, Folder 6.

3 Ibid.

4 Ibid.

5 Ibid.

6 Ibid.

7 Hauke, C.F. to Kneale, May 5, 1916, University of Utah Library, Manuscript Collection, Box 12, Folder 6.

8 Kneale to Sells, May 31, 1916, University of Utah Library, Manuscript Collection, Box 12, Folder 6.

9 Merritt, E.B. to Kneale, June 16, 1916, University of Utah Library, Manuscript Collection, Box 12, Folder 6.

10 Sells to Chipeta, October 2, 1916, University of Utah Library, Manuscript Collection, Box 12, Folder 6.

11 Chipeta to Sells, December 26, 1916, University of Utah Library, Manuscript Collection, Box 12, Folder 6.

12 *Vernal Express,* June 30, 1916.

13 Taylor, Claude, oral history, Doris Duke Collection, Interview #136, University of Utah, Marriott Library.

14 *Grand Junction Sentinel,* August 18, 1924.

15 Ibid.

## Chapter 13
# RECOGNITION COMES

News of Chipeta's death spread rapidly in the world outside the reservation. The *Myton Free Press* reported "Chipeta Is Dead on Bitter Creek." The story stated that she was eighty-one years old, totally blind, and always spent her money taking care of orphaned children, including Mexican and white children.

"Queen Chipeta Rejoins Husband, Chief Ouray, In Happy Hunting Ground," headlined *The Denver Post* the next week. The story that followed, however, was about Ouray and recent Ute history rather than the deceased woman. Chipeta was identified as the youngest and most beautiful of Ouray's several wives. This article was the first to broach the idea that Ouray's body might be recovered so that the great chief and his "queen" could be buried side by side. The writer went so far as to suggest a burial site "on the summit of the lofty peak overlooking the regions wherein they spent their happy youth" and a monument supplied by the white population.[1]

A year earlier Southern Ute Agent McKean and Chief Buckskin Charley had discussed the idea of a monument to Ouray. Buckskin Charlie agreed to identify the location of the grave to see if Ouray's remains could be moved. L.M. Wayt, the agency trader, and Buckskin Charlie's nephew went into the mountains and found the site. The bones of several horses were scattered over the rocks and into the surrounding sage-brush. Digging into the crevice they located two human shoul-der blades, two ribs and one arm bone, which they carefully wrapped and reburied. The location remained a secret.

With news of Chipeta's death, Agent McKean convinced Buckskin Charlie that it was time to remove Ouray's bones from the hills and set in motion a plan for the joint burial of Ouray and Chipeta. On August 24 William L. Tisdell, a Denver photographer, and his wife accompanied Mr. Wayt and Buckskin Charlie to the site. Well into his eighties, Buckskin Charlie rode straight and tall on his horse. His com-panions followed in a car as far as the road allowed. Then they hiked until they located the spot above the arroyo. Tisdell took photographs of the burial site and the bones, which Mr. Wayt

*Chipeta's Utah gravesite near Dragon, Utah. It was very simple but very fitting.*
*Denver Public Library, Western History Department, X-30603*

*Buckskin Charlie at the Consolidated Ute Indian Agency.*
*Colorado Historical Society, F-12855*

removed from their hiding place. They searched the area but found no more human bones or any bits of clothing, blankets, or other items that had been placed with the body. Over the years, water and erosion had disrupted the burial place and dispersed the remains. The few bones were taken to the agency and held for possible reburial along with those of Chipeta.

In November the *Colorado Magazine* published a story, with Tisdell's photos, about the removal of Ouray's bones from their original grave. The article announced McKean's intent to inter Ouray's bones in the cemetery on the reservation. McKean's plans, however, went beyond Ouray's bones. He had already made a request to the government to rebury Chipeta beside Ouray and build a monument at the gravesite. He had contacted Agent Gross in Utah for assistance in recovering Chipeta's remains.

In the meantime the Montrose Chapter of the Daughters of the American Revolution (DAR) had also contacted Agent Gross requesting permission to bury Chipeta at

her old homestead. They had only recently completed a concrete and steel memorial teepee on the site. The freshwater
spring from which Ouray and Chipeta once drank had been
excavated and piped into a bowl in the center of the teepee.
The monument was destined, they said, "to attract interest and
publicity throughout the nation."[2] What more appropriate
place for Chipeta's remains to rest for eternity?

With two requests to rebury Chipeta in two different
locations in Colorado, Agent Gross consulted McCook.
Shortly after Chipeta's death, a white man named Albert
Reagan had discovered her grave. Coyotes had been digging at
the site, and there was a threat the body might be washed away
altogether in the first flash flood. Reagan had suggested to
McCook that Chipeta's remains be moved to a better location.

Agent Gross and McCook discussed options for moving
Chipeta's body to the little cemetery near the church at
Randlett or for reburial in Colorado. McCook chose
Colorado. If her remains were to be disturbed at all, McCook
said, he wanted her buried at the old home place in Colorado.
Gross reported McCook's decision to Southern Ute Agent
McKean and the Montrose DAR. He also said that McCook
wanted the Utes at Ignacio to make the decision about where
to rebury the bones of Ouray. Gross suggested that the old
home place would be a fitting location for Chipeta and Ouray
to be interred together.

With this concurrence from McCook, the DAR in
Montrose mounted a fund-raising campaign to build an
appropriate tomb. Gross reported that $165.70 remained in
Chipeta's account at the agency. He suggested this money
might be used to defray expenses of exhuming the body and
transporting it to Colorado.[3]

On March 10, 1925, the agency farmer, Hugh Owens,
left Ouray for Bitter Creek. Because of ice in the Green River,
he had to travel by way of Jensen, a ninety-mile route, to reach
Dragon, Utah. From there it was twenty-five miles to Bitter
Creek. Accompanied by Yagah Mountain Sheep, he located
and exhumed Chipeta's body on March 12. A Ute who owned

a wagon delivered the carefully wrapped remains to the rail-road station for shipment to Colorado.

On Saturday, March 14, 1925, Owens, McCook, Yagah Mountain Sheep, and Reverend Hersey boarded the Uintah Railway train at Dragon, Utah, with a simple pine box bearing Chipeta's recovered remains. It was her last trip over familiar territory, this time pushing through snow piled higher than the top of the train in some places. They changed trains at Mack, Colorado, as Chipeta had done so often, and arrived in Grand Junction on the D&RGW train No. 4 that evening. Her coffin remained overnight at the station, and the next morning the four men accompanied her on the final leg of the journey by the branch train.

The DAR committee was gathered at the Montrose station to meet the 11:30 Sunday morning train. While the body was taken to White's Mortuary, the committee took the escorts to lunch and explained plans for the afternoon event.

The procession formed at 2:30 p.m. to follow the coffin along the snow-packed four-mile route to Ouray Springs.

*Chipeta's Montrose Funeral — March 15, 1925.*
*Colorado Historical Society, F-44111*

Chipeta's faithful brother, McCook, walked at the front of the line with the Reverends Hersey and Warner and the other dignitaries. They were followed by the Montrose Band and marching units of Company D Colorado National Guard, Boy Scouts, Grand Army of the Republic, Women's Relief Corps, Daughters of Veterans, and the DAR.

At the burial site the DAR chairwoman escorted McCook and party into the concrete teepee. She filled a cup with water from the spring and allowed each man to drink. Rev. Hersey took the cup and pronounced a blessing: "In the name of God, Ouray and Chipeta I sup from this cup, this water emblematic of the purity of your lives. May the memory of your heroic and humanitarian deeds be kept fragrant in the hearts and thoughts of the white people, whom you so faithfully served. Amen." McCook said simply, "Chipeta I have brought you home."[4]

Five thousand people gathered around the burial site. At 3:00 p.m. the band played "America" as the pall bearers placed the coffin in the open vault. Reverend Warner offered the

*Jim McCook at Chipeta's gravesite. It was a grand monument for a grand lady.*
*Denver Public Library, Western History Department, George Beam Photograph, GB-7967*

*Ute Chiefs gathered at the reburial of Chief Ouray at Ignacio on May 24, 1925.*
*Denver Public Library, Western History Department, George Beam Photograph, GB-7914*

invocation. Agent Owens formally presented the earthly remains of Chipeta to the DAR and the people of Colorado. Placing pieces of Chipeta's fine beaded buckskin on top of the coffin, McCook spoke a farewell in Ute. The Honorable John C. Bell, a former member of Congress, accepted the remains on behalf of the people of Colorado and made a speech. Reverend Hersey delivered the Episcopal funeral service. On behalf of the DAR committee, Mrs. J.M. Foster placed a floral arrangement beside the tomb, and Mrs. C.R. Marks added a flag. The band struck up "The Star Spangled Banner." With hands on hearts, everyone joined in the song. Maurice Rhoades, bugler of Company D, sounded "Taps" to close the ceremonies. Although the service was far from the burial any Ute would envision, the white citizens of Colorado had perhaps made peace with themselves.

With Chipeta entombed at the old homestead, the Montrose DAR turned their attention to acquiring Ouray's body to be buried beside her. It was, they said, the right thing to do. They asked McCook to go to Ignacio on their behalf to

*The funeral procession at the reburial of Chief Ouray.*
*Colorado Historical Society, F-28259*

obtain the body. McCook went, but not as an advocate. He reiterated to the Southern Ute chiefs that, while he would like to see Ouray and Chipeta buried together, the placement of Ouray's bones was totally their decision.

Little more than two months after Chipeta was interred, the Southern Ute chiefs buried the bones believed to be Ouray's in the reservation cemetery at Ignacio. The May 24, 1925, funeral was perhaps an effort to outdo the Montrose event. Members of the Southern Ute, Ute Mountain, Jicarilla Apache, and Navajo tribes joined in a parade before the burial. Mounted braves wearing warbonnets rode two abreast followed by blanket-wrapped squaws and papooses. A hearse decorated with evergreens carried the silver-handled hardwood casket draped with a grey cloth. Three hundred-fifty cars filled with local white citizens and tourists followed. A moving picture company filmed the event, and the publicity agent for the Denver & Rio Grande Railroad and members of the press took photos.

In planning the event, one major obstacle presented itself. The cemetery was divided into a Protestant and a

Catholic section, and both denominations claimed the famous chief. In a compromise solution, the fence was lifted, and Ouray's grave was dug lengthwise on the dividing line between the two sections.[5]

Newspapers around the nation picked up the story, including erroneous reports that Ouray and Chipeta were buried together. There were rumors that Ouray was rolled in the hide of a rare white buffalo for burial.

Rumors also began to circulate that the bones buried in Ignacio were not those of Ouray. The authenticity of the bones was so widely debated that in late December 1926, Agent McKean gathered affidavits from those living Utes who had participated in the 1880 burial. McCook, Buckskin Charley, Colorow, and Naneese (George Norris) each stated they buried Ouray in the site near Ignacio where the bones were found.

Some Utes, however, believed — and still believe — that Ouray's bones rested in the mountains, not in the grave at Ignacio. According to the White River Ute Tim Johnson, his son Henry, and a Ute named Corass went to Igancio "that time when the white man's hunt for Ouray to put up stone. They find bones and put up stone. When Corass come back he say to Indian mans, 'No worry. Ouray he all right. White man's never touch him. We make big talk and shake hands and say lots of ho-do-do and have big feast. White mans happy. Me no tell 'em Ouray still in hills. We dig up grave where three Indians buried but Ouray not there. Ouray have ring on finger, gold watch, silver belt. Nobody find these things. White mans happy and Ouray happy too.' "[6]

After her death, stories of Chipeta the heroine grew with each retelling. She became a superwoman profusely honored in stories, books, and poems. "In October 1879 she dashed forth on her pony on a long and dangerous journey. Night and day she traveled through mountain fastness, then virgin forest, and o'er lonely trails, with but one thought in mind — to save mankind. No woman in Rocky Mountain history deserves more praise, or is more worthy of honors that white man may choose to heap upon her."[7]

*TO CHIPETA*
*E. N. Holden*

*You have gone from here. White man's friend,*
*No more will you the white man defend;*
*No more will you answer our helpless call*
*Through the din of the fight at the fort so tall;*
*But our love for you like a thing apart*
*Is treasured and cherished within our heart;*
*Till the threads of life are spun to end*
*We will remember you always, white man's friend.*

People in Colorado spoke of "poor Chipeta" in her lonely life, without home or hearth — or a good bed — for comfort in her last years. To "civilized" white folks, living on the ground under an animal skin wrapped around a few poles seemed like unbearable punishment. For Chipeta, who lived most of her life in a teepee, that was home. The simple, familiar ways were

*Chipeta's lonely fenced-in gravesite about 1930. It looks a lot prettier today.*
*Denver Public Library, Western History Department, George Beam*
*Photograph, GB-7967*

comforting and reminded her of happier times before the white man disrupted her life.

Chipeta was not abandoned by her own people. In fact, she was honored as a wise elder stateswoman. Her devoted brother, McCook, and her extended family surrounded Chipeta with love and attention. In photos from the Utah period, Chipeta always had a child at her side. The Utes were a welcoming society, and families readily accepted orphans, widows, and homeless individuals, calling them "brother, sister, aunt, or uncle" even when there was no blood relationship. J. Monaghan, who interviewed Utes on the reservation in 1933-34, noted that "everyone" on the reservation called Chipeta their grandmother.[8] She lived and died as a Ute, which was always her preference. It is just possible that she was content.

---

[1] *Denver Post,* August 19, 1924.

[2] *Montrose Daily Press,* May 21, 1924.

[3] Gross to Commissioner Indian Affairs, April 1, 1925, NARA Record Group 75, Box 12, Folder 6; McClellan, Val J., *This Is Our Land,* Vol 2, (Jamestown, OH: Western Publishers, 1979), 741-1.

[4] *Montrose Daily Press,* March 16, 1926, "Thousands Honor Chipeta's Homecoming, Regal Rites for Queen of Utes' Return."

[5] *Denver Post,* May 15, 1925; Durango Democrat, May 26, 1925; Ouray stated that he was baptized and raised as a Catholic while in New Mexico. Possibly Rev. Henry Bond, who came to Los Pinos as agent in 1874, convinced Ouray and Chipeta to profess faith in a Protestant denomination.

[6] Johnson, Tim, Interviews by CWA Workers, J. Monaghan Interviewer, Moffat County, 1933-34, page 41, #356/11, collection Colorado State Historical Society.

[7] "Great Heroine of the Colorado Utes," *Pony Express Courier,* Placerville, CA, April 1944.

[8] Monaghan, J., Interviews by CWA Workers, Moffat County, 1933-34, collection Colorado State Historical Society.

## Chapter 14
# EPILOGUE

All native-born Indians became United States citizens in 1924.

The government stopped distributing rations to Indians in 1931.

McCook was buried beside his beloved sister in 1937. The Chipeta Committee of the Uncompahgre Chapter, Daughters of the American Revolution, handled the arrangements.

Through a Works Projects Administration project a monument was erected in 1939 at the Ute Memorial Park in Ignacio to honor Chiefs Ouray, Severo, Ignacio, and Buckskin Charlie.

The site of Chipeta's grave near Montrose became part of an 8.65 acre shrine maintained by the Colorado Historical Society. Ouray and Chipeta's house burned to the ground on October 12, 1944. In 1956 the Colorado Historical Society built the Ute Indian Museum on the property, and in 2000 the society initiated an expansion project to more than double the facility's size to better accommodate the public and especially school groups. The gravesite and monument were also repaired, with much of the work done by Roland McCook, Sr., Chipeta's great-great-grandnephew. The museum contains

Ute artifacts and memorabilia, including many personal items that belonged to Ouray and Chipeta.

The shirt Chipeta made for Ouray's 1880 trip to Washington, D.C., found its way home to the Ute Indian Museum at Montrose. Her gift to Carl Schurz ended up in the collection of the Heye Foundation in New York and was returned in a 1977 exchange of historic materials.

The U.S. government negotiated a settlement with the Utes in 1950, paying the tribe $31.7 million for six million acres of prime Colorado real estate ceded to the government in 1880.[1]

Commemorating Colorado's 1976 centennial, a nine-foot by twelve-foot tapestry was installed in the state capitol rotunda honoring eighteen women who were "integral to the settlement and development of Colorado." With this tapestry Chipeta is honored, like Ouray, as a peacemaker in the seat of the government that claimed their homeland.

In the fall of 1976 a Ute man was fined by Colorado wildlife officials for hunting without a license in western Colorado. The tribes brought suit in federal court seeking

*The Chipeta and Ouray Monument. Denver Public Library, Western History Department, F-30997*

*A concrete teepee was built to cover "Chipeta Springs," which is near the old homestead and Chipeta's grave.*
*Denver Public Library, Western History Department, X-30616*

continuation of their rights under the 1873 Brunot Treaty, which granted them hunting rights in the San Juans "so long as game lasts and the Indians are at peace with the white people." The agreement had been forgotten for more than a century by everyone except the Utes. A negotiated settlement reaffirmed the Utes right to hunt, in any season without license, in their traditional grounds, now defined by towns — Cortez to Pagosa Springs, Ridgway to Lake City.

In a 1995 interview Roland McCook, great-great-grand-nephew of Chipeta, noted that her reburial proved two things — that she was still important in Colorado but that the white people continued to disregard her wishes. He said she certainly would not have wanted her remains moved.

---

[1] "Ute Indians Hit A $31.7 Million Jackpot," *Life Magazine*, July 24, 1950, 37-40.

*Appendix*

# CHIPETA'S NAME LIVES ON

The names of both Chipeta and Ouray are fixtures in Colorado and Utah. Many towns have a Chipeta Street or a community park bearing her name. Place names abound in Colorado: Chipeta Falls, Chipeta Lake, Chipeta Pass, Chipeta State Park, the community of Chipeta Park in El Paso County, and the unincorporated town of Chipeta, in Delta County. The Chipeta Mine is closed. In 1973 the ghost town of Independence, once known as Chipeta, was placed on the National Register of Historic Places.

Today residents of Grand Junction hone their skills on the eighteen-hole Chipeta Golf Course. Travelers in southwestern Colorado find accommodations at the Chipeta Bed & Breakfast or the Chipeta Sun Lodge.

Utah, too, has Chipeta place names: the town of Chipeta in Uintah County; Chipeta Drive, which loops through the University of Utah Campus; and Chipeta Canyon, the gateway to the 15,200 acre Cripple Cowboy wilderness area.[1]

The woman who longed for her own children would be most pleased with the organizations for youth that bear her name. Chipeta Elementary School sits nestled at the foot of the mountains in Colorado Springs, where the Utes once camped and hunted buffalo. Chipeta Girl Scout Troop 80 in

Delta is part of the Chipeta Council, Girl Scouts of America. Lively girls bound in and out of Chipeta Cabin at Cheley Youth Camp near Estes Park, and an older age group resides in Chipeta dormitory at Western State College, Gunnison.

In 1907 an old Ute campground where Willow Creek runs into the Grand (Colorado) River was established as a camp for boys under the auspices of the YMCA. They named it Camp Chief Ouray. By 1908 the first campers arrived: boys age twelve through seventeen, slept in tents with pine bough mattresses, bathed in cold water, and enjoyed fishing, hiking, and nature study. In 1979 Camp Chief Ouray was moved to a new site near Estes Park, where new cabins and the Chipeta dining hall served campers. The new camp welcomed girls and offered camping opportunities for children with special medical needs. The camp continues today operated by the YMCA of the Rockies.[2]

Another designation Chipeta would appreciate is offered by the U.S. Forest Service. In 2001 a proposal was entered for a "Quiet Use Designation" of the Chipeta Roadless Area in Colorado's San Isabel National Forest. This region in the shadow of Pahlone Peak has a single-track trail leading all the way to the Continental Divide near Monarch Pass. Deer, elk, and beaver inhabit the locale, which is filled with mature stands of lodgepole, pine, spruce, fir, and aspen trees. The area remains as Chipeta knew it. Chipeta Mountain (also written as Chapita Mountain), elevation 12,853 feet, sits nearby in Chaffee and Gunnison counties close to Mount Ouray.

Even the dirt of her homeland bears her name. The Chipeta series is described as "shallow, well drained, slowly permeable soils that formed in residuum and colluvium from shale." This soil was first identified in the Uncompahgre Valley of Colorado in 1910.

Dr. Michael Pogue of the Systemic Entomology Lab, U.S. Department of Agriculture, Washington, D.C., labeled a moth common to Colorado and Utah the Tricholita Chipeta.[3]

In 1993 Colorado State University's San Luis Valley Research Center released a new variety of potato called Chipeta. It is described as a "medium to late-maturing chipping potato . . . noted for its excellent chip color during long-term storage . . . considered a good baker."

Chipeta also found her way into the realm of high performance supercomputers. The Cray J90 parallel vector computer was available in two models called ouray and chipeta. When more cost-effective systems were developed, chipeta was decommissioned on January 31, 2002, by its manufacturer, SCD Corporation.

---

[1] <http://w3.access.gpo.gov/blm/utah/pdf/ne142.pdf> (viewed April 5, 2001).

[2] Melton, Jack R., and Lulabeth Melton, *YMCA of the Rockies: Spanning a Century.* (Self published, 1992). <http://www.ymcarockies.org/museum/Books/Camping.html> (viewed April 4, 2002).

[3] <http://www.npsc.nbs.gov/resource/distr/lepid/moths/usa/1374.htm> (viewed April 5, 2001).

# Bibliography

## BOOKS

Bair, Everett. *This Will Be An Empire*. New York: Pageant Press, 1959.

Barton, John D. *A History of Duchesne County*. Salt Lake City: Utah Historical Society, 1998.

Belden, Bauman L. *Indian Peace Medals Issued in the United States*. New Milford, Conn.: N. Flayderman & Company, 1966.

Bender, Harry E. Jr. *Uintah Railway: The Gilsonite Route*. Berkeley, Calif.: Howell North Books, 1979.

Brown, Dee. *Bury My Heart At Wounded Knee*. New York: Holt, Rinehart & Winston, 1970.

Bueler, Gladys. *Colorado's Colorful Characters*. Golden, Colo.: The Smoking Stack Press, 1981.

Clemmer, Richard O., and Omer C. Stewart. *Treaties, Reservations and Claims, Handbook of North American Indians*. Vol. 11. Washington, D.C.: Smithsonian Institution, 1986.

Crum, Sally. *People of the Red Earth*. Santa Fe, N.M.: Ancient City Press, 1996.

Dawson, Thomas F., and F.J.V. Skiff. *The Ute War: A History of the White River Massacre*. Denver: Tribune Publishing House, 1879.

Dunlay, Tom. *Kit Carson & the Indians*. Lincoln, Nebr.: University of Nebraska Press, 2000.

Emmitt, Robert. *The Last War Trail.* Norman, Okla.: University of Oklahoma Press, 1954.

Everrett, George G., and Wendell F. Hutchinson. *Under The Angel of Shavano.* Denver: Golden Bell Press, 1963.

Fanneman, Herbert. *A Ticket To Ride the Narrow Gauge.* Golden, Colo: Colorado Railroad Foundation, Inc., 2000.

Fishell, David. *St. Mary's Hospital A Spirit of Charity Celebrating A Century of Caring.* Grand Junction, Colo.: St. Mary's Hospital, 1996.

Forsee, Aylesa. *William Henry Jackson: Pioneer Photographer of the West.* New York: Viking Press, 1964.

Fremont, John C. *Memories of My Life.* Chicago: Belford, Clark & Co., 1887.

Gardner, Mary Ellen Stewart, *Tales From Indian Country* by George Emery Stewart, Jr. Orem, Utah: SunRise Publishing, 1997.

Guild, Thelma S., and Harvey L. Carter. *Kit Carson — A Pattern for Heroes,* Lincoln, Nebr.: University of Nebraska Press, 1984.

Hafen, Ann Woodbury. *Campfire Frontier.* Denver: The Old West Publishing Company, 1969.

Hafen, LeRoy R., and Ann W. Hafen, eds. *The Diaries of William Henry Jackson Frontier Photographer.* Glendale, Calif.: The Arther H. Clark Company, 1959.

Hill, Alice Polk. *Colorado Pioneers In Picture and Story.* Denver: Brock-Haffner Press, 1915.

Hill, Edward E. *The Office of Indian Affairs, 1824-1880: Historical Sketches.* New York: Clearwater Publishing Company, Inc., 1974.

Horan, James D. *Mathew Brady Historian with a Camera.* New York: Bonanza Books, 1955.

Howbert, Irving. *Indians of the Pikes Peak Region.* New York: Knickerbocker Press, 1914.

Hughes, J. Donald. *American Indians in Colorado.* Boulder, Colo.: Pruett Publishing Co., 1977.

Hunt, Inez, and Wanetta W. Draper. *To Colorado's Restless Ghosts.* Chicago: Sage Books, 1960.

Jackson, William Henry. *The Pioneer Photographer.* New York: World Book Company, 1929.

Jefferson, James, Robert W. Delaney, and Gregory C. Thompson. Edited by Floyd A. Oncil. *Southern Utes, A Tribal History.* Ignacio, Colo.: Southern Ute Indian Tribe, June 1973.

Jocknick, Sydney. *Early Days on the Western Slope of Colorado.* Montrose, Colo.: Western Reflections Publishing, 1913, 1998.

Johnson, Brooks. *An Enduring Interest: The Photographs of Alexander Gardner.* Norfolk, Va.: The Chrysler Museum, n.d.

Kappler, C.J. *Indian Affairs: Laws and Treaties,* II, U.S. Statutes at Large. Vol. 9. Washington, D.C.: U.S. Government Printing Office, 1904.

Katz, Mark D. *Witness To An Era: The Life and Photographs of Alexander Gardner.* New York: Viking Penguin, 1991.

Kunhardt, Dorothy, and Philip Kunhardt. *Mathew Brady and His World.* Alexandria, Va: Time-Life Books, 1977.

Look, Alfred A. *Bits of Colorado History.* Denver: Golden Bell Press, 1977.

Look, Alfred A. *Utes Last Stand.* Denver: Golden Bell Press, 1972.

Lyman-Whitney, Susan. *Worth Their Salt: Notable But Often Unnoted Women of Utah.* Boulder, Colo.: NetLibrary, Inc., 1999.

McClellan, Val J. *This Is Our Land,* Vol. 1. New York: Vantage Press, 1977.

McClellan, Val J. *This Is Our Land.* Vol 2. Jamestown, Ohio: Western Publishers, 1979.

Marsh, Charles S. *People of the Shining Mountains.* Boulder, Colo.: Pruett Publishing, 1982.

Monroe, Arthur W. *San Juan Silver.* Montrose, Colo.: Self-published, 1940.

Nankivell, Major John H. *History of the Military Organization of the State of Colorado.* Denver, Colo.: The W. H. Kistler Stationary Co., 1935.

Pettit, Jan. *Utes: The Mountain People.* Boulder, Colo.: Johnson Books, 1990.

Polley, Rodger. *Uintah Railway Pictorial. Vol. 1 — Mack to Atchee.* Denver: Sundance Books, 1999.

R. L. Polk & Co.'s *Colorado Springs, Colorado City and Manitou City Directory, 1912.*

Rathmell, Ruth. *Of Records and Reminiscence.* Ouray, Colo: Ouray County Plaindealer and Herald, 1976.

Roberts, Dan. *A Story of the Centennial State.* Grand Junction, Colo.: Eagle Tail Press, 1973.

Rolle, Andrew F. *Introduction to A Century of Dishonor by Helen Hunt Jackson.* New York: Harper & Row, 1965.

Saunders, William F. *The Joy of the Frontier.* Unpublished manuscript in possession of author (Smith).

Shaputis, June, and Suzanne Kelly. *A History of Chaffee County.* Buena Vista, Colo.: Buena Vista Heritage, 1982.

Shirley, Gayle C. *More Than Petticoats: Remarkable Colorado Women.* Guilford, Conn.: The Globe Pequot Press, 2002.

Simmons, Virginia McConnell. *The Ute Indians.* Boulder, Colo.: University Press of Colorado, 2000.

Smith, Duane. *Henry M. Teller: Colorado's Grand Old Man.* Boulder, Colo.: University Press of Colorado, 2002.

Southern Colorado Auxiliary of the Territorial Daughters of Colorado. *Pioneers of the Territory of Southern Colorado.* Vol. 1. Monte Vista, Colo.: CBI Offset Printers, 1980.

Sprague, Marshall. *Massacre: The Tragedy At White River.* Boston: Little Brown & Co., 1957.

Tounsend, R. B. A *Tenderfoot in Colorado.* Norman: University of Oklahoma Press, 1968.

Ubbelohde, Carl, Maxine Benson, and Duane A. Smith. *A Colorado History.* Boulder, Colo.: Pruett Publishing Co., 1972.

Underwood, Kathleen Hill. *Town Building on the Colorado Frontier.* Albuquerque: University New Mexico Press, 1987.

Urquhart, Lena. *Colorow: The Angry Chieftain.* Denver: Golden Bell Press, 1968.

Ute Indians of Colorado. Washington, D.C.: U.S. Government Printing Office, 1879.

Vandenbusche, Duane. *The Gunnison Country.* Gunnison, Colo.: B & B Printers, 1980.

Varnell, Jeanne. *Women of Consequence: The Colorado Women's Hall of Fame.* Boulder, Colo: Johnson Books, 1999.

Williamson, Ruby. *Otto Mears: Pathfinder of the San Juan.* Gunnison, Colo.: B & B Printers, 1986.

Wroth, William, ed. *Ute Indian Arts and Culture.* Colorado Springs: Colorado Springs Fine Arts Center, 2000.

# NEWSPAPERS

*Boston Herald.* July 26, 1880.

*Cañon City Times.* Jan. 21, 1875, Feb. 25, 1875, March 11, 1875.

*Central City Register.* July 7, 1863.

*Colorado Springs Free Press.* July 9, 1967.

*Colorado Springs Gazette.* July 16, 2000.

*Commonweel News Bulletin,* Sept. 25, 1914.

*Duchesne Record.* [Myton, Utah]. May, 1914.

*Denver Daily News.* Nov. 4, 1873, Nov. 10, 1873.

*Denver Daily Times.* Oct. 7, 1873, Oct. 9, 1873.

*Denver Post.* Aug. 28, 1880, Aug. 19, 1924, May 15, 1925, June 13, 1957, Nov. 11, 1989.

*Denver Republican.* April 1, 1883, April 2, 1883.

*Denver Tribune.* Sept. 11, 1881.

*Durango Democrat.* May 26, 1925.

*Grand Junction Sentinel.* Aug. 18, 1924, March 15, 1925, Oct. 6, 1974.

*Golden Transcript.* Dec. 17, 1879.

*Greeley Tribune.* Nov. 19, 1879.

*Gunnison Review.* July 10, 1880, July 24, 1880, July 31, 1880, Aug. 28, 1880, Oct. 9, 1880, Oct. 16, 1880, April 2, 1881, June 11, 1881.

*Montrose Daily Press.* May 21, 1924, March 16, 1926, June 4, 1927.

*News.* [Denver]. Sept. 11, 1872.

*New York Times.* Jan. 8, 1880. Jan. 12, 1880, Aug. 22, 1887.

*Ouray Plaindealer.* Aug. 1, 1913.

*Ouray Times.* Oct. 25, 1879.

*Pueblo Chieftain.* Jan. 7, 1880.

*Pony Express Courier.* [Placerville, Calif.]. April 1944.

*Rocky Mountain News.* [Denver, Colo.]. Sept. 3, 1859, Sept. 10, 1859, Oct. 21, 1863, April 19, 1865, July 5, 1865, Oct. 10, 1865, Jan. 22, 1868, Feb. 19, 1868, April 1, 1868, April 17, 1869, June 19, 1872, Aug. 21, 1872, Sept. 7, 1872, Sept. 8, 1872, Sept. 12, 1872, Nov. 27, 1872, Sept. 11, 1873, Sept. 22, 1878, March 19, 1993.

*Salt Lake Tribune.* Sept. 29, 1996.

*Salt Lake Herald.* Nov. 25, 1897.

*Solid Muldoon.* [Ouray, Colo.]. Jan. 30, 1880, March 21, 1990.

*Statesman.* [Boise, Idaho]. May, 25, 1925.

*Steamboat Pilot.* [Steamboat Springs, Colo.]. Sept. 25, 1923.

*Vernal Express.* [Utah]. Dec. 5, 1895, Dec. 26 1895, Oct. 28, 1897, Nov. 11, 1897, Nov. 18, 1897, Nov. 25, 1897, Dec. 30, 1897, Jan. 6, 1898, April 24, 1908, June 30, 1916, July 28, 1916, July 12, 1918, Oct. 11, 1918, Nov. 11, 1937.

*Washington Evening Star.* Oct. 24, 1873, Jan. 12, 1880, Feb. 2, 1880.

*Washington Post.* Jan. 8, 1880, Jan. 12, 1880, Jan. 14, 1880, Jan. 18, 1880, Jan. 20, 1880, Jan. 23, 1880, Jan. 27, 1880, Jan. 28, 1880, Jan. 30, 1880, Feb. 13, 1880, Feb. 17, 1880, Feb. 18, 1880, March 8, 1880, March 27, 1880, May 26, 1880.

## PERIODICALS

Bair, Everett. "Queen of the Utes." *True West,* April 1956.

Bangert, Buckley. "Queen Chipeta." *Journal of the Western Slope, 1986.*

"A Colorado Tragedy." *Harper's Weekly,* Oct. 17, 1874.

Castle, Mrs. Newton. "Chipeta, Famous Ute Chieftain's Wife, Was Friend to Pioneers." *Vernal Express,* Dec. 11, 1941.

Davis, Georgie A. "Illustrated Interview of our lady artist with the Ute Indian Chiefs and prisoners in Washington, D.C." *Frank Leslie's Illustrated Journal,* April 1880.

Dawson, Thomas F., and Major Thompson. "Chief Ouray and the Utes." *The Colorado Magazine,* May 1930.

Downing, Finis E. "With the Ute Delegation of 1863: Across the Plains and at Conejos." *The Colorado Magazine,* Sept. 1945.

Ford, Grant M. "An Indian Christmas: The Spirit of the Missions." *Domestic and Foreign Missionary Society,* May 1907.

Hafen, Ann Woodbury. "Efforts to Recover the Stolen Son of Chief Ouray." *The Colorado Magazine,* March 1939.

Johnston, Shirley. "Fort Crawford: A Symbol of Transition." *Journal of the Western Slope,* Vol. 8, No. 2, 1993.

Parsons, Eugene. "Benton Canon." *The Trail,* July 1923.

Reagan, Albert, and Wallace Stark. "Chipeta Queen of the Utes and Her Equally Illustrious Husband, Chief Ouray." *Utah Historical Quarterly,* July 1933.

Russell, James. "Conditions and Customs of Present-Day Utes in Colorado." *The Colorado Magazine,* May 1929.

Simmons, Virginia. "When Opportunity Knocked on Saguache's Door." *Colorado Central Magazine,* May 2000.

"Ute Indians Hit a $31.7 Million Jackpot." *Life Magazine,* July 24, 1950.

Whittier, Florence E. "The Grave of Chief Ouray." *The Colorado Magazine,* Nov. 1924.

Wood, David Jr. "Chief Ouray and the Washington Hatchet." *Grand Junction Sentinel,* October 6, 1974.

Wright, Coulsen, and Geneva Wright. "Indian-White Relations in Uintah Basin." *Utah Humanities Review,* Oct. 1948.

## WEBSITE URLs

Carlisle Indian School: <http://www.epix.net/~landis/history.html> (viewed Jan. 8, 2002).

Census 1860: <www.npg.org/states/co.htm> (viewed May 6, 2002).

Census 1920, Federal Census, Utah, Uintah County, Enumeration District 131, Line 56, Page 8B: <http://gen.genserver.com/genindex.html> (viewed Sept.10, 2002).

Central America and the Panic of 1857. <http://www.americaslibrary.gov/cgi-bin/page.cgi/jb/reform/goldlost_1> (viewed April 28, 2003).

Fry, Mark, Farmer, Fruita, Colorado, interview by Maggie Mesinger, from *Farm'99* <www.kentart.com/ Mark%20Fry/> (viewed March 16, 2002).

Notarvianni, Philip F. "Mining." Utah History Encyclopedia. <http://historytogo.utah.gov/mining.html> (viewed Sept. 10, 2002).

Nichols, Jeffrey D. "Colorful Sam Gilson Did Much More Than Promote Gilsonite." History Blazer. May 1995. <http://historytogo.utah.gov/sgilson.html> (viewed Dec.19, 2002).

"Gilsonite." Utah Rails. Jan. 28, 2001. <http://www.trainweb.org/ utahrails/mining/gilsonite.html> (viewed Dec. 19, 2002).

Hersey, Rev. Milton J. <http://www.lofthouse.com/ USA/Utah/uintah/pioneers/hersey2.html> (viewed June 14, 2001).

Shan Kive. <www.geocities.com/ Heartland/Trails/8119/ shankive.htm> (viewed Jan. 18, 2002).

Trachoma.<www.spedex.com/resource/documents/veb/trachoma.html> (viewed Aug.16, 2002).

"The Uintah Railway: The Crookedest Railroad in the West, A Short History." <http://home.attbi.com/ !bpratt15/ a_short_history.htm> (viewed Sept. 10, 2002).

# ORAL HISTORIES
Banks, W. A. Doris Duke Collection, Interiew #64, Marriott Library, University of Utah.

Boulter, Edmund. Transcript of June 14, 1884, oral interview. Fort Collins (Colo.) Public Library.

Johnson, Tim. Interviewed by J. Monaghan in Interviews by CWA Workers, Moffat County (Colo.), 1933-34, page 41, #356/11, Colorado State Historical Society.

Monaghan, J. CWA Interviews Moffat County (Colo.), 1933-34, #356/6 and #356/27. Colorado Historical Society.

Richardson, Miss Edith. Doris Duke Collection, Interview #169, Marriott Library, University of Utah.

Taylor, Claude. Doris Duke Collection, Interview #136, Marriott Library, University of Utah.

# INTERVIEWS
Davis, Jim, Taxidermist, Trails End Taxidermy, Pueblo West, Colo. Interview with author (Becker). Jan. 4, 2002.

Fishell, David. Interview with author (Becker). Grand Junction, Colo. Dec. 13, 2001.

Rood, Mrs. A.C. (William Weiser's daughter-in-law). Interview with author (Becker). Jan. 2, 2002.

Sundal, David. Interview with author (Becker). Museum of Western Colorado, Grand Junction, Colo. Dec. 13, 2001.

# CORRESPONDENCE
Brown, Marilyn Hersey, granddaughter of Rev. Milton J. Hersey. Letter to author (Becker). 2002.

Landis, Barbara, Carlisle Indian School, Letter to author (Becker). 2002.

Ochoa, Maria, Director Historic-Artistic Patrimony and Archives of the Archdiocese of Santa Fe. Correspondence with author (Becker). 1996.

# NATIONAL ARCHIVES AND RECORDS ADMINISTRATION
Bureau of Indian Affairs Correspondence, U.S. Government Documents 0246, NARA Record Group 11, M668.

Delegation expense records, NARA Record Group 75, Box 2337-C-1863; Box 1880; Special Case 112.

U.S. Indian Census Rolls, 1885-1940. NARA Record Group 75, M234, Roll 204.

## OTHER RESOURCES

"A Collection Of Signs, Gestures and Signals of Native Americans." Washington, D.C.: Government Printing Office, 1880.

Colorado Commission on Higher Education. Minutes of commission meeting. Nov. 2, 2000.

Exhibit. Fort Garland Museum and Visitor's Center. Fort Garland, Colo. 2001.

Hatch, Edward. Report Regarding the Ute Indians of Colorado. Washington, D.C.: U.S. Government Printing Office, 1879.

Helen Hunt Jackson Collection. Tutt Library, The Colorado College. Colorado Springs.

"Introduction to Study of Sign Language Among Native Americans." Bureau of Ethnology, Smithsonian Institution. Washington, D.C.: Government Printing Office, 1880.

Jones, William C., and Elizabeth B. Jones. "Archaeology of the Eastern Ute: A Symposium." Denver: Colorado Council of Professional Archaeologists, 1998.

Letter from Secretary of Interior transmitting, in compliance with resolution of the Senate of December 8, 1879, concerning the Ute Indians in Colorado. Washington, D,C,: Government Printing Office, 1879.

Lloyd, John B. "The Uncompahgre Utes." Master's thesis, Western State College, 1932.

Montrose Visitors Guide. Montrose, Colo.: Montrose Convention and Visitors Bureau, 2001.

Ouray Collection. Colorado Historical Society. Denver, Colo.

Red Book Guide to Washington, D.C., 1881. Washington, D.C. Historical Museum.

St. Mary's Hospital Patient Register. May 26, 1896 - July 28, 1922. St. Mary's Hospital Library. Grand Junction, Colo.

Territorial Governors Collection, Box 19651. Colorado State Archives. Denver, Colo.

Uintah-Ouray Indian Reservation Records. University of Utah Library. Manuscript Collections. Box 12.

U.S. Congress. Testimony in Relation to Ute Outbreak. 46th Cong., 2nd Sess. HR MIS DOC No 38, 1880.

U.S. Department of Interior. Annual Report of the Commissioner of Indian Affairs. 1868.

U.S. Department of Interior. Report of the Secretary of Interior. November 10, 1863.

Ute Exhibit. El Pueblo Museum. Pueblo, Colorado. August 1995.

Viola, Herman. Research notes for his book *Diplomats in Buckskin.* 1981. Collection of the National Anthropological Archives, Washington, D.C.

# INDEX